BUSINESS ENGLISH

TU GUÍA PARA CONSEGUIR TRABAJO Y TRIUNFAR EN LOS NEGOCIOS **EN INGLÉS**

GETTING THE JOB
COVER LETTERS
JOB INTERVIEWS · CVs
WORKING ABROAD · THE JOB SEARCH

DOING BUSINESS IN ENGLISH
NEGOTIATIONS · EMAIL
PRESENTATIONS · ON THE TELEPHONE
NUMBERS AND MONEY · MEETINGS

ADVANCED BUSINESS TOPICS
ECONOMICS
ACCOUNTING · MARKETING
FINANCE & INVESTING · INSURANCE

Vaughan SYSTEMS

LIBRO
Autor: Kyle Millar
Coordinación del Proyecto: Rubén Palomero y Kyle Millar
Traducción y Edición: Rubén Palomero, Iris Simancas, Marta Campos Sáez, Justin Peterson, Sergio Ortiz, Laura Domínguez Barroso, Víctor Sanabria, Gareth Thomas, Elena Araújo, Alberto Imedio, Nick Keyte
Diseño y maquetación: ZAC diseño gráfico
Fotografías de cubierta: Jaime Arias
Fotografías de interiores: © 2014 Getty Images. Excepto página 1, Jaime Arias.

AUDIO
Locución: Daniel Escudero y Kyle Millar
Sonido: Juan García Escribano y Juan José Durán

VÍDEO
Interpretación: Kyle Millar, Aindrias Fitzgerald, Alberto Alonso, Mary Stabb, Ximena Holliday
Producción: Jaime Arias, Fernando Alarcón, Jorge Malillos, Daniel López

© Vaughan Systems S. L. U.
Calle Orense 69
28020 Madrid
Tel: 91 748 59 50
Fax: 91 556 42 21

www. grupovaughan. com

www.vaughantienda.com

ISBN (obra completa): 978-84-16094-27-1
Dep. Legal: M-9300-2014

ÍNDICE DE CONTENIDOS

Dear reader,

It is with special pleasure that I set aside a few moments to talk about Kyle Millar and, most especially, to recommend his new book... this book... **Business English, *a guide to getting a job and succeeding in the business world in English***.

I have known Kyle Millar since 2003, the year in which he came to Spain as a volunteer to take part in one our Vaughantown residential programs. Two months later, he was a teacher in our organization. Apparently he liked our approach to teaching and learning. He probably noticed a certain affinity between himself and our personality as a company, an affinity that involves intensity, vitality, daring, creativity and thoroughgoing fun. Kyle is a positive person, an optimist, a go-getter and somewhat fearless. He and I share many traits. In addition, he is a true professional in both radio and TV, two bonus skills that he acquired more quickly than anyone I have met.

And now, with **Business English**, Kyle is making a second incursion into the world of publishing, after a first successful foray with his *Verb Circus* series of books and CDs. Having someone like Kyle Millar buzzing around and finding, on his own initiative, ways to be extremely helpful in making Vaughan Systems a solid, profitable outfit is something any company dreams of.

But what is especially interesting for me is that Kyle has finally decided to focus his energy and talents on the business world. It's only logical. He holds an MBA in Finance from Saint Mary's University in Halifax, Canada, and worked both in the Bank of Montreal and the Royal Bank of Canada. In a certain sense, we could say that, up to now, Kyle has been keeping an ace up his sleeve... holding back the best he has to give.

Therefore, I want to encourage anyone who needs to improve his or her command of business English, be it to find a good job or to move up successfully in the business world, to spend some quality time with Kyle Millar, focusing carefully on everything he says. He knows what he's talking about and there are very few people in Spain who can bring together more effectively a persuasive fusion of actual English teaching with business know-how.

Richard Vaughan
President, Vaughan Systems

5

THANKS!

I would like to thank all the people who have helped me with this book and continue to encourage me with all my projects.

To the listeners of my radio show who continually voice their appreciation for my projects, I hope you find this book helpful and interesting.

I would also like to acknowledge the help of various Vaughan Systems collaborators, both past and present who helped in developing some of the materials that appear here, particularly in the Presentations and Negotiations sections and some of the focused translation lists.

I am also grateful to Richard Vaughan for writing the prologue to this book and for his continued support for all my projects, whether they be on radio, television or in print.

A very special thanks to Iris for her encouragement and help with translations and layout ideas, and finally to my parents and my brother Harris, who have always supported me in everything I do.

Kyle Millar

CÓMO DESCARGAR EL AUDIO DEL LIBRO:

Paso 1. Entra en: **http://audios.vaughantienda.com**

Paso 2. Selecciona en Producto: **_"Business English"_** y escribe la clave:**3341VAUGHAN874599**. Pulsa **Entrar**.

Paso 3. Pincha en **el disco** para descargar el audio o en **el triángulo verde** para reproducirlo directamente.

Para cualquier duda puedes consultarnos en **vaughantienda@grupovaughan.com**

CÓMO ACCEDER A LOS VÍDEOS:

Este libro incluye 15 vídeos de una serie llamada **"Top Tips"**. Los vídeos están disponibles en el canal de YouTube **"KyleMillarBusiness"**. Dentro del libro he puesto una serie de códigos QR, que te llevarán directamente al vídeo correspondiente. ¿No sabes usar los códigos QR? Te lo explico: Tienes que bajarte un lector de códigos QR en tu smartphone (hay muchos y son gratis en el *app store*). Usando la aplicación, escanea el código, éste te dirigirá al vídeo de YouTube relacionado con el contenido del libro. Si prefieres ver los vídeos online de una manera más convencional, lo puedes buscar el canal directamente en YouTube y elegir el vídeo con el número que aparece en el libro.

Puedes acceder a los vídeos directamente en el canal aquí:

www.youtube.com/user/KyleMillarBusiness/videos

SOBRE ESTE LIBRO Y CÓMO USARLO:

Este libro ha sido escrito para servir como una herramienta útil para cualquiera que quiera mejorar sus habilidades en el inglés de negocios, o incluso sus habilidades básicas de negocios en general.

Sea una persona desempleada que quiera escribir un curriculum y solicitar un puesto de trabajo en los Estados Unidos, o un profesional experimentado en los negocios buscando un recurso para mejorar su vocabulario de términos claves en inglés, este libro representa una herramienta de referencia definitiva.

Este libro reconoce que hacer negocios con nativos de habla inglesa no solamente significa ser capaz de hablar el idioma. Hay muchas diferencias culturales y de comportamiento que deberían ser aprendidas para interactuar mejor profesionalmente en un entorno laboral inglés.

Business English se divide en las tres partes siguientes:

1. **Getting the job**

2. **Doing business in English**

3. **Advanced business topics**

La sección **"Getting the job"** explica cómo buscar eficientemente puestos de trabajo vacantes, escribir un curriculum y una carta de presentación en inglés para solicitar esos puestos y prepararse para la entrevista de trabajo. También ofrece información y requisitos para trabajar en el extranjero en países angloparlantes.

La segunda parte del libro, **"Doing business in English"** describe las claves del éxito en el entorno del trabajo inglés. Esto incluye tanto tratar con los números y el dinero, inglés por teléfono, por email y en reuniones, como darte las herramientas necesarias para ser eficaz en presentaciones y negociaciones en inglés.

Por último, la tercera sección del libro, **"Advanced business topics"**, incluye el marketing, las finanzas, la inversión, la contabilidad, los seguros y la economía. En cada sección lo esencial del área de negocios en cuestión está explicado con términos clave mostrados también en castellano.

Al leer los textos, el lector gana conocimientos básicos.

SECCIONES QUE PUEDES ENCONTRAR A LO LARGO DEL LIBRO Y CÓMO USARLO:

Secciones de TIP:
Estas secciones ofrecen puntos que recordar relacionadas con términos clave de negocio.

Puntos claves en inglés:
Estas secciones explican la gramática o consejos del idioma inglés relacionados con un concepto dado en el texto.

Secciones de Ejemplo:
Estas secciones muestran ejemplos prácticos del tema explicado en el texto.

Secciones Business Bits:
Estas secciones son clases cortas de inglés, independientes del texto. A menudo incluyen una explicación en español y puede que sea un ejercicio para mejorar la agilidad con expresiones de negocios, una lista de traducciones de jerga típica de oficina, u otras lecciones varias. También incluyen a menudo un audio descargable.

LOS CONTENIDOS DEL MARGEN DE LIBRO:

En el margen puedes encontrar la terminología clave que está marcada en negrita en el texto. **En azul oscuro puedes encontrar los términos que pueden ser vocabulario nuevo** para el lector, mientras que la terminología clave de negocios está en azul más claro.

OTROS CONTENIDOS:

Los "Vocabulary lists":
Hay varias listas de vocabulario específico en este libro, especialmente en la última sección, dedicadas a temas de negocios avanzados.

Los "Translation lists":
Las listas de traducción ofrecen una excelente oportunidad para reforzar el entendimiento de terminología de negocios y vocabulario a la vez que se practican estructuras gramaticales clave. Las listas de traducción también tienen audio descargable.

Audio:
El audio es un compañero importante en el proceso de aprendizaje y acompaña muchas de las secciones de Business Bits, además de las listas de vocabulario y las listas de traducción. Ver la sección de como descargar el audio del libro para encontrar las instrucciones de descarga. Al final del libro se encuentra una guía completa de los archivos de audio.

Vídeos:
Los vídeos complementan el material en este libro, demostrando errores comunes en el ámbito de negocio y cómo corregirlos. Ofrecen ejemplos prácticos de comportamiento, particularmente relacionados con el estar en entrevistas de trabajo, hablar por teléfono, dar presentaciones, y negociar.

SECTION A

GETTING THE JOB!

[Conseguir el trabajo]

CHAPTER 1

THE JOB SEARCH

[Cómo encontrar
el puesto ideal para ti]

THE JOB SEARCH

Finding a job can be challenging and stressful. It can often be difficult to find a job in an area that you are interested in or have studied for. Knowing how to search for job vacancies, apply for suitable jobs and perform well in the job interview are all keys to getting that job you're looking for.

Your path to getting the job begins with a **thorough** and careful job search.

Thorough: *'exhaustivo'.*

ONLINE JOB SEARCH ENGINES

There are many ways you can find job vacancies. Online job search engines can be very effective for helping you find and apply for jobs in your field of interest.

Some of the more common search engines you might want to try are:

- **www.infojobs.com**
- **www.monster.com**
- **www.careerbuilder.com**
- **www.simplyhired.es**
- **www.indeed.com**

Simply searching in Google for "job websites" or "employment opportunities" will also yield numerous results. Depending on where you live, you may also have local web-based job databases.

These websites will typically request that you set up an account with them and upload one or more **CVs**. **Be sure to invest the time to build a good profile on these websites.** A little time invested **up front** will enable you to quickly submit numerous high-quality applications later.

CV: *'currículo', o 'curriculum'.*

Up front - In advance: *'por adelantado'.*

In most cases, these websites will allow you to search for job vacancies according to industry, location, occupation or level of experience. Frequently searching these websites can be an effective way to discover and apply for a high volume of jobs, increasing your chances of finding one suitable for you.

Keep a separate record, in a notebook or on your computer on each job you have applied for and updates on any feedback you may have received. Sometimes applying online can be so quick and easy that you can easily lose track of the jobs you have applied for and what you have searched.

JOB SEARCH AND RECRUITMENT VOCABULARY

Consider the following vocabulary related to recruitment. Knowing these terms will make your online application experience more efficient.

Contratar	To hire
Formación académica	Education
Solicitar un trabajo	To apply for a job
Proceso de contratación	Recruitment process
Candidatos para un puesto	Candidates/Applicants
Referencias laborales	References
Titulaciones, cualificaciones	Degrees, Certificates, Qualifications
Empresas de trabajo (temporal)	Employment agencies
Ubicación	Location
Cazatalentos	Head-hunter
Curriculum Vitae	CV/résumé
Anuncio de empleo	Advertisement
Solicitar	To apply for
Buscar	To search
Profesión	Occupation
Publicar	To post
Apuntarse	To sign up (for)
Sector	Field
Repasar	To review
Vacante	A vacancy or job opening
Subcontratar, Externalizar	To outsource
Fortalezas / Debilidades	Strengths / weaknesses

LINKEDIN

LinkedIn is a very popular social media / professional networking site. Through the website you can create a profile then search and connect to people in your field of employment interest.

LinkedIn has become an important recruiting tool for employers of all sizes, and job seekers should know how to best use the tool to aid their hunt.

According to Nicole Williams, a career expert and LinkedIn's connection director, 85 of the **Fortune 100** companies use LinkedIn to find potential hires. Unfortunately, simply having an account won't do much for your job search. **More and more** hiring managers are being proactive and looking through LinkedIn profiles to fill vacant positions. For this reason, it's important that you make your profile complete.

Skills should be kept up to date and detailed, as should work experience. More detailed and complete profiles are much more likely to get noticed.

To **draw attention** to your profile, you can also use the platform to share news or articles relevant to your industry of interest. This proves that you are actively **in touch with** the industry.

Any positive updates to your profile, such as new skills you are developing or volunteer work will help attract attention.

NETWORKING

Networking is still one of the best ways to find out about job vacancies and get your application to the right person. With successful networking you develop personal contacts who work in different fields. By growing this network, often through social interaction, you can become connected to people who can direct you towards employment vacancies.

For effective networking, it is important to be pleasant, social and interesting. It will become clear if you are only dealing with people for your own personal gain. Be genuine, show interest and use your communication skills.

As a more structured form of networking, you may wish to consider joining an industry association in the industry you would like to work in. Particularly if you have studied in this field, joining an association (which you can find online) enables you to stay up to date with current developments and, more importantly, network with people in the field, which could lead to an employment opportunity.

There are also online discussion groups and social networking groups that can provide similar advantages.

Fortune 100 - "Fortune" magazine's top 100 companies based on annual revenue. Fortune is more famous for its "Fortune 500" list.

More and more: *'cada vez más'.*

To draw attention - To attract attention: *'atraer atención'.*

To be in touch with: *'estar en contacto con'. Es mucho más común decir* "in touch with" *que* "in contact with".

Networking - Social interaction for the purpose of recognizing, creating, or acting upon business opportunities.

"To network": *'hacer contactos'.*

Trade fair: *'feria de muestras'*.

TRADE FAIRS

Trade fairs are also a great way to meet potential employers and ask direct questions to them about their companies and potential vacancies.

You can search online for a list of relevant job fairs in your area or an area that you would like to work in.

To tailor: *'personalizar'*.

At trade fairs you can also ask companies how you should **tailor** your CV and cover letter to best approach them.

We will look at CVs and cover letters next.

BUSINESS BITS

Office Talk!

PISTA DE AUDIO 1

A continuación encontrarás cinco frases típicas de uso corriente que puedes oír en una oficina donde se habla inglés. Tapa la columna de la derecha y traduce en voz alta las frases.

¿Alguna vez has pensado en acudir a una empresa de trabajo temporal?	**Have you ever thought about using a temp agency?**
Nunca he estado tan ocupado en mi vida.	**I've never been this busy in my life.**
Hay un señor al teléfono que quiere hablar con usted.	**There's a gentleman on the line who would like to speak to you.**
¿Podrías apuntar su número?	**Can you get his phone number?**
Dile que le devolveré la llamada.	**Tell him I'll call him back.**

CHAPTER 2

HOW TO PREPARE A CV IN ENGLISH

[Cómo escribir un curriculum ganador en inglés]

HOW TO PREPARE A CV IN ENGLISH

Preparing a good CV (or résumé) is essential to being successful in your employment search. It is important to invest time and care in developing a CV that will make you **stand out** and highlight your suitability for each job you apply for.

To stand out -
To be distinctive or prominent: *'destacar'*.

In addition to language, there are many cultural differences that have to be considered when it comes to preparing a CV or résumé for a specific employer in a specific country.

While they serve a similar purpose, a CV is not the same as a résumé.

A proper CV gives in-depth and structured information about the professional experience and qualifications of a person, whereas the résumé is usually written in a shorter form, **not to exceed two pages**. The résumé format is typical in North America, whereas a more detailed CV is more common in Europe.

From this point on, we will refer to this document simply as a 'CV'. While there are a number of CV formats, we will focus in this book on the most common, chronological CV format as it offers the reader the most logical order of events, showing advancement from one position or life stage to another and the development of your career.

 TIP

Keep it brief! Often managers will have hundreds of CVs to look at and they may only spend 15 – 20 seconds taking an initial look at each. Keep your document short and to the point.

There is no one single template to follow to always create a perfect CV. Here we outline general ideas and points to keep in mind as you build yours.

It is important to remember that the structure and specific content you choose should be dictated by the type of job and company you are applying to.

First, let's consider some general tips to keep in mind when creating your CV.

TIPS FOR WRITING A GOOD CV

1. Prepare several CVs

Prepare several focused CVs, each tailored to a different target job or field.

The odds: *'las probabilidades'.*

While it might seem like a lot of work, this will greatly increase **the odds** of an employer finding your profile suitable for the position they are trying to fill.

2. Length

To the point: *'al grano'.*

In most cases, your CV should not exceed two pages and each page you use should be full. Keep in mind that many managers who will be reviewing CVs may have a hundred or more applicants to choose from. Keep your CV short and **to the point.** Consider that managers may only spend 15-20 seconds initially scanning your CV, so making it concise and eye-catching is very important.

3. Prioritize Your CV Content

Within each section of your CV it's important to prioritize the content so that your most important and relevant experience is listed first, with key accomplishments shown at the top of each position. Once again, use keywords to make each point relevant to the job you're applying for.

To decide what is relevant, put yourself in a potential employer's position and consider if the information on your CV helps convince them that you are a worthwhile candidate to interview for the position in question.

TIP

Quantify as much information as you can - numbers, dollar signs, percentages can all help to make your case for getting selected to interview.

4. Keywords

To draw attention: *'atraer atención'.*

In each version of your CV, include focused keywords to **draw** the reader's **attention** to specific attributes of your profile. Many companies even use software to search CVs for specific terms they may see as desirable.

The keywords you choose should match words found in job descriptions or postings for available positions and help tailor your CV to emphasize these desired attributes. These keywords should include specific technical skills, personality traits, relevant credentials and details of your work with previous employers.

TIP

By using job search engines, you can locate similar job postings and get a good idea of what keywords might be best for the job you are targeting.

In addition to specific qualifications understood within the industry you are applying to work in, descriptive adjectives also serve as important keywords.

Consider the following adjectives to strengthen your CV:

English Adjective	Spanish Translation
Determined	Determinado
Hard-working	Trabajador
Diligent	Diligente
Trustworthy	Digno de confianza
Team-player	Colaborador
Motivated	Motivado
Reliable	Fiable
Self-starter	Emprendedor
Persistent	Persistente
Dynamic	Dinámico
Organized	Organizado
Professional	Profesional
Passionate	Entusiasta

5. Use descriptive adjectives and verbs:

Similar to the keywords suggested above, use descriptive adjectives and active verbs to make your CV and cover letter stronger. When describing your education and work experience, take advantage of the opportunity to use active verbs.

Consider the following list of verbs and choose ones that best relate to the job area you are applying for:

50 SUPER VERBS TO MAKE YOUR CV STAND OUT:

Verb in English	Past tense in English	Spanish verb (infinitive)
Management skills:		
1. To administer	**Administered**	*Supervisar, administrar*
2. To assign	**Assigned**	*Asignar*
3. To contract	**Contracted**	*Contratar*
4. To consolidate	**Consolidated**	*Consolidar*
5. To coordinate	**Coordinated**	*Coordinar*
6. To delegate	**Delegated**	*Delegar*
7. To direct	**Directed**	*Dirigir*
8. To organize	**Organized**	*Organizar*
9. To plan	**Planned**	*Programar*
10. To supervise	**Supervised**	*Supervisar*
Communication skills		
11. To address	**Addressed**	*Dirigirse a*
12. To author	**Authored**	*Crear, escribir*
13. To develop	**Developed**	*Desarrollar*
14. To edit	**Edited**	*Editar*
15. To motivate	**Motivated**	*Motivar*
16. To negotiate	**Negotiated**	*Negociar*
17. To persuade	**Persuaded**	*Persuadir, Convencer*
18. To publicize	**Publicized**	*Hacer publicidad, Publicitar*
19. To translate	**Translated**	*Traducir*
20. To write	**Wrote**	*Escribir*
Technical skills		
21. To assemble	**Assembled**	*Montar*

Verb in English	Past tense in English	Spanish verb (infinitive)
22. To calculate	Calculated	Calcular
23. To engineer	Engineered	Diseñar, Construir
24. To maintain	Maintained	Mantener
25. To operate	Operated	Operar
26. To overhaul	Overhauled	Revisar, Ajustar
27. To program	Programmed	Programar
28. To solve	Solved	Resolver
29. To train	Trained	Entrenar, Formar
30. To upgrade	Upgraded	Actualizar
Financial skills		
31. To allocate	Allocated	Distribuir, Repartir, Asignar
32. To analyze	Analyzed	Analizar
33. To appraise	Appraised	Asesorar
34. To audit	Audited	Auditar
35. To balance	Balanced	Equilibrar, cuadrar
36. To budget	Budgeted	Hacer un presupuesto, Gestionar fondos
37. To calculate	Calculated	Calcular
38. To forecast	Forecasted	Prever
39. To project	Projected	Prever, estimar
40. To research	Researched	Investigar
Creative skills		
41. To act	Acted	Actuar
42. To create	Created	Crear
43. To design	Designed	Diseñar
44. To establish	Established	Establecer
45. To illustrate	Illustrated	Ilustrar, Demostrar

Verb in English	Past tense in English	Spanish verb (infinitive)
46. To introduce	**Introduced**	*Presentar, Introducir*
47. To invent	**Invented**	*Inventar*
48. To perform	**Performed**	*Llevar a cabo*
49. To revitalize	**Revitalized**	*Revitalizar*
50. To shape	**Shaped**	*Dar forma*

TIP

When using bullet lists in any section of your CV, make sure that each item is grammatically formatted the same in terms of tense and structure. Each job should have a minimum of three **bulleted** items with the most relevant duties listed first.

EX

Imagine you have worked as a shop clerk in a clothing store in the center of Seville. In your job, you took payments from customers, handled returns and gave advice on their purchases.

Many people may simply include the job as follows on their CV:

June 2012 – Present: - **K and M Clothing**, Seville, Spain

Store clerk

Job experience listed in this way won't impress anyone. By adding a few active verbs, we can describe the same position much more impressively:

June 2012 – Present: - **K and M Clothing**, Seville, Spain

Customer Service Specialist

- Addressed customer needs and solved their problems
- Worked efficiently both in a team setting and under minimal supervision.
- Trained new staff on best practices and efficient procedures

In this listing, your experience in the clothing store seems much more valuable to almost any employer. Remember, your use of language is essential in presenting your profile as attractively as possible.

THE CV FORMAT:

There are a variety of common styles of CVs you can choose from. The basic sections to include are:

1. **Personal information**
2. **Objective**
3. **Education**
4. **Employment background**
5. **Additional information** (including language skills and specific technical abilities)

1. Personal information

Make sure you include your full name, mailing address, home phone number, cell phone number, and email address. Make sure to use a personal email address, not a current work email address.

Be accessible!

Also, make sure you have a professional sounding voicemail message on your phone to receive messages if you are unable to answer your phone.

Álvaro Álvarez

E-mail- alvaro.alvarez@gmail.com

Av. Diagonal 25, 5, B, Barcelona, 08019, Barcelona, Spain

Phone: +34 935 34 XXXX • Mobile: +34 6XX XX XXXX

2. Objective (or "Summary") Statement

This optional section gives you another chance to make yourself stand out. Including an objective helps the reader quickly see who you are and what you are looking for.

If you include an objective in your CV, it's important to tailor it to match the job you are applying for. The more specific you are, the better chance you have of being considered for the job.

Your academic and work experience will be detailed later in the document, so this section is simply an overview of who you are and what you are looking for in terms of employment.

An alternative to the "Objective" is a "Summary" or "Personal Statement" which communicates specifically what you have to offer for a specific job, including skills and experiences that make you a strong and unique candidate.

1. A young person seeking an entry-level position:
Objective:

A position in a well-established organization with a stable environment that will lead to a lasting career in the field of finance.

EX

2. A young person with three years of work experience:

Summary:

A reliable and hard-working team player with three years of experience in the computer sales field. I have excellent interpersonal and communication skills and work well under pressure. I seek a challenging opportunity for growth within the IT sales field.

3. An applicant with no significant work experience:

Summary:

As a recent graduate from the University of Seville, I have applied my training in media relations and marketing through volunteer work. I am continuing to develop my experience in media relations and seek a position with professional growth opportunities in this field.

3. Education

To go beyond:
'ir más allá'.

Terminology used for education can't always be directly translated because often the type of education differs from country to country, making the differences **go beyond** language. Furthermore, there can be many subtle differences in the terminology used and the education systems themselves are differently structured.

For example, in the United States, the SAT serves a similar purpose as the Spanish *'selectividad'*, but by having completed the *'selectividad'* you can not say on your CV that you have taken the SAT test. The SAT is a standardized test for most college admissions in the United States and has possible scores ranging from 600 to 2400.

The following general guide may be helpful to you in describing your education on your CV:

Spanish	UK English	American English
Educación Primaria y Educación Secundaria Obligatoria	Primary School	Elementary school & middle school / junior high
Formación Profesional	Vocational school	Vocational College or Career College
Bachillerato	A-Levels	High school
Selectividad	Exams	S.A.T. exams
Grado	Bachelor's degree	Bachelor's degree
Máster	Master's Degree	Master's
Doctorado	Ph. D.	Ph. D

When speaking about education, it is important to know how academic qualifications are named in both British and American English. Be sure that your academic background is explained in terminology understandable to the target audience of your CV.

 Commonly confused words:

Career vs. Degree

The word "career" in English refers to your *'vida profesional'*, which may or may not be in the area you studied.

Education vs. Formation

Your "education" refers to your *'formación académica'* while a "formation" is simply *'formación'* in the sense of the process of being formed or shaped. The word "formation" doesn't belong in your CV.

When talking about your education, you can also include programs you are currently studying.

 Consider the following example for someone looking for a job in **IT**:

EDUCATION / CERTIFICATION
Master of Management Information Systems (MMIS), expected 2016
Indiana State University, Indianapolis, Indiana

Bachelor of Science, Business Administration, 2000
University of Atlanta, Atlanta, Georgia

IT - Stands for "Information Technology": *'informática'.*

Notice how this person has not used verbs to actively describe what they accomplished or developed. Using action verbs in this section is optional, but it gives the applicant another chance to stand out and fit with qualifications mentioned in a job posting.

Now let's take a look at some examples using descriptions of each educational experience:

 1. A young person seeking an entry-level position:

Sept. 2011 - Present, University of Navarra

- Candidate for Bachelor in Mechanical Engineering degree
- Academic course highlights: Company Property Management; Marketing; Economics; English
- Achieved top grades in Marketing and Economics classes

2. A young professional with a few years of work experience:

Troy Central College, Troy, NY, May 2008
Major: Computer Science, Minor: Management

- Achieved excellent grades
- Gained experience with a variety of computing languages and applications

4. Employment background

This section can also be called "Work Experience", "Work History" or "Employment History". In it; you should include the names and locations of the companies you worked for, the positions you held, your employment dates for each job and the duties you performed.

Remember:

Detailing the duties you performed is the most important part of the "Work Experience" section. You must be accurate and concise but also highlight the responsabilities that are most relevant to the position you are seeking.

While it is acceptable to write full sentences in paragraph form for each position you held, it is more common to create a bulleted list of the duties you performed.

I work <u>as</u> a businessman. I work <u>like</u> a slave.

¿Entiendes la diferencia entre **"like"** y **"as"**?

As= Esencia/Función/Trabajo

Like= Comparación

Ella trabaja como dentista.

¿Qué palabra usamos: **"as"** o **"like"**?

Ante la duda, siempre hay que hacer la misma pregunta: ¿Es dentista? ¿Sí o no?

Si la respuesta es **sí**, hay que utilizar **"as"**. Si la respuesta es **no**, hay que utilizar **"like"**, ya que se trata de una comparación.

De hecho, en la frase citada, si lo correcto fuera "like", entonces la frase en español tendría que ser "Ella trabaja como una dentista (como si fuera una dentista)".

Nicolás vive como un rey.	¿Es un rey? No.	**Nicholas lives like a King.**
Trabajamos como esclavos.	¿Somos esclavos? No.	**We work like slaves.**
Como orador, es bueno.	¿Es orador? Sí.	**As a public speaker, he's good.**
Me gustaría vivir como ella.	¿Soy ella? No.	**I'd like to live like she does.**
Trabajo como tú.	¿Soy tú? No.	**I work like you.**
Como a él, me encanta el cine.	¿Soy él? No.	**Like him, I love cinema.**

EX

1. A young professional with a few years of work experience:

<u>*June 2011 – Present:*</u> **BBBA Bank**, Madrid, Spain

Lending officer

- Exceeded business lending target figures by 35% in 2012
- Significantly improved profitability on bank branch lending portfolio
- Built and maintained key business relationships with several high-value collaborators

2. A well-experienced professional

SanJuan Electronics, Software Engineer, <u>*August '11 – present*</u>

- Developing current release of Anti-virus software using C++ and Java
- Representing the company internationally at meetings and consumer conferences
- Working closely with new developers in India tech center

**Notice that the format of presentation is different for these two examples. This is fine. What is important is that the format is uniform with the CV.

Carefully consider what you actually accomplished in the job, list the specific activities and duties that you were responsible for, and craft exciting and concise bulleted items representing those activities.

If you have extensive work experience, only include the most recent three or four positions, unless you have a very good reason to include more.

"BA": *significa* **"Bachelor of Arts"**, *una carrera de cuatro años.*

Otras carreras comunes son: **"BS"** - **"Bachelor of Science"**, **"MA"** - **"Master of Arts"** *un máster que suele durar por lo menos 2 años.* **"MS"** - **"Master of Science"** *un máster que suele durar por lo menos 2 años.*

No work experience? Don't worry.

If you are young, or a recent graduate, it is understandable that you might not have any work experience. You can compensate for this by emphasizing other experiences and relevant skills throughout your CV. Be sure to include any internships or volunteer work that you have done.

If you have a job description available, pay close attention to it and try to emphasize the skills it mentions in your CV.

If you don't have experience, it is often a good idea to include a "Summary" in your résumé, instead of simply a statement of "Objective" as mentioned earlier. Consider the following:

Summary:
"Recent graduate with **BA** in economics. Excellent research, time management and problem solving skills. Highly organized with the ability to meet deadlines and manage multiple projects."

5. Additional information and sections (including language and computer skills and specific technical abilities)

Talking about your level of English

This section is an appropriate place to mention your language skills; however, depending on the nature of the job, you may want to have a separate section entitled "Language Skills". When including your English level, be honest and detailed, and mention any certifications you may have (such as Cambridge, Advanced or Proficiency), as well as courses such as the Vaughan MIP "Master en Inglés Profesional".

Be honest!

Don't lie about your English level. The truth will come out in an interview. Hiring managers know a liar when they see one.

Obviously, if you are reading this book, you are aware of the importance of English and other language skills. As a non-native English speaker, it is important to honestly convey your language skills on your CV.

When describing your language skills, consider the following terms and what they REALLY mean:

Conversational: This term indicates basic language ability. You can participate in basic communication, but you get lost in anything beyond a very simple conversation.

Proficient: This term indicates that you have a higher command of verb tenses, and ability with more sophisticated sentence structures. You can modify language to match a situation, and are relatively agile with basic structures.

Fluent: You can follow almost any conversation, and keep up with changing topics. You understand many common expressions and use them appropriately. You can also identify many accents and dialects.

Native: You grew up speaking English at home and use it like other native speakers.

Finally, you may also want to indicate the way in which you're fluent: in speaking, writing, or reading. These three categories of communication count as separate skill sets. If a job specifies language ability of one kind or the other, be sure to indicate that ability on your CV.

Computer Skills

Another section to include if relevant to the job is "Computer Skills".

The way you present computer skills depends on the type of job you are applying for. Obviously, if you are applying for a job in IT, the computer skills section will be prominent. It could even go between "Education" and "Employment History".

Example of a Computer Skills section on a CV of an applicant to an IT job:

 Computer Skills:

Operating Systems: Windows 7/8/2000/NT/XP, Windows 98/95, Macintosh OS.

LAN Administration: Windows 2000 Server, Windows NT 3.51/4.0, Novell 3.12/4.1.

Software: Microsoft SQL, SNA, SMS, Site Server & IIS, CA XCOM, SAS *Certifications:* Candidate for MCDBA, Candidate for CCNA/CCDA, Candidate for MCSE, Microsoft Certified System Administrator, Novell Certified Administrator, Novell Certified Engineer.

For a non-technology job, you may simply include your computer skills in your additional skills section in one point:

Computer Skills:
Comfortable with MS Office Suite (Word, Excel and PowerPoint), Internet and email proficient.

You may wish to include sections such as "Volunteer work" or "Accomplishments and interests" if you feel you have credentials in these areas that could make you a more impressive candidate. Some people also include "Interests and Hobbies". This can serve to show that you are **well-rounded**.

Well rounded:
'bien equilibrado'.

While these additional sections should be kept fairly brief, they can serve to add content to your CV, especially if you have limited work experience or educational background.

Should I include references?

Many employers will want to speak to specific references such as former bosses, employees or clients. Generally, simply stating "references available upon request" is a good starting point, allowing the potential employer to advise you whom they want to contact.

TIP

Apart from your CV, it is a good idea to form a list of reliable people whom you would be prepared to approach to be a reference for you if asked. Be sure to ask references if you can use them before offering their contact details to a potential employer.

FIVE THINGS TO AVOID!

To proofread:
'revisar' o
'corregir'.

1. Spelling mistakes and general lack of attention to detail

Do not expect your computer's spell checking program to find all possible errors. Have someone **proofread** your document.

2. Strange e-mail addresses and unreliable phone numbers

Make sure your address is professional sounding. Even if you are using a free web-based e-mail provider, choose a name that is professional and not shared with anyone else. Make sure that you have a working voicemail on the phone number you provide. If another person, such as a roommate or family member could be answering the phone, make sure they are reliable and prepared to take the message properly.

Are you serious?

Personal e-mail addresses are free and it only takes about five minutes to set up an account with Gmail, so you have no excuse to have one that doesn't seem professional.

If you only have an account that doesn't seem professional, get a new one and include it on your CV.

Consider the following addresses and how a hiring manager would feel seeing them on your CV:

BAD	GOOD
smurfy67@aol.com	john_mcdermid@gmail.com
partygirl100@hotmail.com	cristina.alvarez@gmail.com
tommfs1982@yahoo.com	t.sanderson@gmail.com

The bad addresses show immaturity and a lack of professionalism.

3. Pictures

Believe it or not, in most Anglo-Saxon countries it is strongly encouraged **not** to include a picture of yourself on your CV.

Employers like to avoid the possibility of discrimination based on the appearance of a candidate they hire. Attached images can also make the file size of your document undesirably large or cause complications with the electronic CV sorting programs used by many companies.

4. The use of "lazy" words or phrasing

Do not use terminology such as "etc.", "same as above" or "..." on your CV. Be sure to use customized wording, including key words related to the job available.

Remember: Often CVs submitted by email will be electronically scanned for key words. Be sure your CV contains words describing your skills and experience that have been mentioned in the job posting.

5. Expecting international employers to be familiar with local acronyms or terminology

Be sure to clearly spell out degree programs in full, and include a common acronym afterwards in parenthesis if necessary.

PRESENTATION OF YOUR CV:

If you are presenting your CV on paper, be sure to use quality, solid color paper and that the printing is of high quality. Professional fonts such as 'Times New Roman' or 'Arial' are most common and best used in size 10 to 12 point type. Headings can be in size 14 to distinguish them from the body of the document.

After preparing your CV, be sure to have it read by someone with "fresh eyes" to look for accuracy and check for errors. Ask them to describe you based on the document to see if it has done an effective job of accurately portraying you.

EXAMPLE CVS:

1. Javier Córdoba:

A young professional with a master's degree and a few years' work experience.

Javier Córdoba Ruiz

E-mail: javiercordobaruiz@hotmail.com
Avd. Diagonal 25, 5, B, Barcelona, 08019, Barcelona, Spain
Phone: +34 935 34 XXXX • Mobile:+34 6XX XX XXXX

OBJECTIVE

Challenging employment with opportunities for professional development related to finance or investments in Europe.

EDUCATION

Master's degree, Finance, 2010
Universitat Autónoma de Barcelona, Spain

Bachelor's degree, Business Administration, 2008
Universitat Autónoma de Barcelona, Spain

EMPLOYMENT HISTORY

June 2011 – Present: - **BBBA Bank**, Barcelona, Spain

Lending officer

- Exceeded business lending target figures by 35% in 2012
- Significantly improved profitability on bank branch lending portfolio
- Built and maintained key business relationships with several high-value collaborators

May 2010 – June 2011: - **Bon Systems**, Barcelona, Spain

Payroll assistant, taxation specialist

- Processed payments to over 350 staff members
- Developed and maintained a database to ensure timely payment of all staff payments and payroll taxes

ADDITIONAL SKILLS AND QUALIFICATIONS

- Highly proficient in common accounting software packages, as well as MS Office tools, E-mail and Exchange
- Native Spanish speaker with fluency in English and Intermediate French
- Strong academic and practical knowledge of financial markets and products

Fíjate como los "bullet points" siguen el mismo formato y sangría en todo el currículum.

Utiliza verbos activos para explicar sus logros.

En esta sección, el candidato aprovecha para mencionar cualificaciones especialmente relevantes para el puesto en concreto.

2. Héctor Martínez:

A University student with some internship experience.

Héctor Martínez

hmartinez@gmail.com
Carrer Barcelona 12, 7 B, Girona, 17002, Girona, Spain
Phone: (34) 972 34 XXXX Mobile: (34) 623 45 XXXX

En tu lista vertical, se puede incluir un punto después de cada elemento, pero es más común no hacerlo. Lo importante es la cohesión a lo largo del documento.

EDUCATION

Sept. 2010 - Present, **University of Navarra**
- Candidate for Bachelor in Mechanical Engineering degree
- Academic course highlights: Company Property Management; Marketing; Economics; English
- Achieved top grades class in Marketing and Economics

May 2009, **Certified Public Accounting Training (CPA)**

EMPLOYMENT

July 2009 - Sep 2009, **Intel Products Co**., Zaragoza, Spain
CPU Assembly Engineer (Internship)
- Analyzed yield ratio trends
- Participated in the training of marketing, business process modeling and analysis at Intel University
- Visualized a project review with impressive presentation and multi-media animation, which was highly appreciated by department manager.

June 2008 - July 2008, **GF Fund Management Co., LTD**.
Campus Intern
- Analyzed a variety of investment products
- Formulated an effective scheme for market popularization and network marketing

Aunque no ha tenido un trabajo oficial, aprovecha su experiencia como becario para destacar cualificaciones y experiencias prácticas y aplicables al puesto.

AWARDS

2007-2009, **Second-Class Scholarship for Excellent Students of University of Navarra**

ADDITIONAL SKILLS

Languages:
- *English* –Advanced spoken and written skills. Cambridge advanced certificate.

Computer Skills:
- Professional Certificate of Assistant Information Officer (AIO).
- C++, VBA, Provision, JMP, AutoCAD, 3ds Max, Photoshop, SolidWorks, After Effects

3. Simon Rockwell:
A high school student looking for summer work.

Simon Rockwell

6 Elm Avenue, Stockler, CA 91733
Home: 123.456.7890 Cell: 766.444.1234
simonrocks@email.com

SUMMARY
A hard-working student with experience with children. Interested in a paid summer camp working up to 20 hours per week.

EDUCATION
Stockler Central High School, Stockler, California
High School Diploma anticipated in May 2014
A- average

Electives: Art, Economics, Social Studies

Activities: Band (trumpet) and sports (baseball, football)

SPECIAL SKILLS & INTERSTS
- Love to work with children
- Very creative at making attractive posters and flyers using graphic software
- Able to follow written instructions
- Good with Microsoft Word, Excel, and PowerPoint
- Can do internet research using MS Explorer and Firefox
- Travelling with family

Como Simon no tiene experiencia laboral, usa esta sección para presentar cualidades deseables para el puesto en concreto.

VOLUNTEER & COMMUNITY SERVICE
Stockler Hospital, Stockler CA - **Ongoing**
Pediatric Ward Volunteer
- Read, watch television or play games with children
- Make sure the play area is neat and toys are put away after use
- Run errands or do assignments from staff
- "Run for the cure" Cancer charity, City of Stockler, Summers 2005 - 2008

Volunteer
- **Raised** over $800 for the American Cancer Society
- Assisted in coordinating delivery of donations in three neighborhoods

"Ongoing": significa que 'hasta estas fechas'.

GOALS
Planning to study Psychology or Music as a major in college

Travel and work abroad

"Raise money": significa en este caso 'recaudar dinero' para la caridad.

4. Pamela Sánchez:
A software engineer with several years of experience.

Fíjate como este curriculum sigue un formato un poco diferente. Este formato cuadra bien con su perfil, permitiendo una presentación detallada de su amplia experiencia laboral.

Pamela Sánchez
Av. del Cid, 35, 46018, Valencia, Spain
(555) 555-5555
pamela.sanchez@fakemail.com

EXPERIENCE

SanJuan Electronics, Software Engineer
August '11 - present
Developing current release using C++ and Java,
Representing the company internationally at meetings and consumer conferences.

Working closely with new developers in India tech center.

ABCo Inc., Computer Company Training Program
June '11 - August '11
Member of the "Computer Company Boot camp" program, an intensive three-month training program for select software engineers. The three-month program covered advanced topics in software engineering, SQL, C++, J2EE, XML, Windows 2000 Server, Unix, UML, and various company products.

Consultant
January '08 - June '11
Consultant for high school in the outer Boston area.
Tutored the instructors for the AP programming class in the Java software language.
Helped set up development environment for the classroom.

TECHNICAL
- **Computer Languages**: C++, Java, C, ASP.NET, SQL
- **Applications**: MS Visual Studio, Eclipse
- **Application Server**: JBoss, Tomcat
- **Operating Systems**: Windows, Unix, Linux
- **Database Systems**: SQL Server, MySQL
- **Certifications**: CCNA, Unicenter Certified Engineer

EDUCATION
ABC College, Troy, NY, May 2008
Major: Computer Science, Minor: Management
- Achieved excellent grades
- Gained experience with a variety of computing languages and applications

ACTIVITIES AND INTERESTS
- Volunteer work – 4 years volunteering at the "Georgetown Lung Cancer Awareness Relay" in various capacities.
- Sports – Have played competitive football for 7 years.
- Travel – Have visited 14 countries.

Como busca un trabajo en informática, los conocimientos técnicos merecen su propia sección.

Mencionar estas cosas sirve para mostrar que es una persona bien equilibrada.

5. Amy Broadbent:
College student seeking an opportunity to gain relevant work experience.

Amy Broadbent
amy.b.broadbent@gmail.com - 630-532-7807
64 Pinewood Crescent, Chicago, Illinois, 23427

Summary:
A college student looking to broaden my experiences in the business world while continuing my education.

Experience:
Human Resources Intern in Healthcare - Insurance

June 2011 - August 2011   Blue Cross and Blue Shield Association   Chicago, Ill.
- Recruited new employees based on hiring managers' needs
- Assisted human resources team with event planning
- Analyzed errors in budget reports and fixed them

Sales Associate, Retail/Merchandising

October 2008 - September 2010   Brookstone   Oakbrook, Ill.
- Assisted customers in finding their desired items
- Kept the store clean and presentable throughout the day
- Used sales techniques to encourage the purchase of protection plans on items sold

Education:
Bachelor of Business Administration in Accounting

September 2010 - June 2014   DePaul University   Chicago, Illinois

High School Diploma

September 2006 - June 2010   Downers High School   Downers Grove, Illinois

Additional skills:
Proficient with QuickBooks Accounting software, MS Office software packages (Excel, Access and Word)
Intermediate level of French (written and spoken)

Accomplishments
As a member of DECA (a business/ marketing club in high school) I placed 3rd in the Travel and Tourism competition, which led me to the state competition.

Volunteer work
Oakbrook "children's miracle" program, fundraising assistant coordinator, 2 years.

Office Talk!

PISTA DE AUDIO 2

A continuación encontrarás cinco frases típicas de uso corriente que puedes oír en una oficina donde se habla inglés. Tapa la columna de la derecha y traduce en voz alta las frases.

¿Estás seguro de que el nuevo sistema nos ahorrará tiempo?	**Are you sure the new system will save us time?**
¿Me ha llamado alguien mientras estaba fuera?	**Were there any calls for me while I was out?**
No me apetece nada discutir con él hoy.	**I really don't feel like arguing with him today.**
La economía está empezando a recuperarse.	**The economy is starting to turn around.**
Buenos días a todos. ¿Podrían prestarme atención, por favor?	**Good morning everyone. May I have your attention?**

CHAPTER 3

PREPARING A COVER LETTER

[Cartas de presentación
que te hagan destacar]

PREPARING A COVER LETTER

A cover letter ("covering letter" in British English) is an important tool for you as a job seeker as it allows you to creatively describe yourself and indicate how you would be perfect for the vacant job.

A cover letter may serve to:

- Introduce your application for a known job vacancy.
- Introduce your CV to inquire about potential employment without a position being known to be available.
- General **networking** requesting help with the applicant's job search.

Networking:
'hacer contactos'.

Your cover letter is your first and best chance to make a good impression. It should be tailored specifically to the job you are applying for and contain adjectives and descriptive wording to relate your skills and experience to the job.

TIP

If you have a personal contact or reference within the company you are applying for, be sure to mention this in the letter.

FORMAT

Your cover letter should be one page in length and is generally formatted as follows:

1. **Header**
2. **Introduction**
3. **Body**
4. **Closing**

Header:

The header is the section where you include your own address as well as the recipient's contact information and the date.

After the name of the addressee, it is appropriate to use either a **comma (,) or a colon (:)**.

Immediately above the addressee, you may wish to include a line indicating the purpose of the letter.

Para ver más vocabulario sobre símbolos y puntuación, ver la página 94 de la sección sobre **"Numbers and Money"**.

For example:

Re: Openings in your software development department

Or

Re: New account manager position

The standard format for addressing the letter is as follows:

Your Contact Information:

Name
Address
City, Province, Postal Code
Phone Number
Email Address

Date

Employer Contact Information (if you have it)**:**

Name
Title
Company
Address
City, State, Postal / Zip Code
Date
Salutation to the recipient (e.g. Dear Mr. Jones:)

Whenever possible, use the name of the individual who will be reading the letter (i.e. Dear Mr. Brownlow, Dear Ms. Bartlett). People love to hear their own name. Using it shows that you appreciate their authority.

If you don't know the name of the individual, you may address the letter "Dear Sir or Madam", "To the attention of the hiring manager", or "To whom it may concern".

Mr. and Ms.

In professional writing, it is best to refer to men as "Mr." and women as "Ms.", unless you are certain that a woman is married. If that is the case, you can use "Mrs.".

Introduction:

The introduction should be a short paragraph designed to catch the attention of the reader and state your intentions.

In this section include information on why you are writing. Mention the position you are applying for and where you found the job listing. Include the name of a mutual contact, if you have one.

Body:

The body of the cover letter serves to **highlight** your qualifications and suitability for the job. In this section you include skills, academic and practical qualifications and past experience. Other key information such as licenses or availability for work can be included here as well.

To highlight: *'hacer destacar'.*

Clearly describe what you have to offer the employer. Mention specifically how your qualifications match the job you are applying for. Remember, you are interpreting your CV, not repeating it.

Closing:

Here, you summarize your letter and emphasize your suitability for the position and thank the employer for considering you for the position. It is also important to indicate how you will **follow up.** For example you may mention that you will contact the employer by telephone shortly, or that you **look forward to** hearing from them.

To follow up: *'hacer un seguimiento'.*

To look forward to: *'esperar con ilusión'. Se utiliza mucho en situaciones profesionales.*

You should end the letter with a closing such as "Sincerely", "Yours truly" or something a bit more interesting, such as "I look forward to meeting with you", followed by your handwritten signature, whenever possible.

Much like on your CV, be sure to pay attention to job postings and build the cover letter to mention specific skills or experience requested.

FOLLOW UP LETTERS

You should send a follow-up letter after you have had contact with a potential employer agreeing to grant an interview or after the interview itself.

Before an interview, a letter can serve to:

- Confirm the interview time and place
- Thank the interviewer for their consideration
- Add any additional point that you feel may not have been highlighted enough in your cover letter or CV

After the interview, a letter can serve to:

- Remind the interviewer of you and make a good impression
- Add additional ideas not covered in the interview
- Further thank the interviewer for their time and consideration

USE OF DESCRIPTIVE VERBS AND ADJECTIVES

As with your CV, it is important to use descriptive adjectives and active verbs on your cover letter. See a list of good terms to use on page 27.

Now, let's take a look at some sample cover letters.

SAMPLE COVER LETTERS

Following are some example cover letters demonstrating the format and style mentioned above:

1. Steve Banaducci:

Steve is applying for the job of Event Coordinator with an event organizing company. He has experience organizing events and has been referred to the hiring manager by a friend.

Steve Banaducci

123 Mississippi Street
Memphis, TN 12345
123-555-1234

s.banaducci@gmail.com

April 29, 2014

Mrs. Alexis Spence
Project Supervisor

Edge Productions

123 Margaret Drive
Memphis, TN 12345

Dear Mrs. Spence,

At the suggestion of Charlie Welch, I am submitting my résumé for the position of Event Coordinator. My **forte** is in bringing together exceptional people from a variety of interests to present a well-coordinated and well-attended event.

My interest in your fast-growing consulting firm comes from the creatively planned events your firm is known for. I have tremendous energy and enthusiasm and love to be busy.

One of the most personally rewarding aspects of working in the convention industry is meeting and establishing relationships with others who thrive on the excitement this business inspires. I will contact you early next week to find out when we can meet to discuss the position.

Sincerely,

Steve Banaducci

Forte: *'punto fuerte'.*

2. Sergio Quesada:

In this letter, Sergio Quesada doesn't have a contact in the company, and he is relatively inexperienced. He is writing a "cold-call" letter in reply to an advertisement found in a local newspaper.

Sergio Quesada

24 Birch Street,
Boise Idaho, 12345

May 3, 2014

Mr. Jeff Langille
President

Inline Skates Deluxe

123 23rd St. Boise,
ID 12345

Dear Mr. Langille,

I am writing to express my interest in the junior sales associate position advertised in the Boise News.

As an **avid** skater on both blades and wheels, I cannot imagine a better job than sharing my enthusiasm with your customers. What I lack in sales experience, I more than make up for in knowledge of inline skating and enthusiasm for the business.

I have attached my CV and hope you will consider me for this position. I am available for interviews any day during spring break next week. I will give you a call to see when you can meet with me.

Thank you!

Sergio Quesada

Avid: 'ávido'.

3. Gloria García:

Gloria García is expressing her interest in a job in childcare in a nursery school. She has recently been certified to work in this field.

Gloria García Ramírez
Avenida Islas Filipinas 46, 5 B
28003, Madrid
ggramirez@fakemail.com

June 22, 2014

Director of Human Resources
Kiddy Time Nursery School

Avenida de La Paz 34
28034, Madrid

Dear Director,

A teaching position at your school has long been a career objective of mine. Now that I have become a certified childcare professional, I'm eager to apply for a position on your childcare team.

After reading my enclosed resume, please consider me for any appropriate position in your system. My desire to work with children is strong and I believe that once I join your staff, you will find me to be a productive and creative contributor.

I will call you on Friday to learn what positions are open for the fall. Thank you!

Sincerely,

Gloria García

4. Susan Lane:
Susan Lane is applying for a position as a sales associate in a gourmet food store. She has some retail sales and food industry experience.

June 22, 2014

Evelyn Bathgate

Gateway Gourmet

234 Crowell Street
Hartford, CT 06342

Susan Lane
543 Maple Drive
Hartford, CT 06345
phone: 860-534-0873
email: m.e.little@gmail.com

Dear Ms. Bathgate,

Please accept my enthusiastic application for the position of Sales Associate at your gourmet food store. My passion for customer service, organizational skills and attention to detail make me an ideal candidate for the position.

As a sales associate in the food department at El Corte Canadiense, I provided high quality, knowledgeable service to every customer that walked through the doors. I answered culinary questions, provided information on particular products in the shop, handled inventory and processed purchases.

You state in your advertisement that you want an employee with strong organizational skills. As treasurer for my high school's event fundraising committee, I maintained a detailed, accurate record of our budget. During my time as treasurer, no funds were ever lost or unaccounted for, and we always had extra money at the end of the school year. My responsibility and organizational skills ensured that we had a healthy budget.

I have a keen interest in food and read many culinary books, as well as having worked as waiter at 'Chive Bistro' where I gained an expert knowledge of our dishes and the ingredients that made them so special. I know much of this culinary knowledge is transferrable to the position at Bathgate Fine Foods.

I have enclosed my resume, and will call in the next week to find a time for us to speak.

Thank you so much for your time and consideration.

Sincerely,

Susan Lane

5. Randy Bachman:

Randy has a degree in business administration and experience in sales as well as knowledge in multi-media products.

Randy Bachman

993 Main Street
Winnipeg, Man. B0L 1K6

June 18, 2015

Mr. Gunter Bigsby
General Manager

Bigsby Computer Store
1293 University Avenue
Winnipeg, Man. B0L 1K6

Dear Mr. Bigsby,

After four years as a loyal Bigsby customer, I'd like to apply for your sales management opening. I feel my knowledge of your products and the computer industry in general make me an excellent candidate.

I know the products sold at Bigsby inside and out after having researched them thoroughly before purchasing the multi-media system I now use and love. I have more than six years experience in sales and a bachelor's degree in business administration. I think my professional profile combined with my familiarity of your product offering make me the perfect candidate for the opening.

Because I'm in your store so frequently, I'll ask for you next time I'm there. Perhaps we can set a time to talk about the sales manager position soon. I greatly appreciate your time and consideration of my application.

Best regards,

Randy Bachman

Office Talk!

A continuación encontrarás cinco frases típicas de uso corriente que puedes oír en una oficina donde se habla inglés. Tapa la columna de la derecha y traduce en voz alta las frases.

Me gustaría tener algo más de información antes de comprometerme.	**I'd like to have a bit more information before committing.**
¿Quién va a pagar la factura?	**Who's going to foot the bill?**
Mi correo era un poco agresivo ahora que lo he leído por segunda vez.	**My email was a bit strong now that I have read it the second time.**
Susan estará de baja por maternidad a partir de la semana que viene.	**Susan will be on maternity leave starting next week.**
Todavía no tenemos a nadie que la reemplace.	**We still don't have anyone to take over for her.**

CHAPTER 4

IN THE JOB INTERVIEW

[Claves para el éxito en una
entrevista en inglés]

IN THE JOB INTERVIEW

A job interview can certainly be a stressful experience. **Prepare, prepare, prepare**. The more prepared you are, the more comfortable and confident you will be. Keeping a few things in mind and preparing intelligently can help you increase your chances of impressing a potential employer and getting the job.

HOW TO PREPARE

In addition to preparing for potential questions it is essential to create in image of professionalism in the interview. Be sure to show up early and dress formally.

TIP Whenever possible, try to learn the names of the people that will be interviewing you beforehand. Be sure to greet them personally and with a firm handshake.

Consider possible questions, and prepare your answers in advance.

Many companies may even include potential interview questions on their website to reward those who do research in advance. Be sure to do your homework, researching the company carefully and understanding the skills desired for the position.

TYPICAL INTERVIEW QUESTIONS

Consider the following typical interview questions and some ways to answer them:

Question 1: What is your greatest strength?

This is a very common question and one that you should certainly be prepared to answer.

Here you have the opportunity to emphasize qualities that the employer is sure to value.

If possible, consider the qualities mentioned in the job posting and emphasize them as your strengths.

Imagine the position of "risk calculator" for an insurance company, requesting strong analytical skills. You would want to stress your mathematical background and academic achievements in analytical tasks in the past.

Consider the following 10 **traits** that are greatly desired in the workplace, and how you can make a few of them strengths of yours:

Traits: *'características'.*

1. **Motivation** - Employers want to see that you are driven towards goals. Show them that you are! Prove that you are motivated to do your job well, even if it means working long hours towards specific goals.

2. **Enthusiasm** - Employers want employees that are excited about the company, and the opportunities within it.

3. **Communication skills -** Communication and language skills are essential in the modern workplace. Give concrete examples of how you are a great communicator face to face, on the telephone and via e-mail.

4. **Resilience -** Demonstrate how you persevere when tasks are tough. Employers don't like complainers.

To strive: *'luchar'.*

5. **Ability to learn** - Are you willing and able to learn on the job? Give concrete examples of how you have done so in the past and how you **strive** to constantly improve.

6. **Integrity -** High personal values and ethics are always a key hiring trait. Don't be afraid to explain that you are an ethical person.

To go the extra mile: *'ir más allá de lo esperado'.*

7. **Pride -** Prove that you are proud of a job well done and not just interested in arriving when you have to and leaving when you can. Employers like people who **go the extra mile**!

8. **Task accomplisher** - Prove that you get the job done. Give specific examples of how you worked on a challenging task and got it completed.

9. **Technologically comfortable** - These days all jobs use technology on some level. Indicate how you can use relevant technology with ease.

10. **Logical -** There's great value in being logical. Show that you are good at reasoning particularly when it can lead to solving problems in the workplace.

Question 2: What is your greatest weakness?

This is another common question and one that MUST be prepared for in advance.

Consider how you can turn a weakness into a strength.

Consider the following example answer:

"I am quite reserved and like to take time making important decisions. On the other hand, this trait has kept me from jumping into decisions that could prove to be harmful to the company. Sometimes I like to play it safe."

Question 3: What were your responsibilities in your last job?

With this question, think of specific details you can mention and try to connect them to the job you are interviewing for. Considering the responsibilities listed in the job description will help you do this.

Giving the employer the idea that you already have relevant work experience will be very beneficial.

 TIP
If you haven't worked before, consider aspects of your life where you have held responsibilities, including at school, in clubs or on sports teams or even family responsibilities.

Question 4: What was your greatest accomplishment and your greatest failure in your last position?

Again, try to relate lessons learned from your past job to the one you are interviewing for. You may wish to review your CV and choose points that appear in the **job posting**. You can then comment on accomplishments in areas that are important to the employer.

When commenting on a failure, always be sure to explain what you have learned and how learning through that failure was a valuable experience for you.

Question 5: Why are you leaving your job?

If you were **fired** from your last job, this question can be particularly difficult to answer.

Job posting:
'oferta de trabajo'.

To be fired:
'ser echado de una empresa'. Se dice **"laid off"** *o* **"made redundant"** *para decir despedido por reducción de plantilla o motivos económicos.*

It is always important not to speak negatively about your past supervisors. Employers typically don't want to hire people who are particularly difficult to keep happy.

Criticizing a past boss or company may make you seem demanding or excessively selective.

Following are some good answers that may apply to you:

- *You found yourself not challenged with the work.*
- *You felt there was a lack of room for growth.*
- *You were laid-off from your last position when your department was eliminated due to corporate restructuring.*
- *You are looking for a new challenge and an opportunity to use your technical skills and experience.*
- *You recently received your degree and want to utilize your educational background in your next position.*
- *You are seeking a position with a stable company with room for growth and opportunity for advancement.*
- *This position seemed like an excellent match for your skills and experience and you are not able to fully utilize them in your present job.*
- *The company was cutting back and, unfortunately, your job was one of those eliminated.*

TIP

If you are asked this question, be sure not to speak negatively about your past employers. This could make you look like a complainer.

VIDEO 1

TOP TIPS – BUSINESS ENGLISH VIDEOS
Never speak negatively about past employers
No hables mal de tus jefes anteriores

No está bien hablar mal de jefes anteriores. Puedes dar la imagen de ser una persona envidiosa o no respetuosa que siempre echa la culpa de su fracaso a otro.

Habla siempre con respeto de otros empleadores o clientes si quieres ganar el respeto de los demás, incluyendo al entrevistador.

En este vídeo, vemos un ejemplo en el que se muestran maneras respetuosas de hablar de una mala experiencia laboral.

Question 6: What have you been doing since your last job?

It's important to be honest but prepared for this question. Be sure to prove that you were active and busy in your time between jobs or after graduating from university or school.

You may want to indicate that you have done things such as the following:

- *You worked on freelance projects.*
- *You volunteered with charity programs.*
- *You worked to improve your education or language skills.*

Question 7: How would you describe yourself?

Once again, be sure to make this answer fit well with the company and the job you're interviewing for.

Depending on the nature of the job, you might want to say for example:

- *"I like challenges, solving problems, and coming up with solutions".*
- *"I am a very social person and I think that shows in my work life. I love working with a lot of different people".*
- *"I'm a very creative thinker. I have an open mind and like to explore alternative solutions to problems".*
- *"I'm very organized in both my personal and professional life. I think this is a good trait as it enables me to be very productive on the job".*

When you talk about yourself, use descriptive adjectives and active verbs, as explained in the section on CV writing. Consult a list of these words on page 27.

Question 8: What motivates you?

While there may not be an exact right or wrong answer to this one, it is an opportunity for the employer to gain a better understanding of your character.

You may want to consider this as an opportunity to mention past successes in the workplace and the satisfaction you got from those successes.

Question 9: Are you self-motivated?

While teamwork and a team attitude are important, it is also very important to indicate that you can initiate and work on your own.

Give an answer that implies that you seek new challenges in the workplace and aren't afraid to work hard.

Question 10: Do you prefer to work independently or on a team?

With this question it is often best to give an answer that implies that you are comfortable in both situations.

To tailor:
'personalizar'.

Of course, if the job is known to be one that requires work in teams or unsupervised work, be sure to **tailor** your answer accordingly.

Question 11: Give some examples of teamwork.

Although not really a "question" this one is very typical in interviews along with other "give me an example of....." questions.

Sample Answers:

"I was part of the team responsible for evaluating and selecting suppliers for key components in our company's manufacturing process. We worked very well together to ensure acceptable pricing, quality and delivery, helping our company improve sales and reduce costs".

Or, remember you can still answer similar questions even if you haven't had a job before. For example:

"While I haven't had a job yet, teamwork has always been an important part of my life. I played competitive football in high school and needed to follow my coach's guidance and work in line with my teammates to succeed on the field".

Question 12: Why do you want this job?

Once again this question represents an opportunity to emphasize how you fit the profile described in the job posting. Having reviewed it carefully, you can say that you are interested in developing professionally in the job areas that you will gain experience with in the position.

Bank teller:
'cajero de banco'.

For example, if you are interviewing for a position as a **bank teller**, you can say that you would like to learn more about the banking industry and that

you see this as an excellent way to gain hands-on experience in the financial
services industry.

TIP

Regardless of the position, you should convey your enthusiasm for the opportunity to interview, along with
your solid ability to do the job.

Question 13: Do you have any questions?

The answer to this question should always be **yes.** You should **always** have questions.

Use your questions as an opportunity to show your knowledge about the company.

Example questions to ask:

"I know you have recently expanded operations into Portugal and France. Do you expect the company to offer international opportunities for employees in the coming years?"

"There have been a lot of mergers in this industry lately. Do you think this company could merge in the coming years? If so, what could that mean for new employees?"

TIP

Remember to ask questions and use them as an opportunity to show what you know about the company.

Question 14: What are your goals for the next five years?

The best way to answer this type of question includes a reference to the company you are interviewing for. This gives the interviewer the idea that you are committed to working in this position.

Interviewers will want to see that you are committed to working with the company. You may want to imply that you would hope to advance beyond the particular position you are interviewing for, but suggesting that you plan to go back to school or move to another company in the industry may discourage the interviewer.

You may also use this question as an opportunity to ask what career possibilities are available to a person who gets this position and wants to advance within the company.

OTHER PREPARATIONS FOR THE JOB INTERVIEW

In addition to preparing for specific questions, it is of course essential to present yourself professionally for the interview. Be sure to dress professionally and greet the interviewer with a confident handshake.

TOP TIPS – BUSINESS ENGLISH VIDEOS
The proper handshake
Dar la mano, ¡no dos besos!

En las culturas anglosajonas, no tenemos la costumbre de dar besos al presentarse a alguien. Además, una entrevista de trabajo, al ser una situación formal requiere sin duda un apretón de manos.

Para dar la mano con confianza, ten en cuenta los siguientes consejos:

1. Extiende la mano derecha con el pulgar arriba y la palma plana.

2. Coge la mano del otro con firmeza, palma contra palma.

3. Sacude la mano dos o tres veces en una moción vertical mirando a los ojos del otro.

4. Suelta la mano.

Escanea el código y podrás ver un ejemplo en el vídeo.

Be sure you arrive on time for the interview. If you aren't sure where the office is located, you may want to try finding it the day before the interview to avoid any confusion on the interview day.

Research the company and position as much as possible.

In addition to answering the interviewer's questions, the interview is an opportunity to give the potential employer an indication of your "people skills" and confidence as well as to prove your genuine interest in the job.

TOP TIPS – BUSINESS ENGLISH VIDEOS
Be prepared!
Estate preparado y conoce la empresa

Es imprescindible que te informes sobre la empresa con la que tengas la entrevista y que uses la entrevista como plataforma para demostrar que tienes suficiente conocimiento sobre ella y el sector en general.

Demostrar que lo que buscas es este trabajo en concreto, no solamente un trabajo cualquiera.

Si no demuestras que sabes algo sobre la empresa, va a parecer que no te tomas en serio la empresa y el puesto.

Escanea el código y podrás ver un ejemplo en el vídeo.

Be sure to demonstrate personal skills, good character and professionalism.

Consider positive adjectives of character such as the following and how you can use them describing yourself:

Ambitious	*Ambicioso*
Confident	*Seguro / Con Confianza*
Hard-working	*Trabajador*
Honest	*Honesto*
Loyal	*Leal*
Motivated	*Motivado*
Organized	*Organizado*
Trustworthy	*Digno de confianza*
Independent	*Independiente*
Team-player (noun)	*Persona que sabe trabajar en equipo*

TOP TIPS – BUSINESS ENGLISH VIDEOS
Don't talk too much
¡No hables demasiado!

Hay que respetar al entrevistador. Hay gente que cuando está hablando, se anima y se deja llevar, hablando mucho y a veces demasiado. Presta atención a los gestos del entrevistador y si parece querer avanzar, déjale avanzar y nunca interrumpas.

Es importante que el entrevistador esté cómodo contigo y tu manera de conversar.

Escanea el código y podrás ver un ejemplo en el vídeo.

Money phrasal verbs!

¿Cómo se construye el castillo?

Ladrillo a ladrillo...Es decir, poco a poco. La misma regla se puede aplicar al aprendizaje de los "phrasal verbs". Aunque hay miles, aquí tratamos algunos "phrasal verbs" relacionados con el dinero y de uso común. El secreto es ir poco a poco, priorizar su aprendizaje y centrarse primero en las estructuras más habituales. Te presento dos de ellos por ahora, relacionados con "gastar dinero" y "acumular deuda" de uso bastante informal. Luego veremos más.

To splash out	*Gastar más de lo necesario en "caprichos".*	To spend a lot of money on something you don't need, but is very pleasant, usually for a luxury.
To run up	*Acumular deuda, facturas etc.*	To accumulate a bill or debt.

¡A practicar! Para ganar soltura con estas estructuras, tapa la columna de la derecha y contesta afirmativamente a las siguientes preguntas con respuestas completas.

Did she splash out a lot of money on fancy shoes?	Yes, she splashed out a lot of money on fancy shoes.
Have they splashed out on technology lately?	Yes, they've splashed out on technology lately.
Are they splashing out on their honeymoon?	Yes, they're splashing out on their honeymoon.
Is he going to splash out when he buys his new car?	Yes, he's going to splash out when he buys his new car.
Did they run up a lot of debt on their vacation?	Yes, they ran up a lot of debt on their vacation.
Has the government been running up too much debt lately?	Yes, the government has been running up too much debt lately.
Do they always run up huge debts?	Yes, they always run up huge debts.
Will they continue running up debts next year?	Yes, they will continue running up debts next year.

CHAPTER 5

WORKING ABROAD

[Lo que tienes que saber sobre trabajar en el extranjero]

WORKING ABROAD

Following is a brief outline of some of the details you will want to be aware of if you would like to work in an English-speaking country, specifically the United Kingdom, Australia, the United States or Canada. Of course, this book only provides a very brief outline of things you might want to have in mind if you are looking to work abroad.

It is recommended that you look for further information online as well as contact a country's immigration office to get up-to-date details on work requirements and potential opportunities for foreigners.

THE UK

Assuming you are a European passport holder and therefore a member of the European Economic Area (EEA), you do not need further permission to work in the United Kingdom.

You can:

- Seek and accept offers of work
- Work as an employee and/or in self-employment
- Set up a business
- Manage a company
- Set up a local branch of a company

Office Talk!

Aquí te ofrezco cinco frases típicas de uso corriente que puedes oír en una oficina donde se habla inglés. Tapa la columna de la derecha y traduce en voz alta las frases.

Estoy sentado al otro lado de la fuente de agua.	**I sit just on the other side of the water cooler.**
No nos queda margen con ese precio.	**There's no margin for us at that price.**
Tendrás que hablar con John sobre eso.	**You'll need to talk to John about that.**
No tienen nada que ganar en ese acuerdo.	**They have nothing to gain from the deal.**
Será mejor que no digamos nada hasta que sea oficial.	**We'd better not say anything about it until it's official.**

AUSTRALIA

If you are interested in working in Australia, there are a few options that you may find interesting. A great resource for learning about the details of obtaining the necessary documentation and different programs that you may be eligible for can be found at:

http://www.workingin-australia.com/

As you will see on the website, passing an English test will be an important part of the eligibility process.

Much like most other countries, Australia is open to accepting skilled people with the qualifications and attributes to succeed and help the Australian economy prosper.

"SkillSelect" is an online service that enables skilled workers and business people interested in migrating to Australia to record their details to be considered for a skilled visa through an Expression of Interest (EOI). You can access SkillSelect here: **http://www.immi.gov.au/skills/skillselect/**

Australia has a shortage of skilled workers in some areas. You can find a list of jobs that are in demand here, on Australia's "skills occupation list":

http://www.immi.gov.au/skilled/general-skilled-migration/skilled-occupation-list.htm

One option you may find interesting is the "Temporary Work Visa", which allows workers to come to Australia and work for an approved business for up to four years.

To be eligible for this, you must be sponsored by an approved business that cannot find an Australian citizen or permanent resident available to do the skilled work.

With this visa, you will be able to travel to Australia to work in a nominated occupation, which appears on the above mentioned "skills occupation list":

http://www.immi.gov.au/skilled/general-skilled-migration/skilled-occupation-list.htm

To qualify, you also must speak English to an acceptable level, meet certain licensing obligations and be nominated by an approved business.

More details on this visa and how to apply can be found at:

http://www.immi.gov.au/Visas/Pages/457.aspx

USA

Every year, the United States offers working documents to thousands of workers in a wide variety of occupations. There are several employment categories, each with different requirements for admission, conditions and authorized periods of stay.

Temporary (Non-immigrant) Worker

These workers are non-immigrants who may work in the US for a limited period of time and must work within the employment activity defined by their visa.

Permanent (Immigrant) Worker

These workers can live and work permanently in the United States.

Students and Exchange Visitors

Students may be allowed to work if they have special permission from their school's Designated School Official (DSO) for students and the Responsible Officer (RO) for exchange visitors.

Temporary Visitors for Business

A visa as a temporary visitor for business (B-1 visa) is necessary to visit the United States for business purposes unless you qualify for admission without a visa under the Visa Waiver Program.

All the details on these classifications and eligibility requirements can be found on the U.S. Citizenship and Immigration website: **http://www.uscis.gov/**.

The Green Card lottery

Every year, the US State Department randomly grants 50,000 permanent resident visas (Green cards) to applicants of the Diversity Visa, or "DV Program". With this visa, you can live, study and work in the US like any other American resident.

Green card holders have the freedom to move in and out of America while keeping their native country's citizenship documents.

You can find more information and register for the DV Program here: **http://www.usa-greencards.org/**.

CANADA

Canada is one of the world's wealthiest nations and a member or the Group of Eight (G8). The economy is driven by the service sector, but also has a very strong oil and gas industry along with strong automotive, aircraft and software industries.

There are employment opportunities in Canada for qualified people, providing they are legally eligible to work.

Tens of thousands of people come to Canada each year either to work and become permanent residents or to start new businesses or temporarily to help Canadian employers address short-term requirements for employees in specific occupations.

Temporary work in Canada

Canada's "Temporary Foreign Worker Program" exists to help Canadian employers deal with shortages of people with particular skills or experience.

For temporary work in Canada, you will typically need a work permit and you may also need a temporary resident visa. To find out whether you need a visa, and how to qualify for one, you can view the requirements at: **www.cic.gc.ca/visit**.

Your application will include some documents from your employer, including a job offer, and possibly special permission from the Government to hire you.

You will find more details on the Temporary Foreign Worker Program at **www.cic.gc.ca/work** and more information on what employers need to do to hire a temporary foreign worker at **www.cic.gc.ca/employers**.

Often, opportunities exist for temporary foreign workers to become eligible to apply for permanent resident status in Canada. Temporary workers in certain occupations can apply for permanent residence after gaining experience in a Canadian workplace through the "Canadian Experience Class". You can find more information at **www.cic.gc.ca/cec**.

Becoming a permanent resident

It may be possible to become a permanent resident of Canada through either Canada's immigration programs for skilled workers, or the Provincial Nominee Program operated by many of Canada's provinces and territories, or Canada's Business Immigration Program.

If you decide to apply to come to Canada through any of the programs described below, all the information and forms you need are available at no charge on the Citizenship and Immigration Canada (CIC) website at: **www.cic.gc.ca.**

Skilled workers

To qualify for permanent residence under Canada's "Federal Skilled Worker Program" you will have to have skills and experience that meet the country's labor needs. Other factors are considered including education and your ability to speak English or French.

You can find specific information on Citizenship in Canada at Citizenship and Immigration Canada's (CIC) website: **http://www.cic.gc.ca/ENGLISH/INDEX.ASP**.

You can also find a specific interactive tool to help you determine whether you meet the basic requirements for permanent residence status by answering a few questions to determine eligibility. You can find the interactive tool at **www.cic.gc.ca/cometocanada**.

The Provincial Nominee Program

Another possible avenue for permanent residence is through the "Provincial Nominee Program" in which you would apply to an individual province, then if accepted, you would make a separate application to CIC for permanent residence.

You can find more information on the Provincial Nominee Program, including links to provincial and territorial government websites at: **www.cic.gc.ca/pnp.**

Are you qualified?

Canada's Foreign Credentials Referral Office (FCRO) can best advise you on whether or not your qualifications and experience will be recognized in Canada.

You will find the FCRO website at **www.credentials.gc.ca.**

There is also a workbook called *"Planning to Work in Canada? An Essential Workbook for Newcomers"*, which can be helpful to gather information about living and working in Canada. It is available at **www.credentials.gc.ca/immigrants/workbook**,

Also, to learn about general requirements for different occupations or sectors, you may find the "occupational fact sheets" helpful. They are available at: **www.credentials.gc.ca/immigrants/factsheets**.

Business Immigration Program

Business people, entrepreneurs and investors may be eligible to work in Canada through the "Business Immigration Program", which is designed for newcomers who have financial resources to invest in Canada, as well as for businesspeople who will own and operate businesses that can contribute to Canada's economic prosperity and create jobs for Canadians.

There are three categories for business immigrants to Canada:
- investors
- entrepreneurs
- self-employed people

There are different experience and financial requirements for each category. Visit **www.cic.gc.ca/immigrate** to learn more about the Business Immigration Program.

More money phrasal verbs!

Ya que hemos visto unos "phrasal verbs" en otras secciones de "Business Bits" te presento tres más por ahora, relacionados con "gastar dinero" y de uso bastante informal. Luego veremos otros.

To fork out / over	*Pagar algo por obligación.*	To pay for something, usually something you would rather not have to pay for.
To shell out	*Pagar algo por obligación.*	To pay for something, usually something you would rather not have to pay for.
To cough up	*Pagar una cantidad específica que se te obliga.*	To provide money for something when you do not want to.

¡A practicar! Para ganar soltura con estas estructuras tapa la columna de la derecha y contesta afirmativamente a las siguientes preguntas con respuestas completas. También escucha el audio e intenta contestar en voz alta con la voz grabada.

Did he fork out a lot for his new car?	Yes, he forked out a lot for his new car.
Have they forked over more than a thousand dollars?	Yes, they've forked over more than a thousand dollars.
Do they fork over the fees every month?	Yes, they fork over the fees every month.
Is John going to fork over what he owes me?	Yes, John is going to fork over what he owes you.

Did he shell out more than necessary for the supplies?	Yes, he shelled out more than necessary for the supplies.
Have they shelled out all the fees?	Yes, they've shelled out all the fees.
Does the company always shell out for the Christmas dinner?	Yes, the company always shells out for the Christmas dinner.
Will his mother shell out for his trip to the beach?	Yes, his mother will shell out for his trip to the beach.

Did John finally cough up the money?	Yes, he finally coughed up the money.
Has she coughed up the money for the premium subscription?	Yes, she has coughed up the money for the premium subscription.
Do they always cough up the full price?	Yes, they always cough up the full price.
Will she cough up the money if the program works?	Yes, she'll cough up the money if the program works.

SECTION B

DOING BUSINESS IN ENGLISH

[Claves para hacer negocios en inglés]

CHAPTER 6

NUMBERS AND MONEY

[Expresándote correctamente en el idioma de las cifras]

NUMBERS AND MONEY

In the business world, it's essential to be able to pronounce numbers correctly.

THE RULES!

Following are a few simple rules to pronounce numbers correctly:

Rule # 1. When reading numbers, we don't say "hundred**s**", "thousand**s**" or "million**s**", instead, we pronounce these words without the "S".

Examples: two thousand, six million, four hundred etc.

Rule # 2. We always pronounce the word "and" after "hundred" and not after "thousand" or "million"*.

- 123 = "One hundred **and** twenty-three"
- 456 = "Four hundred **and** fifty-six"

*"And" can only be pronounced without the word "hundred" when a zero falls in the hundred position, such as 1,034 – "One thousand and thirty-four".

Rule # 3. We don't say "thousand million". In English to say *'mil millones'* we say "one billion". To say *'un billón'* we say "one trillion".

Rule # 4. Remember that the use of commas (,) and decimal points (.) are the opposite in English of what they are in Spanish.

Imagine the following number:

"and"   "and"
↓   ↓
123,456

According to these rules, this number would be pronounced "one hundred and twenty-three thousand four hundred and fifty-six".

PISTA DE AUDIO 7 **LET'S PRACTICE:**

Practice with the following numbers to make sure you can pronounce them properly.

324,365	Three hundred and twenty-four thousand, three hundred and sixty-five.
1,354,880	One million, three hundred and fifty-four thousand, eight hundred and eighty.
23,340,533	Twenty three million, three hundred and forty thousand, five hundred and thirty-three.
50,123,070	Fifty million, one hundred and twenty three thousand, and seventy.
170,324, 170	One hundred and seventy million, three hundred and twenty-four thousand, one hundred and seventy.

 Intonation Tip:

A lot of people have difficulty clearly marking the difference in pronunciation between numbers such as 14 and 40, 15 and 50 etc.

The secret to making the difference clear is in the intonation.

With numbers ending in "teen" we stress the final syllable, whereas with multiples of ten, we place the intonation on the first syllable.

Consider the following examples:

	14	40
	fourteen	forty
Pronounced	fourTEEN	FORty
	15	50
	fifteen	fifty
Pronounced	fifTEEN	FIFty
	16	60
	sixteen	sixty
Pronounced	sixTEEN	SIXty

In the "On the telephone" section on page 103 we will take a further look at number pronunciation as it appears specifically in telephone numbers.

Let's set a date!

Es importante saber pronunciar las fechas en inglés. Para hacerlo, hay que entender los números ordinales (primero, segundo, tercero). En inglés, pronunciamos los números ordinales de la siguiente manera:

The first - 1st (ferst) *'primero'*

The second - 2nd (second) *'segundo'*

The third - 3rd (zerd) *'tercero'*

The fourth - 4th (forz)

The fifth - 5th (fifz)

The sixth - 6th (siksz)

The seventh - 7th (sevenz)

The eighth - 8th (eiz)

The ninth - 9th (nainz)

The tenth - 10th (tenz)

The eleventh - 11th (elevenz)

The twelfth - 12th (tuelvz)

The thirteenth - 13th (zertinz)

The fourteenth - 14th (fortinz)

The fifteenth - 15th (fiftinz)

The sixteenth - 16th (sikstinz)

The seventeenth - 17th (seventinz)

The eighteenth - 18th (eitinz)

The nineteenth - 19th (naintinz)

The twentieth - 20th (tuéntiez)

The twenty-first - 21st (tuenti-ferst)

The twenty-second - 22nd (tuenti-second)

etc.

Thirtieth - 30th (zertiez)

Fortieth - 40th (fortiez)

Cuando pronunciamos las fechas en inglés, hay dos maneras comunes:

La manera británica: The 9th of February, the 23rd of June.

La manera americana: February 9th, June 23rd.

PRONOUNCING MONEY:

Remember

Money itself is uncountable, while euros, dollar or pounds are countable.

When we talk about money, we have a countable number of euros, dollars or pounds and a separate, countable number of cents.

$16.34 — Sixteen dollars and thirty-four cents.

€24.65 — Twenty-four euros and sixty-five cents.

$254.23 — Two hundred and fifty-four dollars and twenty-three cents.

So, we will say:

How much money <u>does</u> he have?   – *'¿Cuánto dinero tiene* él?'

How much money <u>is</u> in the account? – *'¿Cuánto dinero hay en la cuenta?'*

And, talking about the existence of money in an account, in your wallet etc:

There <u>is</u> $25.47 – There is twenty-five dollars and forty-seven cents.

There <u>is</u> €1,354.18 – There is one thousand, three hundred and fifty-four dollars and eighteen cents.

It's also important to know how to pronounce terms related to punctuation and symbols that you may use in presentations or on the telephone. Following is a list of some of the most common terms you should know:

Punctuation	Spanish	English
.	*Punto*	Period / Full stop
,	*Coma*	Comma
:	*Dos puntos*	Colon
;	*Punto y coma*	Semicolon
-	*Guión*	Dash or Hyphen
_	*Guión bajo*	Underscore
'	*Apóstrofe*	Apostrophe
?	*Signo de interrogación*	Question mark
!	*Signo de admiración*	Exclamation mark
" "	*Comillas*	Quotation marks
()	*Paréntesis*	Parentheses or Brackets
[]	*Corchetes*	Square Brackets
/	*Barra*	Slash
\	*Barra invertida*	Back slash

Symbols

Symbol	Spanish	English
@	*Arroba*	At
#	*Almohadilla*	Pound or number sign
&	*Et*	Ampersand (means "and")
*	*Asterisco*	Asterisk
. (as in "i")	*Punto*	Dot
%	*Porcentaje*	Percent sign
$	*Dólar*	Dollar sign

Figures

Figures	Spanish	English
+	*Suma*	Addition or plus sign
-	*Resta*	Subtraction or minus sign
* or x	*Multiplicación*	Multiplication sign
/	*División*	Division sign
=	*Es igual a*	Equal sign
. (as in 0.25)	*Punto*	Decimal point
x^2	*Al cuadrado*	Squared or to the 2nd power
x^3	*Al cubo*	Cubed or to the 3rd power
$\sqrt{}$	*Raíz cuadrada*	Square root
$\sqrt[3]{}$	*Raíz cúbica*	Cube root

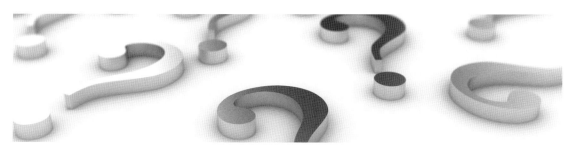

Consider the following vocabulary as we put mathematical terms to use.

Symbol	Operation	Verb	In use	Example
+	Addition	To add	Plus	One plus two equals three.
-	Subtraction	To subtract	Minus	Five minus three equals two.
X	Multiplication	To multiply	Times	Three times two equals six.
÷	Division	To divide	Divided by	Six divided by three equals two.

Note: The word subtraction only has one "S". We don't say "substraction".

Numbers

Number	Spanish	English
½	Una mitad	One-half
$\frac{1}{3}$	Un tercio	One-third
¾	Tres cuartos	Three-fourths
1,000,000	Un millón	One million
2,000,000,000	Dos mil millones	Two billion
5,000,000,000,000	Cinco billones	Five trillion
3.1415926535	Tres con uno, cuatro...	Three-point-one four...

Money

Amount	Pronunciation
$98.00	Ninety-eight dollars
$37.52	Thirty-seven dollars and fifty-two cents
$7,921.05	Seven thousand, nine hundred and twenty-one dollars and five cents
$1,523,948	One million, five hundred and twenty-three thousand, nine hundred and forty-eight dollars
€398,735,096	Three hundred and ninety-eight million, seven hundred and thirty-five thousand and ninety-six euros
€120,867,142,003	One hundred and twenty billion, eight hundred and sixty-seven million, one hundred and forty-two thousand, and three euros

It's all in the preposition

"By" o "To"

Cuando hablamos de cambios de valor, sea de precio, temperatura, edad, etc. hay que considerar la diferencia entre aumentar (o disminuir) en un valor o aumentar hasta un valor final.

Es decir:

"increasing (or decreasing) by" or "increasing to" a final value.

Imagina que el precio de unos vaqueros en 2005 era de 35$ y en 2010, de 45$

The price increased by $10.

The price increased to $45.

Imagina que la temperatura en Toronto fue de 23 grados el viernes y 18 grados el sábado.

The temperature dropped by five degrees.

The temperature dropped to 18 degrees.

CHAPTER 7

ON THE TELEPHONE

[Claves para conversar
con seguridad]

ON THE TELEPHONE

Needless to say the telephone is a key tool for business communication. Over the years of teaching in Spain, I have had so many students tell me that they absolutely **dread** dealing on the telephone.

To dread - To fear: *'temer'*.

Telephone conversations are often more challenging than face-to-face encounters since we cannot see the other party and take advantage of gestures and expressions that help us understand the conversation. Also, native English speakers tend to speak very quickly on the phone.

First of all, let's consider some tips for successfully doing business on the phone.

TIPS FOR SUCCESS ON THE TELEPHONE

1. Prepare well

Plan ahead and consider specific questions you are going to ask, and how you will phrase them in English. Make sure you know whom you have to speak to. Also keep things **handy**. Having relevant files open on your computer or reports in front of you will make it easier to find the information you may need. Finally have a piece of paper and a pen ready to take notes.

Handy - Available, nearby: *'a mano', 'cerca'*.

2. Ask the other person to speak slowly

Knowing that English isn't your native language, they won't mind doing this.

3. Repeat key information out loud

When key information is given, repeat it **out loud**. This way you will both know if you have understood the information correctly.

4. If you don't understand, tell them!

It doesn't do any good to lie and say that you understand when you don't. This may sound obvious, but people make this mistake all the time.

5. Be polite and friendly

This will help establish an understanding tone in the conversation and will be appreciated.

20 OF THE MOST IMPORTANT TERMS RELATED TO THE TELEPHONE:

To call	Llamar
To dial	Marcar
Dial tone	Señal de llamada
To ring	Sonar
To pick up	Coger el teléfono
To answer	Contestar
Busy signal	Ocupada
To be busy	Comunicando
Voicemail	Buzón de voz
To leave a message	Dejar un mensaje
To take a message	Tomar un recado
To call back	Volver a llamar
To hang up	Colgar
Hold on	Esperar
Speak up	Hablar más alto

Bad line	*Mala señal*
To put through	*Pasar la llamada*
Mobile phone / Cell	*Móvil*
Operator	*Operadora*
Wrong number	*Nímero equivocado*

PRONOUNCING TELEPHONE NUMBERS:

Remember, we pronounce telephone numbers in English according to the individual digit, that is:

902 354-2188 = "nine – oh – two – three – five – four – two – one – eight – eight"

When we pronounce the number "0" in phone numbers, we typically say "Oh".

We also do this with:

Years: 1905: "Nineteen-oh-five".

Times: 12:05: "Twelve-oh-five".

Room numbers: 302: We're staying in room "Three-oh-two"

EXPRESSIONS TO USE ON THE TELEPHONE

Let's look at some common telephone expressions through translation.

Answering the phone and introducing yourself:

The introduction we choose for each call depends on the degree of formality of the call and how well we know the person on the other end of the line.

When answering the phone, it is important to always be polite and clearly identify yourself and your company.

In 2000 I worked at the Bank of Montreal in Canada. I often was responsible for answering the telephone when people called the branch. I always answered the phone as follows:

"Good morning, thanks for calling Bank of Montreal. Kyle speaking. How can I help you?

While it isn't necessary to always be as detailed as this, it is important to always make sure the caller knows who you are and what you can do for them.

If you are answering an internal call, within your company, you may wish to just say:

Hello, this is David. How can I help you?

Consider the following examples and video below of how to answer the phone properly in English.

Hola, soy Juan García.	Hello, this is Juan Garcia.
Hola, soy Juan García de Bing Industries.	Hello, this is Juan Garcia calling from Bing Industries.
Buenos días, soy Juan García de Bing Industries.	Good morning, this is Juan Garcia calling from Bing Industries.
Hola, soy Juan.	Hello, this is Juan.

Notice how we don't say "I'm Juan Garcia" but rather "This is Juan Garica" or "It's Juan Garcia calling.

VIDEO 5

TOP TIPS – BUSINESS ENGLISH VIDEOS
Answering the phone
Contestar al teléfono

Saber contestar al teléfono es algo fundamental. El típico "dígame" no tiene traducción al inglés común, ni tiene lugar en situaciones profesionales en inglés.

Es imprescindible que te identifiques y también identifiques tu departamento o empresa de una manera cordial.

Escanea el código y podrás ver un ejemplo en el vídeo.

Asking for someone:

It's important to be polite, and in English communication and culture we usually seem to be more polite than in Spanish. Sometimes when we call an office or residence we don't immediately reach the person we would like to talk to.

Here are some ways to ask for someone else:

¿Podría hablar con George, por favor?	May I speak to George please?
¿Podría hablar con George, por favor?	Could I speak to George please?
Querría hablar con George Stevens, por favor.	I'd like to speak to George Stevens, please.
¿Podría pasarme a George Stevens, por favor?	Could you put me through to George Stevens, please?
¿Podría hablar con alguien del departamento de finanzas, por favor?	Could I speak to someone in the finance department, please?

Connecting to other people

Now let's look at some terminology for connecting to other people on the telephone:

Le paso.	I'll put you through.
Le paso al Sr. Smith.	I'll put you through to Mr. Smith.
Le paso en seguida.	I'll put you through right away.
Un momento, por favor.	Just a moment, please.
¿Puede esperar, por favor?	Could you hold the line please?
Espere, por favor.	Hold the line, please.

Put through vs. Get through

These are two related, but different phrasal verbs.

The receptionist may put you through, which means to actually pass the call to another telephone, and the person you are trying to reach may or may not be available to pick it up.

If you get through, it means you actually managed to connect to the other person by phone.

When someone is not available

Sometimes the person you are trying to reach isn't available. In that case, you may hear the following:

Me temo que el Sr. Smith no está en este momento.	I'm afraid Mr. Smith isn't in at the moment.
Lo siento, esta fuera en un viaje.	I'm sorry, he's away on a business trip.
Lo siento, está reunido en este momento.	I'm sorry, he's in a meeting at the moment.
Está comunicando ahora.	The line is busy at the moment.
Me temo que no está disponible en este momento.	I'm afraid he's not available at the moment.

Remember

We say "at the moment" and not "in the moment".

> **To take a message:** *'tomar un recado'.*
> **To leave a message:** *'dejar un recado'.*

Leaving and taking messages:

¿Quiere que le dé un mensaje?	Can I take a message?
¿Quiere dejar un mensaje?	Would you like to leave a message?
¿Hay algún mensaje?	Is there any message?
¿Quiere que le dé algún mensaje?	Can I give him a message?
Por favor, dígale que llame a Jeff cuando llegue.	Please ask him to call Jeff when he gets in.
Por favor, que me llame.	Please have him call me.
Le diré al Sr. Jones que ha llamado.	I'll tell Mr. Jones that you called.
Le diré a ella que le llame tan pronto como sea posible.	I'll ask her to call you as soon as possible.

Recording a voicemail message:

Sometimes you will call a phone number and reach voicemail. Don't be afraid to leave a message. Keep your messages short, but detailed. Be sure to include your full name, company, reason for calling and your telephone number.

Consider the following examples:

A formal message:

 EX

"Hello this is Javier Cordoba calling. I would like to ask you about the new changes to your course schedule for this month. Please call me back at 643 321 213. Thank you."

Or a less formal example:

EX

"Hello, this is Javier calling for Randy. Could you please return my call as soon as possible? My number is 643 321 213. Thank you."

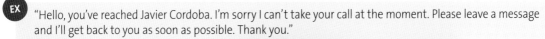

VIDEO
6

TOP TIPS – BUSINESS ENGLISH VIDEOS

Leaving a message
Dejar mensajes por teléfono

Al dejar un mensaje por teléfono, pensad en las tres C:

Claro
Conciso
Completo
Es imprescindible que quien recibe el mensaje entienda quién eres, qué quieres y cómo puede ponerse en contacto contigo.

Escanea el código y podrás ver un ejemplo práctico en este vídeo.

If you expect to be receiving calls from native English speakers, you may want to record a voicemail greeting in English. The following is a standard greeting style you can use:

EX

"Hello, you've reached Javier Cordoba. I'm sorry I can't take your call at the moment. Please leave a message and I'll get back to you as soon as possible. Thank you."

If English is not your first language, it is very understandable that you may want to ask for clarification. Here are some common ways to ask for clarification:

Lo siento, no te entiendo. ¿Podría repetirlo, por favor?	I'm sorry, I don't understand. Could you repeat that please?
¿Puede repetir el nombre, por favor?	Could you repeat the name, please?
Déjeme repetir el número para asegurarme de que la he entendido bien.	Let me repeat the number to make sure I got it right.
¿Podría hablar un poco más despacio, por favor?	Could you speak a bit more slowly, please?
¿Le importaría repetir eso?	Would you mind repeating that?
Lo siento, no he entendido lo último que ha dicho.	I'm sorry I didn't understand the last thing you said.

Common Mistake!

Remember - We say "repeat it for me" or "repeat the number" and NEVER "repeat me"

SAYING DATES

If you work on the phone regularly, it is important to be able to say dates correctly, pronouncing the days, months and ordinal numbers correctly, as well as using the correct prepositions;

Following are the common British and American forms:

05/05/2013

British   The fifth of May, two thousand and thirteen

American   May fifth, two thousand and thirteen

Notice the use of the preposition "of" before the month in the British form.

17/12/ 1987

British   The seventeenth of December, nineteen eighty-seven

American   December seventeenth, nineteen eighty-seven

03/03/1997

British   The third of March, nineteen ninety-seven

American   March third, nineteen ninety-seven

06/04/2004

British   The sixth of April, two thousand and four

American   April sixth, two thousand and four

THE ALPHABET

It is important to know the alphabet well and to be able to spell words out if asked. Following is a pronunciation guide:

Letter	Pronounced
A	ei
B	bi
C	si
D	di
E	i
F	ef
G	chi
H	eich
I	ai
J	chei
K	quei
L	el
M	em

Letter	Pronounced
N	en
O	ou
P	pi
Q	kiú
R	ar
S	es
T	ti
U	iú
V	fi
W	dábaliu
X	eks
Y	ouai
Z	si (U.S) or sed (U.K.)

VIDEO
7

TOP TIPS – BUSINESS ENGLISH VIDEOS
Spell it out
Deletréalo claramente

Tanto si estamos hablando de direcciones de correo electrónico, como apellidos, o referencias a productos, hay siempre casos en los que debemos deletrear palabras para que nos entiendan claramente.

En el vídeo disponible con el código de arriba, vemos un ejemplo de cómo deletrear claramente en inglés.

Pronunciation:

To pronounce many sounds correctly, it is important to understand the difference between vocalized or "voiced" sounds and non-vocalized sounds. Some sounds are pronounced with the vocal chords muted, and the sound being created in the mouth. Others rely on the vibration of your vocal chords. Keep this distinction in mind when practicing pronunciation.

The letters "G" and "J" when pronounced in words like *George*, or *Jam* or *Jerry* begin with a "ch" with the vocal chords activated. The "J" is not pronounced like the Spanish "ll".

The "V" sound is not related to the letter "B". The "V" sound is created pronouncing the "F" and activating the vocal chords.

The "X" sound should be pronounced as "eks", otherwise it can be confused with the "S" sound.

The letter "Z" is pronounced like an "S" sound but with the vocal chords activated.

Following is the American system for clarifying letters when dictated. Use it to make yourself better understood on the telephone.

A as in Alpha	H as in Hotel	O as in Oscar	V as in Victor
B as in Bravo	I as in India	P as in Papa	W as in Whisky
C as in Charlie	J as in Juliet	Q as in Quebec	X as in X-ray
D as in Delta	K as in Kilo	R as in Romeo	Y as in Yankee
E as in Echo	L as in Lima	S as in Sierra	Z as in Zulu
F as in Foxtrot	M as in Mike	T as in Tango	
G as in Golf	N as in November	U as in Uniform	

What does that stand for?

Cuando usamos acrónimos en inglés en muchos casos comunes solemos pronunciarlos según cada letra individual, es decir:

La CIA, se pronuncia **C. I. A.** *es decir* **"si, ai, ei"**, *y no "cia" como se hace en español.*

Igual pasa con otros ejemplos comunes como:

ASAP, DIY, LOL, or UCLA

ASAP stands for **"as soon as possible"**

DIY stands for **"do it yourself"**

LOL stands for **"laughing out loud"**

UCLA stands for the **"University of California at Los Angeles"**

* *"to stand for" = 'significar' cuando hablamos de acrónimos.*

ORGANIZING MEETINGS AND APPOINTMENTS

To arrange meetings there are also specific structures that are commonly used.

Quisiera concertar una reunión.	I'd like to arrange a meeting. / I'd like to set up a meeting.
¿Cuándo está disponible?	When are you free?
¿Cuándo le viene bien?	When is good for you?
¿Cuándo esta él disponible?	When is he free?
¿Qué tal el martes a las dos de la tarde?	How about Tuesday at 2 pm?
¿Qué tal en algún momento mañana?	How about sometime tomorrow?
¿Qué hora le viene bien?	What time would suit you?
¿Le importaría si lo dejáramos para otro día?	Would you mind if we left it for another day?
Entonces nos vemos la semana que viene.	So, we'll see you next week then.

EX

Now that we have seen an overview of telephone terminology, let's see it all put into practice in a conversation:

Robert Brown: Hello, Thanks for calling Brown Brokers International, how can I help you?

Susan Green: Hello, my name is Susan Potter. I'm calling regarding the promotion contract I had been negotiating with Alex Brown. May I speak to him please?

Robert Brown: I'm sorry, but Alex is out of the office today, is there any way I could help you?

Susan Green: Alex sent me a detailed service plan, but he wasn't clear on the number of distributors you deal with. If I agree to work with you, how many distributors will my products be able to reach and in what parts of the country?

Robert Brown: Well, that depends on the nature of your business. To be honest, I think Alex has all the details of your account, so it would be best to speak with him.

Susan Green: Could you tell me when he'll be back in the office?

Robert Brown: Certainly. He'll be back first thing tomorrow morning. If you'd like to give me your phone number, I'll have him call you right away.

Susan Green: That would be great, it's 902 675 234.

Robert Brown: Let me make sure I've got that. 902 675 234.

Susan Green: That's right. I look forward to hearing from Alex. Thank you very much.

Robert Brown: You're welcome. Thanks for calling.

Susan Green: Good-bye

Robert Brown: Good-bye

Notice how Robert and Susan are professional and courteous in the conversation. While speaking on the phone might be intimidating, just remember to prepare ahead of time, stay relaxed and don't be afraid to ask for repetition or clarification. Treat the person you are speaking with like a friend and they will too.

BUSINESS BITS

Office Talk!

PISTA DE AUDIO 9

A continuación encontrarás cinco frases típicas de uso corriente que puedes oír en una oficina donde se habla inglés. Tapa la columna de la derecha y traduce en voz alta las frases.

¿Por qué no organizamos una reunión sobre eso?	**Why don't we call a meeting on that?**
¿Dónde deberíamos tener la reunión?	**Where should we hold the meeting?**
Estoy muy contento con los comentarios.	**I'm really happy with the feedback.**
Él pide un descuento.	**He's asking for a discount.**
Tendremos que ver las últimas cifras de ventas.	**We'll need to see the latest sales figures.**

CHAPTER 8

EMAIL

[Cómo redactar el mail perfecto]

EMAIL

Being able to communicate effectively via email is essential in the modern workplace. Although email has only become common on the job within the last 20 years, it seems almost impossible to think of offices functioning without it.

Let's take a look now at how to write an effective email.

THE SUBJECT LINE

The subject line of an email serves an important role as it must capture the reader's attention and clearly tell the reader what the email is about.

An effective subject line is complete, concise and clear. For example, if the email is to set up a meeting, be sure to include the date and time in the subject line. If the purpose is to suggest another action, state it specifically and clearly.

If possible, include a keyword that will make the email content easier to remember and/or search for in a crowded inbox.

Some sample subject lines:

• October sales results
• Meeting scheduled for Thursday, October 12 at 3:30
• Fancy Food Show 2014 registration information

ADDRESSING THE RECIPIENT

Begin your email with a greeting. Choosing the type of greeting depends on the level of formality. Using the word "Dear" is almost always an excellent choice for starting your email.

For an informal email, a typical greeting such as "Dear Steven," would be perfect. If the recipient is a friend or relative and you can be very casual, you could simply say "Hi Ralph,".

To whom it may concern: *'a quien corresponda' o 'a quien pueda interesar'.*

In a more formal email, including most professional business emails, you would address the recipient by their last name, such as "Dear Mr. LaRocque".

Finally, if you are writing to a company and don't have the name of a specific recipient, you can say **"To Whom It May Concern"**:

We don't refer to an email as simply a "mail" in English. If you tell someone you will send them a "mail" they may confuse it with regular mail sent through the postal system.

BEGINNING YOUR EMAIL

The tone you choose to begin the content of your email depends on what the purpose of the email is. There are a few ways you may wish to start the email.

To express your purpose:

Particularly if this is your first email correspondence, you will most likely want to begin by expressing its purpose.

Consider the following:

- "My name is Lance Bigglesworth. I'm contacting you to apply for the administrative assistant position listed on your website".
- "I am writing to express my interest in Vandelay Industries' products...".
- "I am writing with reference to an advertisement posted in the Queens County Advance...".

To thank the recipient:

You may wish to begin by thanking them for their interest in your company, or for their reply to a previous email.

- "Thanks for your interest in RomCo products and services...".
- "Thank you for your prompt reply...".

It is important to clearly and concisely express the purpose of the email before elaborating in the email body.

DON'T MAKE TOO MANY POINTS IN EACH EMAIL

When you write the actual message be sure to get your point across without rambling. If you use too many unnecessary words, the reader may miss important details. Try to break up the message into paragraphs according to topic to make your message clearer.

To ramble: *'irse por las ramas'.*

It doesn't cost any more to send multiple emails compared to sending just one. If you have a lot of different points to make, consider sending multiple emails so that each point gets the attention it deserves.

In terms of formatting, the email should be no more than five paragraphs long and each paragraph should be no more than five sentences long. Insert a line break between each paragraph. Indenting isn't necessary and is often lost during the email transfer anyway.

BE CLEAR ON THE TYPE OF RESPONSE YOU WANT TO RECEIVE

Is the purpose of your email to inform, to persuade or to request something? If you are looking for a specific response, be sure to make that clear.

Consider the following requests for a specific response:

- "Please get back to me by Friday afternoon so we can finalize the details."
- "Please let me know what you think of the proposal and whether or not we can begin the shipment."
- "Can you confirm that you agree with the proposal we have outlined?"

CLOSING YOUR EMAIL

It is also important to end your email politely. Of course, the specifics of how you would end the email depend on the purpose of the email itself, but a few common lines include:

- "Thank you for your consideration."

- "I look forward to hearing from you."

To look forward to

"To look forward to" is essentially a way of saying *'esperar con ilusión'*, and indicates a strong desire and anticipation for an upcoming event. It is very common in business and is a good term for business writing, conversations and emails.

Sometimes the expression is used so much that it isn't always as heartfelt as the speaker could simply be *'haciendo la pelota'* when saying he is looking forward to "the next meeting" or "seeing you again at the conference".

"To look forward to" is always followed by a noun or the gerund verb form (ing):

- I look forward to seeing you.
- I'm looking forward to the party.
- She's looking forward to meeting you!

Be sure to end your email with the appropriate wording. "Best regards", "Kind regards" (more common in Britain) and "Sincerely" are all very professional and appropriate for almost all kinds of emails.

Common informal options include "Best wishes," or "Cheers" which is more common in Britain.

If the email is formal, be sure to sign with your full name and include your job title. This may be done with an automatic signature, which should also include your contact information.

Remember:

Before clicking the send button on your email, be sure to proofread it, ensuring there are no spelling mistakes and that the email flows logically and conveys your message in the appropriate tone.

ATTACHING FILES

If you are attaching files along with your email, you can mention this as follows:

- "Please find attached the sales results for the first quarter…".
- "I have attached a document showing…".

BEFORE SENDING

Be sure to **proofread** your email for content, spelling and grammar. You may wish to even read it aloud to make sure that the email flows properly and addresses all the key points. Don't trust spell check programs, as they can mistake the words that you intended to use for others with a different meaning. If the email is detailed and very important, you may also wish to paste the body into a word processor, revise it if necessary, and copy and paste it back into your email.

Proofread:
'revisar'.

PUTTING IT ALL TOGETHER – A FEW EXAMPLES

Following are three example emails. In them you can see several common structures and wordings that you may find useful for your own professional emails.

EX

Sample email 1: Formal request

Subject: Performance at the Seagrove folk music festival

Dear Mr. Brathwaite,

I am writing to thank you for your interest in performing at the Seagrove Folk music festival and request a meeting to discuss scheduling and financial details.

As you know, this year will be the biggest festival to date and we are counting on a number of new acts to make it a memorable experience for everyone in attendance.

Are you available to meet in our downtown office this Thursday, May 12 at 1:00?

I look forward to hearing from you.

Best regards,

Lilly Martin

Volunteer coordinator

Seagrove folk music festival

EX

Sample email 2: Formal apology

Subject: Apology and return of television remote control

To whom it may concern:

My name is Greg Millman. I stayed at your hotel with my family April 8-12, 2014. We had a wonderful stay, but I recently learned that my six-year-old son took the television remote control from our hotel room with him when we left.

I apologize for my son's actions. He is very sorry and apologizes as well. I have had a long discussion with him about private property. I would like to know what address I should mail the remote control back to. Please let me know the preferred address, and I will send the remote (and my son's letter of apology) as soon as possible.

Sincerely,

Greg Millman

EX

Sample email 3: Informal information request

Subject: Moe Hornsby's address

Dear Rick,

It was great seeing you at the banquet last night.

In line with our conversation about our search for a new chef, I was wondering if you could send along Moe Hornsby's contact information as you mentioned.

Moe clearly has a lot of experience in the Barbeque restaurant business and I would like to talk to him about the possibility of joining our team.

I look forward to hearing from you.

Best regards,

Harris

More money phrasal verbs!

PISTA DE AUDIO 10

Ya hemos visto unos "phrasal verbs" en otras secciones de "Business Bits". Te presento dos más...ahora enfocados en la idea de tener el dinero justo y necesario , es decir "having just enough money."

To get by	Apañarse económicamente	To have just enough money for your needs.
To scrape by	Apañarse económicamente con dificultades	To manage to live on very little money.

¡A practicar! Para ganar soltura con estas estructuras tapa la columna de la derecha y contesta afirmativamente a las siguientes preguntas con respuestas completas.

Did he get by with his part-time salary?	*Yes, he got by with his part-time salary.*
Have they gotten by so far?	*Yes, they've gotten by so far.*
Do all the workers get by with their *wages?	*Yes, all the workers get by with their wages.*
Do you think the young people be able to get by with these wages?	*Yes, I think young people will be able to get by with these wages.*

*wage = 'salario'

Was he able to scrape by?	*Yes, he was able to scrape by.*
Has she scraped by this month?	*Yes, she has scraped by this month.*
Do most students scrape by?	*Yes, most students scrape by.*
Will he scrape by with an allowance* from his mother?	*Yes, he'll scrape by with an allowance from his mother.*

*allowance = 'paga'

CHAPTER 9

MEETINGS

[Claves de comportamiento y
comunicación en
tus reuniones en inglés]

MEETINGS

Business meetings are an essential part of most office jobs. Face-to-face meetings put your communications skills to the test.

In this section you can learn specific vocabulary and terminology that will help you communicate effectively and professionally in English in a typical meeting.

WHY ARE YOU HAVING THE MEETING?

It is important to be confident and professional in a business meeting and also clearly understand the goal of the meeting.

Much like a presentation, where you must understand your audience, in meetings it is essential to understand the other party, their goals and their motivation.

Is the purpose of the meeting:

- To inform or train?
- To persuade?
- To sell or impress?

Obviously, the tone of a meeting will be different if it is with colleagues working together on a project, than it will be, say, if it is with a potential buyer of your products.

By understanding the position you want to take and the people you will be dealing with, you can appropriately prepare for the business meeting.

Know your culture – greetings

There are many behavioral differences to consider when dealing with different cultures in business. An interesting one is the way people greet each other.

The typically "Spanish" greeting of two kisses is not known in American or British cultures, although some forms of giving kisses are common in other areas:

- **Holland:** 3 kisses. 3 kisses, beginning and ending on the right cheek.
- **Italy:** Often a handshake is used, but kissing is used with family and close friends.
- **Belgium:** One kiss on the cheek is common. Three kisses for an older person as a sign of respect.
- **Austria and Scandinavia:** Follow the same customs as Spain – 2 kisses beginning on the right cheek.
- **Germany:** No kissing except for family and very close friends. Handshakes are much more common and all meetings begin and end with them.

When meeting someone for business, it is best to greet them with a firm handshake lasting about 2 seconds. While other regional variations exist, this is a safe and standard greeting.

Throughout face-to-face conversations keep in mind that, in Anglo-Saxon countries, people tend to stand physically farther apart than is common in Mediterranean cultures.

TOP TIPS – BUSINESS ENGLISH VIDEOS
Know the names of the people you're meeting with
Saber con quién estás hablando

Aunque parece obvio, es sorprendente la cantidad de gente que se olvida de los nombres de las personas con quienes quedan.
La palabra que más nos gusta es nuestro propio nombre. Es importante saber los nombres de la gente y usarlos cuando te presentas, como en los siguientes ejemplos:
Good morning, Mr. Jones. It's nice to finally meet you.
Thanks for coming, Ms. Rodgers. We have plenty to talk about today.
En este vídeo, veremos presentaciones correctas para tus reuniones.

MEETING TERMINOLOGY

Let's now consider the relevant terminology and typical phrases that you could use at various stages of a business meeting.

Starting the meeting

Let's take a look at some terms you can use for starting the meeting:

Pongámonos manos a la obra.	Let's get down to business.
Más vale que empecemos.	We'd better start.
Me gustaría empezar por....	I'd like to begin by...
Hay tres puntos que me gustaría destacar.	There are three points I'd like to make.
Me gustaría empezar diciendo.	I'd like to kick off by saying...

Following an agenda

In a formal meeting, having a printed agenda will help you stay on track and ensure all relevant points are discussed. Particularly if you are controlling the meeting, you will want to use specific terms to introduce points of discussion:

Como verán en el orden del día...	As you'll see from the agenda...
En primer lugar, tenemos que considerar....	First of all, we must consider/examine/ bear in mind...
Para empezar...	To begin with...
Sugiero que empecemos por este punto primero.	I suggest we take this item first.
Empecemos con el asunto de...	Let's start by looking at the issue of...

Introducing points

As you move through the agenda, it is important to know relevant phrases to introduce new points of discussion and add additional information:

Pasando a....	Turning to... / Moving on to... / Turning our attention to...
Ahora centrémonos en...	Let's now focus on...
Además...	In addition... / Additionally...
También deberíamos pensar en...	We should also think about...

Introducing your arguments

As you present your points, just as in presentations, it is important to use examples to strengthen your arguments. Consider the following phrases to introduce your points:

Déjeme darle un ejemplo...	Let me give an example...
Para mostrar este punto, centrémonos en...	To illustrate this point, let's consider...
Veamos el caso de...	Let's look at the case of...

Considering alternatives

When considering possible alternatives, there are several ways to weigh options:

Por un lado...y por otro...	On one hand..., but on the other hand...
Aunque....tenemos que recordar que...	Although..., we must remember that...
A pesar de... aún así creo que...	In spite of..., I still think that...
A pesar de que...no deberíamos olvidar que...	Despite the fact that..., we mustn't forget that...

Sharing opinions

To keep information flowing freely in the meeting, it's important to use the right terminology both for giving opinions and for asking for them. Here are some useful phrases:

¿Qué piensas?	What do you think?
¿Cuál es tu opinión?	What's your opinion?
¿Cuál es tu punto de vista sobre...?	What are your views / thoughts on...?
Creo que...	I strongly / firmly / really believe that...
Realmente creo que...	I really think / feel / believe that...
En mi opinión, deberíamos...	In my opinion, we should...
Como yo lo veo...	As I see it...
En cuanto a mí...	As far as I'm concerned...
Desde mi punto de vista...	From my perspective / point of view...
Que yo sepa...	As far as I know...
Entiendo lo que quieres decir.	I see what you mean.

Expressing agreement and disagreement

It is important to be able to express different degrees of agreement in a meeting. Consider the following phrases to express how you **agree** or disagree with the comments you hear in a meeting. The list progresses from strong agreement, through tentative agreement, polite disagreement and then to strong disagreement.

REMEMBER:
"To agree" is a verb. We say "I agree", and not "I am agree".

Estoy completamente de acuerdo contigo.	I entirely agree with you.
Creo que tienes razón.	I think you're right.
Hasta cierto punto, estoy de acuerdo contigo.	To a certain extent, I agree with you.
No puedo estar de acuerdo contigo sobre...	I really can't agree with you about...
No estoy convencido sobre...	I'm not convinced about...
Creo que necesitamos más tiempo para considerar...	I think we need more time to consider...
Sinceramente...	Frankly...
Para ser sincero...	To be blunt...
Entiendo tu punto de vista, pero...	I understand your point, but...
No estoy para nada de acuerdo contigo.	I totally / completely disagree with you.
No estoy de acuerdo en absoluto.	I don't agree at all.
Lo que dices es imposible.	What you are saying is unfeasible / impossible.

Introducing questions

Depending on the formality of the meeting, it may be important to introduce questions in a careful manner. Following are some ways to introduce questions:

¿Has pensado en...?	Have you considered...?
¿Se te ha ocurrido que...?	Has it occurred to you that...?
¿Te das cuenta de que...?	Do you realize / know that...?
¿No estarías de acuerdo en que...?	Wouldn't you agree that...?
¿No deberíamos considerar...?	Shouldn't we consider...?

Seeking clarification

Paraphrasing:
'parafrasear'.

There are many ways you can ask questions, each with a different level of formality, or particular purpose. Often **paraphrasing** can be used in a question to seek clarification. Carefully study the following list to improve your ability to ask questions in business meetings:

¿Podrías decirnos...?	Could you tell us...?
¿Qué clase de...?	What sort of...?
¿Podrías decirnos un poco más sobre...?	Could you tell us a little more about...?
¿Podrías entrar en un poco más de detalle sobre...?	Could you go into a little more detail about...?
A ver si te he entendido. Quieres...	Let me see if I've understood you. You want to...

If you aren't entirely clear on something, be sure to seek clarification. Doing business in a language that is not your own always presents additional challenges. If you don't understand something, be sure to seek clarification. Even if you do understand, hearing others express their ideas again, perhaps in other words gives you time to think and consider important details.

Don't hesitate to ask for clarification if you don't understand something in the meeting!

VIDEO
9

TOP TIPS – BUSINESS ENGLISH VIDEOS
Don't be afraid to ask questions!
Si tienes dudas, ¡pregunta!

Hablando en un idioma que no es el 'tuyo' es normal que encuentres momentos en los que no entiendas algo. Los interlocutores lo entenderán. Lo importante es no tener miedo de pedir la repetición o clarificación de términos claves.
Aquí en este vídeo, vemos cómo se puede buscar una clarificación de una manera profesional.

Consider the following lines that we use to seek clarification and correct misunderstandings:

¿Podrías repetirnos eso otra vez más, por favor?	**Could you run that by us again please?**
Me temo que no te sigo. ¿Podrías repetirlo?	**I'm afraid I don't quite follow. Could you repeat that?**
¿Te importaría repetir eso otra vez, por favor?	**Would you mind repeating that again, please?**
Me temo que no te entiendo.	**I'm afraid I don't see what you mean.**
Ha habido un malentendido.	**There's been a misunderstanding.**
Eso no es exactamente lo que quería decir.	**That isn't quite what I meant.**
Lo siento, quizás no me he explicado bien.	**Sorry, perhaps I didn't make myself clear.**

Emphasizing

When you have a strong or important point, it is key to be able to emphasize it properly. Using the correct terminology will draw attention to the point you would like to emphasize.

Déjame enfatizar...	Let me emphasize...
¿Puedo atraer tu atención a...?	Can I just draw your attention to...?
Me gustaría destacar...	I'd like to point out...
Preferiría...	I'd rather...

Interrupting and dealing with interruptions

Interruptions are common in meetings. If you feel the need to **interject** with a point, or get the conversation back on track it is important to do it politely and using appropriate wording. Following are some terms to help you in these situations:

To interject: *'interrumpir'.*

Perdóname, ¿puedo interrumpir aquí?	Excuse me, may I interrupt here?
¿Puedo decir algo aquí?	Can I say something here?
Perdona la interrupción.	Sorry to interrupt.
Si os parece bien, me gustaría aprovechar la oportunidad para...	If it's alright with everyone, I'd like to take this opportunity to...
Como yo decía...	As I was saying...
Volviendo a lo que decía...	Coming back to what I was saying...
Para continuar... (Para continuar con)	To resume... / To return to...
Déjame terminar, por favor.	Just let me finish, please.

Expressing certainty

Expressing different "shades" of certainty is also important in business meetings. Consider the terminology below to properly express how certain you are of different pieces of information or options in your business discussions.

Estoy 100 por cien seguro de que...	I'm 100 percent certain that...
Estoy absolutamente seguro de que...	I'm absolutely sure that...
No hay duda...	There's no doubt...
Es posible que...	It's possible that...
No es imposible que...	It's not impossible that...
Hay una posibilidad de que...	There is a possibility that...

Es muy improbable que...	It's very unlikely that...
No creo que haya ninguna posibilidad de que...	I don't think there's any chance that...
No estoy seguro de que...	I'm not sure / certain that...
Tengo dudas sobre...	I have doubts about...
No estoy seguro sobre...	I'm uncertain about...

Reassuring

To make the other side understand your confidence and have them feel calmer about details you have discussed, you may use reassuring phrases, such as the following:

Te puedo asegurar...	I can assure you...
Déjame asegurarte...	Let me assure you...
Entiendo tus dudas sobre...	I understand your concern about...

Summarizing

When it seems that you have covered most of the main issues, or even periodically throughout a long meeting, it is important to confirm everyone understands. To summarize agreements in your meeting, consider the following terms:

Entonces, resumiendo...	So, to sum up...
En resumidas cuentas...	In short...
Resumiendo, creo que estamos de acuerdo en que...	To summarize, I think we are in agreement on / that...

Concluding the meeting

When the meeting is coming to a close, you may wish to have closing remarks or make a statement on the conclusion of your talks. Here are a few ways to introduce it:

En conclusión...	Concluding...
Déjame concluir diciendo...	Let me wrap up by saying...
En conclusión, me gustaría reiterar...	In conclusion, I would like to restate / reiterate...
Me gustaría concluir mis comentarios con...	I would like to conclude my comments by...

FOUR TIPS TO ENSURE THE SUCCESS OF YOUR MEETINGS

1. Use an agenda

A printed agenda will show participants where they are going, and help make sure all important issues get discussed. Distribute the agenda and any other documents in advance. This way, participants can prepare for the meeting ahead of time. They will be immediately engaged in the business of the meeting, and waste less time.

2. Call a meeting only when it is necessary

Before you call a meeting, consider whether you can achieve your goal in some other way, perhaps through a discussion with someone in your organization, a telephone conference call, or email. As you reduce the number of meetings you have, be sure to improve their quality.

3. Maintain focus

Meetings can easily get off track. Meeting leaders and participants must actively work to keep meetings focused on the agenda items. Whenever you see the meeting drifting off track, encourage other attendees to refocus.

4. Capture and assign action items

If the meeting is a formal one, and requires actions to be taken by participants afterwards, be sure that someone keeps record of everything discussed and decided. After the meeting, summarize the outcome of the meeting, as well as assignments and timelines, and email a copy of this summary to all attendees.

TOP TIPS – BUSINESS ENGLISH VIDEOS
Don't make promises that you shouldn't make or can't keep
No hagas promesas sin la investigación adecuada

Aunque quieras resolver problemas en las reuniones y cerrar las cosas cuanto antes, es importante no hacer promesas ni ofrecer precios si no están bien pensados o no son beneficiosos para ti o tu empresa.

No dudes en tomarte más tiempo si te hace falta para tomar decisiones con calma y contemplando tus intereses.

Escanea el código y podrás ver un ejemplo en el vídeo.

Office Talk!

PISTA DE AUDIO 11

A continuación encontrarás cinco frases típicas de uso corriente que puedes oír en una oficina donde se habla inglés. Tapa la columna de la derecha y traduce en voz alta las frases.

Ella está nerviosa por el informe de ventas.	**She's nervous about the sales report.**
Llevo toda la mañana intentando hablar por teléfono con él.	**I've been trying to get through to him all morning.**
Avísame cuando sepas las cifras.	**Get back to me when you know the figures.**
La grapadora está atascada.	**The stapler is jammed.**
Ven a verme si necesitas ayuda.	**Come see me if you need help.**

CHAPTER 10

PRESENTATIONS

[Hablar en público con confianza]

PRESENTATIONS

Presentations are very important in business and often common in the workplace. Having good presentations skills means being able to make people understand your ideas and the importance of what you have to say.

Preparation is the key to a good presentation. In this section of the book, we will look at how to plan and execute your presentation in a way that is appropriate for the circumstances and that you can execute with confidence.

"He who fails to plan, plans to fail." - Winston Churchill

WHY ARE YOU GIVING A PRESENTATION?

To establish the most appropriate presentation style it is very important to understand why you are going to give a presentation.

Presentations can be used to:

- Inform or train
- Persuade
- Sell or impress

A successful presentation means communicating your message effectively. The techniques, styles and vocabulary in English are quite different from those of Spanish, so gaining knowledge and fluency with these terms makes your presentations much more effective.

DIFFERENT TYPES OF PRESENTATIONS

Most presentations can be divided into three categories. There are presentations that are used to inform or train, to persuade and to sell or impress. How do you approach the three different styles?

"hook" word or term: 'gancho'.

- For an **informative presentation**, the key is to transmit benefits without getting involved emotionally. The more you are emotionally tied to a product or idea, the harder it is to inform your audience in an effective way.
- For a **persuasive presentation** you really have to know who you audience is. As a result, you will know what their needs are. Once you demonstrate how to deal with their needs, you will stimulate their interest or reasons for listening to you. This is a presentation where examples and visuals aids are extremely useful in convincing your audience.
- For a presentation that is used to **sell or impress**, it is important to explain the benefits and weaknesses of your products or ideas. You must tell the audience what they want to hear. It is a style of presentation where rhetorical questions, **"hook"** words that catch the audience's attention ("important", "new", "surprising"), voice and body language all make a difference.

Know your audience

In 2007 I finished my MBA, (Master's in Business Administration) degree from Saint Mary's University in Halifax, Nova Scotia, Canada.

One of the most challenging requisites of the course was the completion of a major research paper, essentially a master's thesis. Given my background and interest in finance and investments, I researched the performance of emerging investment markets in a diversified portfolio, and the effectiveness of diversification in these international markets.

Thesis presentations to a variety of professors and the MBA program director were to begin a few weeks before the end of the term. When the time came, I still felt that I had a few weeks before my thesis would be ready.

It was a Friday afternoon when the program director approached me and told me that my name had been selected to present on Monday afternoon.

I was shocked and worried.

I simply wasn't ready and couldn't think of how I would be able to deliver my presentation. My topic was analytical, but I know the audience would be primarily managerial and marketing people.

That's when I remembered the motto KISS – **K**eep it **S**imple, **S**tupid

I decided to build the presentation to be very specific for the audience in question. I decided not to dig too far into the numbers, but rather simply explain the concept, why it was relevant and what my findings were. **The last thing I wanted to do was confuse the audience.**

By keeping my presentations simple and at a level that everyone in the room could understand, I was able to keep the audience engaged and interested. I remembered the important fact that this was my research and that I was the expert. By conveying passion in the content and enthusiasm for the findings, even though the final figures hadn't even been calculated, I won over the audience.

Keeping the content simple, showing enthusiasm and being confident throughout proved to be the keys to success.

After that experience, I felt I could handle almost any public speaking situation.

STRUCTURE

Make your structure clear so that the audience can follow along easily. Organize your points in a logical order and in the following three parts:

1. Introduction: "Tell the audience what you are going to tell them"

A short introduction welcomes your audience, introduces your subject, explains the presentation structure and **sets down** the rules for questions.

To set down
- To establish: *'fijar' con reglas, normas etc.*

You only have one chance to make a first impression.

The following is a good example:

"Good morning ladies and gentlemen. As most of you know, my name is Rob Wilkinson. I am going to talk about our expansion into the North Eastern United States. To start, I'll describe our progress this year opening new branches. Following, I'll mention some of the problems we have encountered and how we overcame them. Finally, I'll consider possibilities for further growth and expansion in the next five years. I'll summarize my presentation with some more general recommendations for the company. I'll try to answer all of your questions after the presentation since our time is limited".

2. Body: "Tell the audience"

With a good introduction, you are now ready for the main part of your presentation. The body needs to be well structured and divided up logically. Space your visuals so that your audience does not get overwhelmed.

Remember the following while delivering the body of your presentation:

- Don't rush. Relax and slow down.
- Be enthusiastic.
- Give the audience time to look at your visual aids.
- Maintain eye contact.
- Modulate your voice for variety.
- Look friendly and smile.
- Keep to your structure and say what you said you were going to say!
- "Signpost" throughout your presentation.

TIP

Three – The magic number

As a general rule, three is the ideal number of major points to cover in a presentation. By addressing three points, you are able to go into depth with each, yet the presentation stays short enough that you can keep the audience's attention throughout.

3. Conclusion: "Tell the audience what you told them"

The conclusion is a summary of your presentation, a word of thanks to your audience and an invitation to questions.

Consider the following example:

EX

"I would just like to recap what I've talked about this afternoon. My recommendations are to collaborate with Nelson Consultancy who really are at the cutting edge of the field. I also would like to thank you for your attendance and attention. Now I'll try to answer your questions. We have only ten minutes left so I'll have to be quick with each one."

Question and Answer Session (The Q&A):

This part of your presentation is a good opportunity to interact with your audience. Many speakers find questions and answers difficult or **nerve-racking** because they are afraid they will not understand or be able to answer the posed questions. While preparing for your presentation, try to anticipate the audience's questions. This will help you feel better prepared and alleviate some of the anxiety.

Nerve-racking: 'angustioso', 'estresante'.

Depending on how you feel, how much time you have and the overall reception of your presentation, you can choose to answer questions during or only after the presentation. After all, it is your presentation and your decision. Be polite with the people who ask you questions, even the difficult ones. At the end of this chapter, you have some tricks to deal with tough situations.

It's time to be PC!

Aunque la corrección política es algo relativamente nuevo y en desarrollo en España, en los países angloparlantes está ampliamente establecido. La corrección política tiene que ver con el uso de lenguaje, ideas o políticas que tratan sobre la discriminación contra la gente desventajada políticamente, socialmente, o económicamente.

Los títulos de los puestos de trabajo han cambiado con el tiempo para ser más neutrales con respecto al género, para indicar que cualquier género puede ser perfectamente cualificado por un puesto dado.

Abajo vemos una lista de términos tradicional, y su equivalente más moderno y políticamente correcto:

Old term	Politically correct alternative	Spanish
Chairman	Chairperson	*presidente de la junta*
Spokesman	Spokesperson	*portavoz*
Police man	Police officer	*policía*
Barman/barmaid	Bartender	*camarero (de barra)*
Fireman	Firefighter	*bombero*
Fisherman	Fisher	*pescador*
Salesman / Saleswoman	Sales worker or Sales associate	*vendedor*
Steward / Stewardess	Flight attendant	*asistente de vuelo*
Secretary	Administrative assistant	*secretaria*
Waiter / Waitress	Server	*camarero (de restaurante)*
Weatherman	Meteorologist	*meteorólogo*

KNOW YOUR MATERIAL AND REHEARSE IT

Make sure you have a strong understanding of the material you are going to be talking about, and how it fits together in your presentation.

Practice, practice, practice. The more you practice, the more comfortable you will be in your presentation and the easier it will be.

To wing it -
To improvise:
'improvisar'.

Use a mirror or family members as an audience to dress rehearse your entire presentation. Give the presentation as if it were the real thing. Perhaps the exercise sounds silly or you feel you can **"wing it"**, but you will be surprised by how relaxed you are during the actual presentation. By addressing all these issues, you will be more confident and enthusiastic.

Practice makes perfect

In his book, *Outliers*, Malcolm Gladwell estimates that it takes ten thousand hours to achieve mastery of a challenging skill, such as becoming a successful recording artist. Eric Clapton is known to have practiced guitar alone in his room for twelve or more hours each day for a long time, before feeling good enough to play professionally.

When you look at people who are great at anything, they generally have one thing in common – they have worked incredibly hard to achieve what they have.

Whether it's learning a language, mastering the guitar, or hitting a golf ball, practice will make you better. If you repeat your presentation enough, it will come much easier and you will be more comfortable.

USING NOTES

Do **NOT** read your presentation off a script or the slides you prepared. Instead, use NOTES. By writing down the titles of each section of your talk you can later refer to them as you speak. The notes will give you confidence and if you go blank momentarily will serve as, a way to get back on track. Again, **the key is preparation.**

TOP TIPS – BUSINESS ENGLISH VIDEOS
Don't read directly from your notes during your presentation
No leas directamente tus apuntes durante tu presentación

Aunque tener apuntes es importante y puede ser una herramienta útil, sobre todo para combatir los nervios, no deberías leerlos directamente de ellos o de una hoja de papel.
Quédate con apuntes cortos, con palabras clave y términos generales para que te sirvan como guía si te olvidas de algo o pierdes el ritmo en tu presentación.
Aquí veremos un de vídeo sobre el uso correcto de apuntes en una presentación.

PRESENTATION DESIGN

There are several considerations to be made when designing your presentation. Consider the following:

1. Audience: Whom am I giving this presentation to?

How many people are there? Who are they? Is your audience professional, political, expert or non-expert? How much do you know about them and what will they be expecting from you?

Remember that the audience is on your side. Generally, a business audience will be interested and understanding. They want you to succeed because they benefit from a presentation that is carried out successfully.

Notice: We use "whom" here and not "who", since the question word represents the object, not the subject of the sentence.

2. Venue: Where am I giving this presentation?

Consider how a small hotel room or a large conference hall will affect your presentation. What facilities and equipment are available to you? How will your audience be seated?

3. Time and Length: When will I give this presentation? How long will it last?

Ten to fifteen minutes is usually a good duration for most presentations. The time of day is also important to consider with regard to the style of your presentation. In the morning, an audience is often less alert and in the evening they are often tired after a long day. Around 11 in the morning is usually an ideal time as the audience is awake and more receptive to your efforts to connect with them.

4. Method: How should I give this presentation?

The presentation can be given in a formal or informal way. You also have to consider how you will use visual aids or if you will include anecdotes, props and humor to provide some variety.

5. Content: What am I going to say?

You can start by brainstorming, which will give you ideas. Nevertheless, be selective by including information that is relevant for your audience and your objective. Remove everything else.

Less is more:

In general, less is better for your audience and you can always give more information after you finish your presentation.

CHOOSING A TITLE

A good title will help get the attention of your audience and have them focused from the beginning. To get the audience to listen, your title should be interesting.

Some ideas for choosing a title are as follows:

1. Promise benefits

A clear title explaining that participants will benefit from the presentation will get their interest.

Consider one of the best-selling communications books in the world, Dale Carnegie's "How to Win Friends and Influence People". The title of the book is a big part of its success because it promises benefits.

Rather that titling your presentation:

"How to make ice cream".

A more attractive title would be:

"How to make ice cream that will have your friends and family asking for more."

or

"How to make the best ice cream you'll ever taste."

2. Introduce a story

Everyone loves stories. Imagine the following titles and how they would capture your interest:

"How a poor immigrant boy started one of America's greatest empires."

or

"How the world's great empires came to be."

3. Create concern

People like to know that they aren't making mistakes. Using this strategy can draw interest from people looking to learn and avoid mistakes.

Consider the following:

"Major flaws in traditional supermarket design"

or

"Common mistakes of amateur managers"

These titles are clear, concise and will capture the interest of people dedicated to the field of work being discussed.

WHAT TOOLS SHOULD I USE IN MY PRESENTATION?

Think about what is available for you and what is best for your audience and room.

Here are some things to consider:

Whiteboard

A classic tool for simple presentations.

Whiteboards are very useful for interactive presentations, where you may want to **jot down** notes, to brainstorm and to illustrate examples.

To jot down: *'apuntar'.*

TIP

Sometimes the eraser or markers are old and do not work. It is a good idea to carry your own.

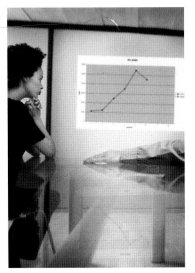

PowerPoint presentations

Probably the most common tool in business presentations, PowerPoint can be very effective for conveying a great deal of information in a structured, logical way.

• Get comfortable with PowerPoint so you do not become nervous if there are technical difficulties.
• Do not read directly from your PowerPoint slides.

"Prezi" and other new presentation software

New, attractive alternatives to PowerPoint, such as "Prezi" (see: www.prezi.com) are available and can help you make eye-catching presentations. Learn about them and how they can add to the quality of your presentation.

Keep in mind that any aids shouldn't serve to dazzle the audience, but rather to reinforce your message. Remember: **YOU** are the star of your presentation.

Handouts

Handouts serve two important purposes in a presentation. They are a way to offer visual information if you don't have other resources and they also reduce the audience's need to be taking notes throughout the presentation, allowing them to focus more on you.

TIP Do not hand these out right before your presentation because they will read them instead of listening to you.

VISUAL AIDS

A huge portion of what your audience will learn will be learned visually. Visual aids are therefore extremely effective at conveying your message and at helping the listener overcome the language barrier by relying on visual comprehension.

It is worth developing visual aids but keep the visual information quite simple. Some PowerPoint **slides** come loaded with information or text and are often difficult to decipher. Give the audience time to look at and absorb the information. They need time to study and understand what the visual aids mean. Generally, the most useful aids are graphics such as pie charts, bar charts, graphs or flow diagrams.

Slides: 'diapositivas'.

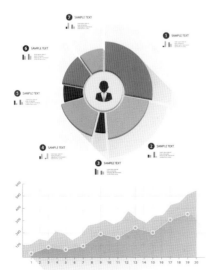

Choose the most appropriate visual aids for the information you would like to explain.

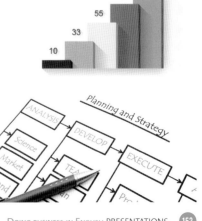

Keep your visual aids simple

If you are using PowerPoint, be sure not to put too much information on your slides.

Your slides should have no more than **four** points and be quick and easy to understand.

In your presentation, YOU should be the center of attention, not the slides. Consider the following example slide and how easy it is to follow, compared to slides full of long texts that the audience won't be able to read in full.

Import and Export statistics for last year:

Imports have increased by 11% due to more favorable labor rates abroad.

Exports have declined due to wages and the rising dollar.

Overall demand growth continues to be promising.

Notice how each comment is brief. Reading it won't completely distract the audience from the speaker.

TOP TIPS – BUSINESS ENGLISH VIDEOS

Don't rely entirely on technology

No uses demasiada tecnología.

La tecnología forma parte de nuestras vidas hoy en día, y sirve como un buen apoyo a la hora de presentar información. Es importante que la estrella de la presentación seas tú, y que las herramientas no distraigan demasiado del mensaje comunicado personalmente.
Además, la tecnología tiene el riesgo de crear problemas y dejar de funcionar. Asegúrate de que eres capaz de dar tu presentación sin tus PowerPoints u otros recursos audiovisuales si hace falta.
Aquí veremos un ejemplo en el vídeo disponible con el código de arriba.

DESCRIBING CHARTS AND GRAPHS:

If you have charts or graphs in your presentation, it is important to know the vocabulary you can use to describe them. Using a variety of verbs and adjectives can **"spice up"** your presentation and keep the attention of your audience.

To spice up - To make something more interesting or lively: *'animar'*.

	Spanish verb	English Verb	English noun
decrease	Disminuir, descender	decline	A decline
	Disminuir,	decrease	A decrease
	Caer, bajar	drop	A drop
	Caer, bajar	fall	A fall
	Quebrar	crash	A crash
	Desplomarse	collapse	A collapse
	Caer en picado	plummet	A plummet
	Desplomarse, hundir, zambullirse	plunge	A plunge
increase	Ascender	climb	A climb
	Subir	rise	A rise
	Incrementar	increase	An increase
	Dispararse	soar	A soar
	Dispararse como un cohete	skyrocket	A skyrocket
stabilize	Allanar, alisar	flatten out	A flattening out
	Mantenerse	hold steady	A steady hold
	Nivelar, estabilizarse	level off	A leveling off
	Estabilizar	stabilize	A stabilization
recover	Rebotar	bounce back	A rebound
	Rally, Recuperarse	rally	A rally
	Recuperar	recover	A recovery
	Fluctuar	fluctuate	A fluctuation

	SPANISH ADJECTIVE/ADVERB	ENGLISH ADVERB
Change	Ligeramente, levemente	Slightly
	De manera significativa	Significantly
	Bruscamente, repentinamente	Sharply
	Considerablemente	Considerably
	Drásticamente	Dramatically
Speed	Rápidamente	Rapidly
	Rápidamente, deprisa	Quickly
	Rápidamente	Swiftly
	Poco a poco	Gradually
	Constantemente	Steadily

Let's practice by looking at a graph and seeing how we could use this vocabulary.

Consider "Kyle's Farm Market", which sells ice cream all year round. The price fluctuates constantly throughout the year as Kyle tries to charge the highest price he can get for his ice cream at a given moment.

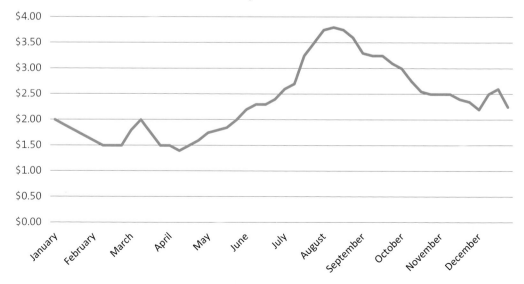

Price of ice cream at Kyle's Farm Market

Ice cream price fluctuations over the course of last year:

January: Ice cream prices fell steadily through the month after Christmas.

February: Prices continued to fall then leveled off.

March: Prices rose sharply for a short period as students on their spring break demanded more ice cream.

April: Prices fell again, then bottomed out at the end of the month.

May: Prices began to rise steadily as the weather got better.

June: Prices continued to rise significantly.

July: Prices skyrocketed as temperatures rose, causing great demand.

August: Prices peaked and leveled off.

September: Prices began a sharp decline as the summer ended and people felt they wanted less ice cream.

October: Prices leveled off then began another slow decline.

November: Prices declined sharply at the end of the month.

December: Prices shot up temporarily as people bought ice cream for Christmas. After Christmas demand and prices began to decline again.

KNOW THE AUDIENCE

Take a moment before your presentation to speak informally with audience members. Introduce yourself and make "small talk" with a few of them. This will help you feel more comfortable presenting to them shortly after.

Enthusiasm is contagious, so if you are enthusiastic, you audience will be too. During your presentation establish eye contact with each member by looking at each listener one by one.

Also, consider the type of audience. Why are they there? Who are they and what do they already know? Prepare your presentation with your audience in mind.

Visualize your success

Before you begin, imagine yourself succeeding and getting a good response from your audience. This will help you make it a reality. Remember, the audience wants you to succeed as well. They aren't the enemy!

NERVES

Almost everyone gets nervous when speaking in public. It is absolutely okay, even good for you to be a little nervous. Remember that no one is going to be as critical as you of your performance in the presentation.

The beginning of the presentation is usually the most challenging part. Once you break the ice and begin speaking, you will gradually feel more comfortable.

By heart: *'de memoria'*.

At the beginning of the presentation, make an effort to speak slowly. You can even memorize your introduction **by heart**.

Consider the following tips for dealing with nerves:

Practice deep breathing - By breathing deeply your brain will get the oxygen it needs and the slower pace will trick your body into believing you are calmer. It also helps stabilize your voice.

Smile - This will naturally relax you. Smiling sends positive chemicals through your body.

Drink water - Adrenalin can cause a dry mouth, which in turn leads to getting tongue-tied. Have a glass of water handy.

Move around during your presentation - This will use up some of your nervous energy.

Use visualization techniques – Imagine your audience as interested, enthusiastic, and positive. Fix this positive image in your mind and recall it right before you are ready to speak.

Speak slower than you would in a conversation, and leave longer pauses between sentences - This pace will calm you down, and make you easier to hear, especially at the back of a large room.

Don't apologize for being nervous

Your audience probably won't realize how nervous you may be. Don't tell them that you're nervous. It adds nothing and only makes you feel more self-conscious.

KNOW THE ROOM

Become familiar with the area where you are going to give your presentation. This includes understanding how any visual

aids can be best used and allows you to consider and solve any potential problems the audience may have seeing or hearing you.

BODY LANGUAGE

Your body language communicates a message to your audience even before you open your mouth to speak. Your clothes, your walk, your glasses and your expression all help the audience form their first impression of you. Keep the following in mind:

- It is better to stand than sit when giving a presentation.
- Be aware of any irritating habits or gestures such as swaying or touching your hair.
- Movement should be made with purpose. If you need to move from one part of the stage to another, then take three firm steps in that direction.
- Smile! If you are enthusiastic, it will show on your face.

Move with purpose:

When you are going to move around, be sure that your movements are deliberate, and not movements that could be seen as the result of nervousness or insecurity. Moving with confidence will help you feel more confident in yourself.

TOP TIPS – BUSINESS ENGLISH VIDEOS
Controlling your movements during a presentation
¡No te muevas!

Con los nervios la gente tiende a moverse sin control, tocarse el pelo o mecerse delante del público. Estas manías no añaden nada positivo a la presentación e indican nervios, hay que hacer un esfuerzo consciente para no hacerlos.
Cuando te muevas, hazlo con intención. Si te mueves da dos o tres pasos pronunciados.
Veremos un ejemplo en el vídeo disponible con el código arriba.

CULTURALCONSIDERATIONS

Be sensitive to cultural matters that may be misinterpreted by your audience. For example, in the Unites States, Canada and the UK it is considered rude to point at a person. Some Anglo-Saxon audiences might feel uncomfortable around a person who is "touchy" or "invades" their personal space, which is perhaps the **norm** in some Mediterranean cultures.

The norm: *'lo normal'.*

VOICE QUALITY

Be sure to speak clearly and directed towards the audience. If you need to write something on a whiteboard, write it and then explain it. You should not speak to the audience with your back facing them. In general, you should speak slightly louder than usual.

Punch line: *'frase clave', 'remate'.*

Vary your voice to make your speaking style more interesting.

Tips for attracting attention with your voice:

Speed	Vary the pace of your voice and use pauses to gain the audience's attention. For example, pause briefly before and after your **punch line**.
Intonation	You can change the pitch by speaking in a high or low tone.
Volume	You can speak at a normal level, loudly or quietly. Speaking loudly can wake your audience up and speaking softly can pique their curiosity.

LANGUAGE

If you want your audience to understand your message, use simple and clear language.

Jargon: *'jerga profesional'.*

TIP

Here are some more tips for language use in your presentation:

- Only use **jargon** if your audience understands it.
- Use concrete facts instead of abstract ideas.
- Use active verbs instead of passive verbs. Active verbs are easier to understand and make more of an impact. Just as with the subject "YOU", the active voice is a more powerful tool in making your message heard.

SIGNPOSTING

Help your audience navigate through your presentation by putting up "signposts" throughout. By using specific words to mark transitions and signal where you are in your presentation, you help your audience follow along and know what to expect.

Signposting: 'señalización'.

During your introduction, briefly explain the structure of your presentation. For example:

*"I'll **start** by describing the current European portfolio. **Then**, I'll move on to some of the achievements we've made in Europe. **Thirdly**, I'll consider the opportunities we see for further expansion in Europe by 2020. **Lastly**, I'll quickly recap before concluding with some recommendations."*

These terms will help your audience members structure your presentation in their heads as they recognize the introduction, the body and the conclusion. Throughout your presentation it is a good idea to indicate where you are and what point you have reached.

The following table provides useful signpost expressions you can use in your presentation.

Signposting		Grammar	
To introduce the subject	• I'd like to start by...	+	"ing" verb
	• Let's begin by...		
	• I'll begin by...		
	• Starting with...	+	"ing" verb / noun
	• First of all, I'll...	+	Present simple
To finish a subject	• Well, I've told you about...	+	"ing" verb/noun
	• That's all I have to say about...		
	• We've looked at...		
	• So much for...		
...and to link to another subject	• Now we'll move on to...	+	"ing" verb/noun
	• Let me turn now to...		
	• Turning to...		
	• Now let's look at...		
	• I'd like to discuss...		
	• This brings me to my next point, which is...		
	• Next, ...	+	Phrase
Analyzing a point and giving recommendations	• Where does that lead us?		
	• Let's consider this in more detail.		
	• What does this mean for the company?		
	• Translated into real terms...		
Adding and supporting data	• On top of that,	+	Phrase
	• In addition,		
	• Moreover,		
	• Furthermore,		
	• As a matter of fact,		

Giving an example	• For example, • A good example of this is • As an illustration, • To give you an example, • To illustrate this point,	+	**Phrase**
Using rhetorical questions	• What was the reason for this? • How can we explain this? • Why did we achieve these results? • What can we do about it?		
Contrasting	• In contrast, • However, • On one hand,...On the other hand,... • Despite this, • Whereas	+	**Phrase**
Reporting causes	• Due to • As a result of • This was because • This was caused by	+	**"ing" verb / noun**
Dealing with questions	• We'll be examining this point in more detail, later on. • I'd like to deal with this question later, if I may. • I'll come back to this question later in my talk. • Perhaps you'd like to raise this point at the end. • I won't comment on this now.		
Using past information	• As I said earlier, • As mentioned before, • As we've already seen,	+	**Phrase**

Stressing data	• I would like to point out that	+	**"ing" verb / noun**
	• I'd like to emphasize that		
	• I want to highlight the fact that		
	• It's worth mentioning that		
	• Regarding		
	• With respect to		
	• On the issue of		
Summarizing and concluding	• In conclusion…	+	**Phrase**
	• Right, let's sum up, shall we?		
	• I'd now like to recap.		
	• Let's summarize briefly what we've looked at.		
	• Finally, let me remind you of some of the issues we've covered.		
	• If I can just sum up the main points.		
Ordering	• Firstly…secondly…thirdly…lastly.		
	• First of all…then…next…after that…finally.		
	• To start with…later…to finish up.		

ANSWERING DIFFICULT QUESTIONS

Consider the following tips to help you with difficult questions during your question and answer (Q&A) session:

When you don't know the answer, admit it

- *"I'm not sure of that at the moment, but I'll find out and let you know…".*
- *"That's an important question and I'm coming to that problem shortly…in the next part of my speech".*

In this last example, you then have two alternatives:

- You can try to answer the question, or
- Leave it out, in which case you hope your questioner will forget about having asked you in the first place!

Turn the question back to the questioner

- *"Do you have an opinion on that yourself?"*
- *"Well, what would you say?"*

Answer a different question

This is typical of politicians.

- Supply information you hope will satisfy the questioner.
- Avoid giving information that either you do not know or do not want to reveal.

Refuse to answer

You will normally have to give at least an apparently acceptable reason.

- *"Unfortunately, that is information which is not mine to give."*
- *"Would you perhaps like to have a word with the financial director who may be prepared to say more than I can".*

Request that the question be discussed privately

- *"That is a very important question, but it really is one that is particular to you and to your business. Would you be kind enough to have a word with me afterwards and I will try to answer it for you?"*
- *"I am sorry, but I have so little time left to complete this speech. Would you mind discussing that later?"*

Referring the question to a committee

- *"This is a very complex question. I am going to ask Jeff, Mary and Bill to meet and discuss it and then to report back to us."*
- *"Let's set up a subcommittee to look into that question. It is really unsuitable for a gathering of this size. We need to do some serious research, don't we?"*

Ask your audience

- *"Now, that's an interesting question. Does anyone know the answer to it?"*

If someone knows and tells you, you have won.

If no one knows, you can say:

- *"Well, we have a lot of experienced people here and no one has come across the answer. I don't know it either. But we must find out. I will make inquiries and let you know."*

You may not have won, but at least you will not have lost!

TOP TIPS – BUSINESS ENGLISH VIDEOS
Honesty is the best policy
Ser honesto en tus respuestas

A veces te pueden hacer preguntas difíciles en una presentación, y puede que hasta no sepas la respuesta a algunas.
Es importante no mentir. Si no sabes la respuesta, no inventes una. Aquí en el libro presentamos unas alternativas para tratar este problema. Lo más fácil y correcto siempre es ser honesto y abierto pero siempre mostrando interés y ofreciendo opciones para resolver cualquier duda.
El vídeo disponible con este código, muestra un ejemplo interesante.

Office Talk!   PISTA DE AUDIO 12

Aquí te ofrezco cinco frases típicas de uso corriente que puedes oír en una oficina donde se habla inglés. Tapa la columna de la derecha y traduce las frases en voz alta.

Creo que el taxi está esperando abajo.	**I think the cab is waiting downstairs.**
Teníamos que empezar a las 16.00, pero parece que él no llegará hasta y cuarto.	**We were supposed to start at 4:00, but it looks like he won't be here until a quarter past.**
Necesitaré que me reserves un vuelo a Amsterdam.	**I'll need you to book me a flight to Amsterdam.**
No sé cómo funciona este teléfono nuevo.	**I can't figure out this new phone.**
El Sr. Alfredson no está. ¿Podría llamar dentro de media hora?	**Mr. Alfredson isn't in at the moment. Could you call back in half an hour?**

PRESENTATION CHECKLIST

To summarize everything we have covered presentation, consider the following 20-point checklist before giving yours.

1.	Have you allowed yourself plenty of time for preparation?
2.	Do you consider the all-important question-words? • Why? • Who? • Where? • When? • How? • What?
3.	Is your presentation clearly structured into introduction, body, conclusion and questions?
4.	Have you rehearsed your presentation and modified it as necessary?
5.	Have you selected the right equipment for the job, and can you use it effectively?
6.	Will you make use of clear, powerful visual aids that do not overload your audience?
7.	Do you use clear, simple language, avoiding too much jargon?
8.	Does the presentation use active verbs and concrete facts?
9.	Do you explain the structure of your presentation at the beginning so that your listeners know what to expect?
10.	Do you signpost your presentation throughout so that your listeners know where they are?
11.	Do you say what you are going to say, say it, and then say what you have just said?
12.	Can you overcome your nerves?
13.	Will you try to establish audience rapport?
14.	Are you aware of your body language?
15.	Do you understand cultural differences?
16.	Can you control the quality of your voice?
17.	Do you maintain interest by varying the speed, volume and pitch of your voice?
18.	Do you deal with listeners' questions politely?
19.	Do you respond to your audience positively?
20.	Does your presentation have an interesting title?

By considering the items discussed in this section, you can prepare and deliver a presentation effectively.

A final tip:

Remember, no one will be as critical of your presentation as yourself. Relax, don't be afraid of the audience and have fun!

CHAPTER 11

NEGOTIATING

[Llegando al "Sí" en inglés]

NEGOTIATING

Negotiation is a process of **bargaining** where agreement is reached between two or more parties. We all negotiate every day in a wide range of work and social situations. It is important to know how to negotiate effectively so we can reach agreements that are better for us.

Bargaining:
'regateo' /
'negociaciones'.

Remember

The general goal of a negotiation is to give away things that are less valuable to you in exchange for things that are more valuable to you.

Keep in mind that not everyone places the same value on every concession, product or service.

The most important thing to understand in a negotiation is the value of potential **concessions** not only to you, but also to the party you are negotiating with.

Concession:
'concesión'.

Imagine the following example:

Let's say you have a farm with a lot of hens that lay several hundred eggs per day.

For you, eggs are plentiful, and therefore you don't mind trading some for other things that you would otherwise have to buy. To your neighbor, who has no hens, the eggs are more precious or "valuable", so you gladly trade some of your eggs to him for some of the cheese he produces.

He produces tons of cheese each year, so for him cheese is an easy product to give away, so he is happy to trade it for a regular supply of eggs.

Here we see how essential it is to understand how the other party in the negotiation may appreciate each concession you may be able to give them.

There doesn't have to be a "winner" and a "loser" in negotiation. In general, in the long term, it will be easier to **foster** long-term business relationships if the companies and people you deal with are genuinely happy with the relationship they have with you.

To foster - To promote:
'fomentar' /
'promover'.

STYLES OF NEGOTIATION – "ADVERSARIAL" VERSUS "COOPERATIVE BARGAINING"

Generally speaking, bargaining styles can be considered either cooperative or adversarial. Depending on the circumstances, and whom you are dealing with, you must find the balance between these two ends of the negotiation spectrum.

In the case of **adversarial bargaining** the two sides take more rigid positions where each side defends their position and gives as few concessions as possible. They often open negotiations with unrealistic requests, either too high or too low, in order to maneuver the negotiation. Tactics or "tricks" may be used to gain short-term advantage and progress is generally slow.

Information sharing is limited and each side truly tries to get the better end of the deal.

Cooperative bargaining is more likely to lead to both parties being satisfied not only with the deal they make but with the other party, which is particularly important if they plan to develop a long-term business relationship. With this style each side recognizes the needs and general situation of the other. They accept implicit rules and acknowledge what is reasonable.

With cooperative bargaining the sides tend to trust each other, share information, and more openly gain an understanding of concessions. The sides are more willing to work together to solve problems with the goal of developing a mutually profitable relationship. The sides work towards a "win-win" **outcome**.

Adversarial bargaining - A bargaining style where each side gives as few concessions as possible and tries to "defeat" the other side.

Cooperative bargaining - A bargaining style where sides work together towards a more mutually beneficial outcome.

Outcome: 'resultado'.

To end up: 'acabar'.

PLANNING YOUR NEGOTIATION

In any kind of negotiation the planning stage is extremely important. Too often we go into the negotiation poorly prepared and **end up** making concessions that reduce the overall profitability of the final deal. Effective planning will give us a very clear idea of what is desired before entering the negotiation.

PREPARATION CHECKLIST
Consider the following points to be prepared for the negotiation:

Objectives

- What exactly do I wish to achieve from this negotiation?
- Which of my objectives:
  - would I like to achieve?
  - do I intend to achieve?
  - must I achieve?
- What options would be acceptable to me?
- What are the other side's objectives?
- How does the other side see the negotiation?

Information

- What information do I need to know about this negotiation?
- What information does the other side need to find out?
- What information does each side have that will influence the outcome of the negotiation?

Concessions

- What is the best deal I could realistically achieve in this negotiation?
- What is the likely outcome of the negotiation?
- What is the limit of my authority?
- At what point should I walk away?
- What concessions are available to me?
- What is the cost of each concession and what value does each concession have to either side?

Strategy

- How am I going to achieve my objectives in this negotiation?
- What is the strategy of the other side likely to be?
- What tactics should I use within the negotiation?
- What tactics is the other side likely to use?

Tasks (team negotiations only)

- What role should each team member play in the negotiation?
- How can we work together in the most effective way?

HOW TO STRUCTURE NEGOTIATIONS

Successful negotiators have a well-constructed strategy before going into the negotiation. They are well prepared, self-confident and structure the negotiation so that they remain in control of the negotiating process.

A recommended structure for negotiations is the following, involving three stages:

1. Establish the issues being negotiated
2. Gather information
3. Build a solution

Stage 1. Establish the issues being negotiated

Begin by agreeing on an agenda for the negotiation. What needs to be discussed and agreed on? Who will be involved and what will their role be? What timescales are we working towards? What are the major issues that need to be agreed on?

Consider the following:

- Many negotiators make the mistake of negotiating too quickly. Skilled negotiators spend more of their time asking questions and looking for alternatives.
- Professional negotiators will often want to obtain your commitment on issues, such as price, early on in the negotiation.
- You should never commit yourself to anything until you have established everything that is being negotiated.
- Negotiators will often bring up an issue at the end of the negotiation, when you are vulnerable and likely to agree to a "one-sided" concession in order to conclude the deal.
- Skilled negotiators will often ask the other side for their "shopping list" before beginning the negotiation and refuse to accept any last minute additions to the list.

- Issues will include things like price, delivery schedule, payment terms, packaging, quality of product, length of contract, etc.
- At this stage, issues are kept general, no concessions are made and no agreements are reached.

Stage 2. Gather information

This is a vital part of the negotiation. There are four kinds of information.

The four kinds of information in negotiations:
- Information you have that you are willing to give to the other side
- Information you have that you are unwilling to give to the other side
- Information the other side has that they are willing to give you
- Information the other side has that they are unwilling to give you

You need to decide before the negotiation how much information you are willing to share and what your own information requirements are. Skilled negotiators are able to ask a range of open, closed and follow-up questions and are able to listen effectively. Be patient. Skilled negotiators wait until they have all their information requirements before making concessions.

Stage 3. Build a solution

Having gathered information, the next stage is to begin to put together a solution. Usually this will take the form of the selling side putting forward a proposal, or an opening **bid**.

Bid: *'puja'.*

Remember the following:

- The opening bid should be ambitious, but realistic.
- You should always challenge an opening bid.

Wary - Cautious: *'receloso'*, *'cauto'*.

- Concessions should not be given away for free and you should be **wary** about conceding on issues you are not prepared for.

IMPORTANT POINTS TO REMEMBER

1. Never let emotion get in the way of making the right decision.

The "other side" in a negotiation is made up of people just like you. They have emotions, values and different backgrounds. They may be unpredictable and are never perfect.

People may get angry, depressed, frustrated or offended during negotiations.

Trigger - To cause: *'causar'*.

It is essential that the behavior of the other party not **trigger** irrational decision making on your part due to emotion.

One example of this could be if the other party doubts your authority in the decision making process. This may frustrate some people, leading them to make an unnecessarily firm decision simply because they can.

2. Taking your position

It is important not to take positions that are so strong that you lose sight of the truly best available agreement, simply for the sake of remaining "strong".

Firm: *'firme'*.

3. Focus on interests, not firm, inflexible positions

A **firm** position may initially seem like the only way to achieve your goals, but sometimes the initial positions presented may obscure what the parties really want. By asking questions to gain an understanding of the other side's

interests, and clearly explaining your own interests, you may find a way to achieve a solution that is satisfactory to all.

Getting to Yes

The famous book *Getting to Yes*, by Roger Fisher and William Ury, tells the story of two men arguing in a library. One man wants the window open and the other wants it closed. They argue about how much to leave it open: a crack, halfway, three quarters. No solution satisfies them both.

The librarian comes in and asks one man why he wants the window open. "To get some fresh air", he replies. She asks the other man why he wants it closed. "To avoid the draft", replies the second man. After thinking for a moment, she opens the window in the next room bringing in fresh air without a **draft**.

Draft: *'corriente'.*

Here we see an example of how, by not worrying about firm positions such as "I want the window closed" vs. "I want the window open", and rather focusing on the interests of each party the two parties were able to reach an **amicable** solution.

Amicable: *'amistoso'.*

4. Listen actively and ask questions

It is important to listen closely in a negotiation. This may seem obvious, but complementing careful listening with actively acknowledging what is being said and even asking the other party to repeat and clarify details will make them feel satisfaction that they are being heard and understood. In a way, you are already giving them a small concession.

To make sure your understanding is clear, you may wish to repeat their comments back to them, clearly including the benefits to them, so they see how it could be a concession in their favor.

Be sure to ask questions when something isn't clear. You want to understand the details of a discussion before committing to anything or accepting anything. When negotiating in a language other than your mother tongue, some people make the mistake of nodding in agreement or even saying "yes", despite not understanding. Don't let this happen.

VIDEO 15

TOP TIPS – BUSINESS ENGLISH VIDEOS
Not asking enough questions
No dudes en preguntar

La información es poder y una negociación es una calle de doble sentido. Antes de tomar decisiones u ofrecer concesiones, es imprescindible entender los detalles de lo que se está ofreciendo y saber exactamente lo que el otro espera de ti.

Haz muchas preguntas en la negociación para evitar compromisos de los que te puedas arrepentir en el futuro.

Aquí vemos un vídeo sobre la importancia de conseguir información.

5. Look for mutual gain and find options to achieve it

As mentioned in the library example above, often we can have mutual gain or "win-win" outcomes in negotiations. To achieve this, it is important to be open-minded and prepared to work to develop options.

The main obstacles that limit the development of options are:

- Premature judgement
- Searching for a single answer
- Assumption of a fixed reward
- Believing that solving someone else's problem is not your responsibility

To jump to a conclusion
- To reach a conclusion prematurely: *'llegar a conclusiones precipitadas'.*

It is important not to **jump to conclusions** and not to make decisions about the options available until your options and interests have been clearly discussed.

It is also important to be open-minded about potential solutions. How often have you had a solution in mind that you know would be satisfactory to the other party, but never had the chance to explain it? Now imagine how many times you have been on the other side of that same situation. **Don't be close-minded.**

Brainstorming: *'tormenta de ideas'.*

6. Brainstorming:

Brainstorming is often a common first step. It helps you understand your options, the other side's desires and the value of concessions. In a brainstorming session, participants produce as many ideas as possible to solve the problem. In the session itself, all ideas are included without evaluation or pause, as they will be analyzed in detail later.

Depending on the type of negotiation, you may even brainstorm together with the other side. Afterwards, each idea is considered and a list of realistic options is formed.

Mutual gain: *'De mutuo beneficio'.*

Identifying **mutual gain** will become easier as you have more open dialogue with the other side, gaining a better understanding of their needs.

7. Be fair and objective

Unfortunately, it isn't always possible to reach a simple "win-win" outcome in a negotiation.

Sometimes the other side, or you yourself, must be **firm** on certain concessions or details of the negotiation. It is important to communicate with the other side to develop objective criteria that can be acknowledged by both sides and established as being non-flexible in negotiations. For example, if a request from a supplier is against the law or logistically impossible, you clearly have a right to explain that you can't be flexible in that area.

Establishing the "rules of the game" early can help keep your negotiations **on track**.

To be firm: 'ser firme'.

To be on track: 'ir por buen camino'.

WHAT TO DO WHEN A TRULY GREAT DEAL IS IMPOSSIBLE:

Sometimes things can be out of your hands and a truly good deal may not be possible for you, but making a deal is necessary. In these cases, it is important to consider how you can protect yourself from making a clearly bad deal that you will regret, and help you make the most of the assets and possibilities that you do have.

One of the simplest ways to avoid making a truly bad deal is to clearly know your worst-case scenario, or worst acceptable offer. If you are selling, this could be your absolute lowest price or if you are buying, it could be your absolute highest.

It is also important to consider the options you have outside of the negotiations. Are there other suppliers or buyers you could consider? Are there other people you could be dealing with? What alternatives do you have to making this deal? Unfortunately, sometimes making a poor deal is better than making no deal at all. On the other hand, sometimes options are available but we let our emotions get in the way and we get so determined to make the deal that we don't consider other alternatives. **In short, understand your choices.**

In short: 'en resumidas cuentas'.

As mentioned before, understanding your assets and how they are valued by the other side can help you get the most out of a negotiation.

NEGOTIATING TACTICS

We can now look at negotiating **tactics**. Whether or not you choose to use these tactics, it is vital to understand that they can be used by you but also on you. Once they are recognized as tactics, their effects are reduced or eliminated.

There are many tactics available to negotiators. Here are ten tactics that you may find useful.

1. Pre-conditioning

This tactic involves establishing an important point before the negotiation even begins. It can begin before you even get together to start your negotiations with the other party. Let's take a sales example:

Tactics: *'trucos'.*

You telephone to make the appointment and the other side says, aggressively:

"Don't bother coming if you are going to tell me about price increases. You'll be wasting your time and I'll be forced to speak to your competitors."

2. The monkey on the back

Some negotiators have the irritating habit of handing their problems over to you so that they become your problems. This is the "monkey on their back" that they want you to carry around for them.

A classic example is the person who says, *"I only have €10,000 in my budget"*. This is often used tactically to force a price reduction. Here is what you can do in response.

When one side says *"I only have €10,000 in my budget"*, you can look worried and say for example:

"That's a problem. As you are no doubt aware, the cost of our systems can be up to €20,000 and I really want to help you choose the best system that meets your needs. Does that mean that if one of our systems has everything you are looking for...but costs €17,000, you would rather I didn't show it to you?"

The "monkey" is now on the other person's back and they have to make a choice. If the objection is genuine and the budget figure is correct, you must try to look for an alternative that meets your needs as well as theirs.

If they can really only spend €10,000, then it is not a tactic but the truth. In dealing with tactics, the first decision you must make is whether it is a tactic or a genuine situation. If it is genuine, you have a problem to solve, rather than a tactic to overcome.

3. The use of higher authority

This can be a very effective way to reduce pressure in the negotiation by introducing an unseen third party and can also be effective in bringing the negotiation to a close. *"I need to have this agreed on by my Board of Directors. If they agree to the terms we have discussed, do we have a deal?"* Make sure to use this device sparingly so that the other side does not begin to feel you have no decision-making authority yourself.

One way of countering this tactic is to say before the bargaining begins, *"If this proposal meets your needs, is there any reason you would not give me your decision today?"*

If the other side still wishes to resort to higher authority, appeal to their ego by saying, *"Of course, they will go along with your recommendations, won't they?"* or *"Will you be recommending this proposal?"*

4. Nibbling

Negotiations can be a long process. As the end approaches, both sides naturally look forward to finishing.

At this point, you may be vulnerable to conceding items that do not significantly affect the final outcome. *"Oh, by the way, this does include free delivery, doesn't it?"* or *"Oh, by the way, the price of the car does include a full tank of gasoline, right?"*

Nibbles work best when they are small and are asked for at the right psychological moment. Like peanuts, eat enough of them and they get fattening.

To nibble: *'mordisquear'.*

Good negotiators will often keep back certain items on their "want list" until the very last minute when the other party is vulnerable. **Watch out for this**!

5. The good guy and the bad guy

You may have come across this tactic before or else have seen it used in films or on television. This is a tactic designed to "soften you up" in the negotiation.

For example, you are negotiating the renewal of your service contract with the Purchasing Director and his Finance Director. You present your proposal and the Purchasing Director suddenly gets angry and walks out in disgust, claiming you have been unreasonable and how the business relationship is finished.

You pick up your briefcase and are being shown the door when the Finance Director smiles at you sympathetically and says:

"I'm sorry about that. He is under a lot of pressure. I would like to help you renew your contract, but he really will not consider the price you have suggested. Why don't I go and talk to him for you and see if we can make a compromise? What is the bottom line of the contract? If you give me your very best price, I will see what I can do".

The bottom line: *'el resultado final'.*

The best way of dealing with this tactic is to recognize the game that is being played and assess the level of familiarity you have with this person. You may be able to say something such as:

"Come on, you are using good guy, bad guy. You're a great negotiator, but let's sit down and discuss the proposal realistically..."

To stand firm: *'permanecer firme'.*

If you do not have this kind of relationship, **stand firm** and insist on dealing with the bad guy. Or else **bluff** and give a figure that is within your acceptable range of alternatives.

To bluff: *'farolear'.*

Sometimes, you can combine the "good guy, bad guy" technique with "higher authority" such as in the following example:

"Well, I'd love to do a deal with you on that basis, but my manager refuses to let me agree on terms of this nature without referring back to him. Frankly, he just refuses to talk to salespeople. Give me your best price and I will see what I can do..."

6. Body language

It is important in negotiation to react verbally and visually when offers are made. If you show no reaction, they may be tempted to ask for more and more. Also, it is almost certain that their opening offer is higher than the figure they are prepared to settle for, so it is essential that you clearly signal your unwillingness to accept their opening position.

If you reach the point where you refuse to go further, it is important that you show this with your body language. For example, television broadcasters have the habit of picking up their script and tidying their papers when they have finished reading the news. This indicates to the viewing audience that they have finished the broadcast and are preparing for exit.

Similarly, when you make your final offer, it can be very powerful to collect your papers together and indicate with your body that it really is your final

offer. Put your pen away, sit back in your chair and remain silent. Look concerned and keep quiet. If your voice says final offer but your body is saying, "let's keep talking", the other party will disregard what you say and keep negotiating.

7. The use of silence

During the negotiation, you may make a proposal and find the other party remains silent. This can be very difficult to handle and often signals "disapproval" to the inexperienced negotiator.

If you have a proposal to make, make it and ask the other side how he or she feels about it. Having asked the question, sit back and wait for the answer. Whatever you do, don't change your offer as this could seriously weaken your position.

8. The squeeze play or **"The vice"**

A common technique used by negotiators when presented with a proposal is to say, *"You'll have to do better than that"*.

The most powerful way of dealing with this is to ask them to be more specific. Whatever you do, don't weaken your negotiating position in response to the vice by giving anything away too easily. This will only encourage repeat behavior.

9. The power of legitimacy

People believe what they see in writing. We all assume that if a thing is printed or written down, it is non-negotiable. This is what can make price lists so powerful. If you have to present a customer with a price increase or you wish to encourage an early order to beat a price increase, show something in writing such as an office memo from your boss announcing the increase. This will have a far greater impact than just saying your prices are about to go up.

Vice: *'torno de banco, abrazadera'.*

When presented with a price tag in a shop, ask to speak to the manager and make him an offer. You could be surprised at the results.

10. The low-key approach

Never appear too enthusiastic during negotiations. Over-enthusiasm during negotiations can encourage skilled negotiators to review their strategy and demand more.

If you are in a negotiation and the other side is not responding to your proposal, recognize this could be a tactic and avoid giving concessions just to cheer them up. Salespeople like to be liked and will often give money away in a negotiation, if the other side appears unhappy.

For example, if you are buying a car, avoid saying to the seller:

"This is exactly what I'm looking for. I really like the engine capacity and the overall appearance".

Develop a low-key approach. Say:

"Well, it may not be exactly what I'm looking for but I may be interested if the price is right".

WHAT TO DO WHEN TACTICS (OR TRICKS) ARE USED ON YOU:

Understanding these and other possible tactics will help you identify them when they are used on you and decrease the chance of you falling victim.

Recognition of the tactics used is the first step to avoid being victim to them. You may also choose to draw attention to the fact that they are using a tactic, so that they will stop.

USEFUL NEGOTIATION PHRASES:

Review the following list of useful negotiation phrases and consider how you could use them in your negotiations.

	TYPE OF PHRASE	EXAMPLES OF PHRASES FOR EACH TYPE
1.	**Opening statements and beginning the negotiation**	• Today we're going to talk about... • We're glad that you could come today.
2.	**Adding extra points** *Use these phrases when you wish to reinforce your arguments.*	• There are other things/issues/ considerations; for example the price... • Let me elaborate on this further...
3.	**Asking for clarification of further information**	• Could you expand on that? • Could you clarify the first point please? I don't understand it completely.
4.	**Asking for confirmation**	• Basically, what you are saying is that..., right? • Could you confirm that you feel...?
5.	**Asking for repetition**	• I didn't quite catch that. What did you say? • Sorry, what was the figure?

	TYPE OF PHRASE	EXAMPLES OF PHRASES FOR EACH TYPE
6.	**Correcting a misunderstanding**	• That isn't quite what I said; you see all the items we sent are... • With all due respect (name), the information is wrong (Formal)
7.	**Rephrasing a point**	• Perhaps I haven't made myself clear • To be more specific, I think the data...
8.	**Suggesting**	• So why don't we look at ways of increasing your net sales? • How about cutting down the volume? • Are you willing to consider new payment terms?
9.	**Making proposals**	• I'd like to propose that... • I hope you all agree that... • I strongly recommend that...
10.	**Expressing disagreement**	• I can't say I share your view on this... • I respect your opinion, of course, but on the other hand... (More formal)
11.	**Expressing total or partial agreement**	• Well, I agree with you on the whole, but then again... • I agree in principle that all of us...; however,...
12.	**Playing down a point**	• Yes, I see your point, but let's take into account that... • OK, but that's a just minor issue.
13.	**Playing for time**	• I'm afraid I'm in no position to comment on that... (Formal) • You have certainly raised an important point there... (More formal)

	TYPE OF PHRASE	EXAMPLES OF PHRASES FOR EACH TYPE
14.	**Avoiding answering**	• I'm afraid I don't have the exact numbers here. • Sorry I can't discuss that at the moment. • In our case, that's confidential information. I'm sorry.
15.	**Rejecting an offer**	• I'm afraid that those conditions are unacceptable because...
16.	**Reassuring the communication partner**	• You needn't worry about this, really. We are going to fix all the details later. • We do understand your concern, it's not always easy to....
17.	**Tying concessions to conditions**	• Provided that you..., I would consider...
18.	**Summing up**	• It's been a pleasure doing business with you. • The main points that have been made are...

More money phrasal verbs!

Está bien ayudar a nuestros amigos cuando lo necesitan, ¿verdad? Ahora vamos a ver otra tanda de "phrasal verbs" en esta sección. Aquí hablamos de verbos relacionados con la idea de rescatar o apoyar a personas u organizaciones.

To bail out	Rescatar	To help a person or organization out of a difficult financial situation.
To tide over	Apañar temporalmente (Ayudar)	To help someone with money temporarily until they have enough.

¡A practicar! Para ganar soltura con estas estructuras tapa la columna de la derecha y contesta afirmativamente a las siguientes preguntas con respuestas completas. También escucha el audio e intenta contestar en voz alta con la voz grabada.

Were they bailed out in the 90s?	Yes, they were bailed out in the 90s.
Have you bailed out your brother yet?	Yes, I've already bailed out my brother.
Do they bail out banks when needed?	Yes they bail out banks when needed.
Will they bail out their daughter?	Yes, they'll bail out their daughter.

Did the bonus tide you over until after Christmas?	Yes, the bonus tided me over until after Christmas.
Have the payments tided over the workers?	Yes, the payments have tided over the workers.
Can his loan tide you over for now?	Yes, his loan can tide me over for now.
Will 50 dollars tide you over until tomorrow?	Yes, 50 dollars will tide me over until tomorrow.

TRANSLATION LISTS:

Following are five translation lists with useful terminology and common structures you may find in negotiations:

Negotiations Translation List 1

PISTA DE AUDIO 14

1.	¿Cómo inicio la negociación?	How do I start the negotiation?
2.	Hay una regla de oro.	There's one golden rule.
3.	Hay que tenerle respeto a la otra parte.	You have to have respect for the other party.
4.	Es una regla fundamental.	It's a fundamental rule.
5.	Esto facilita el llegar a un acuerdo.	This makes it easier to reach an agreement.
6.	La otra parte no es el enemigo.	The other side isn't the enemy.
7.	No tienes por qué vencerles.	You have no reason to defeat them.
8.	Muy al contrario, hay que verlo como a un colaborador.	Quite the contrary, he has to be seen as a collaborator.
9.	Es con él con quién trabajarás codo con codo.	He's the one you'll be working closely with.
10.	Superemos las diferencias existentes.	Let's get over the existing differences.
11.	Es posible llegar a un acuerdo aceptable.	It's possible to come to an acceptable agreement.
12.	No conoces realmente cuál es mi posición.	You don't really know what my position is.
13.	Busco un acuerdo que satisfaga las necesidades de todos.	I'm looking for an agreement that satisfies everyone's needs.
14.	¿Quiénes son los implicados?	Who are the people involved?
15.	Él sólo busca obtener el máximo beneficio a costa de los demás.	He's only looking to get the most benefit at everyone else's expense.
16.	No están dispuestos a negociar contigo nunca más.	They're not willing to negotiate with you ever again.
17.	Ni siquiera consideraron nuestros intereses.	They didn't even consider our interests.
18.	Queremos encontrar una solución.	We want to find a solution.
19.	Busco una solución racional.	I'm looking for a rational solution.
20.	Las dos partes están involucradas en el problema.	Both sides are involved in the problem.
21.	No veo una solución satisfactoria.	I don't see a satisfactory solution.
22.	Siento que son dos ideas contrarias.	I feel like they're two opposing ideas.
23.	No quiero un enfrentamiento.	I don't want a confrontation.
24.	Tratemos de establecer una solución.	Let's try to establish a solution.
25.	Hagamos un trato.	Let's make a deal.

Negotiations Translation List 2

#		
1.	*Hay muchas diferencias entre ambas partes.*	There are many differences upheld by both parties.
2.	*Quiero eliminar esas diferencias.*	I want to get rid of those differences.
3.	*No intenta acercar posiciones.*	He isn't looking to draw positions closer together.
4.	*No sabes escuchar.*	You don't know how to listen.
5.	*Quiero resaltar estos dos puntos.*	I want to emphasize these two points.
6.	*Hay que tenerle respeto a la otra parte.*	You have to have respect for the other party.
7.	*Sólo funciona la profesionalidad.*	Only professionalism works.
8.	*Aprecio tu franqueza.*	I appreciate your being frank with me.
9.	*Siempre estoy preparado antes de sentarme a la mesa de negociación.*	I'm always prepared before sitting down to the negotiating table.
10.	*Sé anticipar los movimientos de la otra parte.*	I know how to anticipate the other side's movements.
11.	*Entonces tomo las medidas oportunas.*	Then I take timely measures.
12.	*Consigo una buena comunicación entre las partes.*	I get channels of communication open between the two sides.
13.	*¿Eres capaz de comunicar de forma clara?*	Are you able to communicate in a clear way?
14.	*¿Cuáles son tus planteamientos?*	What is your plan of execution?
15.	*¿Cuáles son tus objetivos?*	What are your objectives?
16.	*No captas el mensaje que pretendo transmitir.*	You don't get the message I am trying to convey.
17.	*Busquemos puntos de encuentro.*	Let's look for some common ground.
18.	*Podemos adaptar nuestra oferta.*	We can readjust our offer.
19.	*Quiero que se satisfagan los intereses mutuos.*	I want both parties' interests to be satisfied.
20.	*Veo que corremos ciertos riesgos.*	I see we're running certain risks.
21.	*Puede que luego no cumplan lo acordado.*	Later, they might not carry out the agreed agenda.
22.	*No están dispuestos a negociar contigo nunca más.*	They're not willing to negotiate with you ever again.
23.	*No fue una solución equitativa.*	It wasn't an egalitarian solution.
24.	*Ni siquiera consideraron nuestros intereses.*	They didn't even consider our interests.
25.	*Tengo varias fuentes de información.*	I use several sources of information.

Negotiations Translation List 3

1.	Seamos directos.	Let's be straight with one another.
2.	Yo no quiero tratar contigo.	I don't want to deal with you.
3.	No tengo interés en mantener esta relación profesional.	I have no interest in maintaining business relations.
4.	No me ha resultado muy beneficiosa.	It hasn't turned out to be very beneficial for me.
5.	Su estilo de negociación está basado en la confrontación.	Her negotiation style is based on confrontation.
6.	No significa no.	No means no.
7.	¡Que no! Lo digo en serio.	I said no and I mean it.
8.	No debes seguir el juego.	You mustn't play along.
9.	Sigue intentándolo.	Keep trying.
10.	Trata de convencer a la otra parte de las ventajas.	Try convincing the other side of the advantages.
11.	No es un negociador nato.	He's not a born negotiator.
12.	Me doy cuenta de que necesito desarrollar otro estilo de negociación.	I realize that I need to develop another negotiating style.
13.	¿Cuáles son las estrategias?	What are the strategies?
14.	¿Me enseñas algunas tácticas útiles?	Can you teach me some useful tactics?
15.	Mantén abiertas todas las vías de comunicación.	Keep all channels of communication open.
16.	El lenguaje corporal es extremadamente importante.	Body language is extremely important.
17.	No tengas miedo a mantenerte firme.	Don't be afraid of asserting yourself.
18.	¿Has elegido un lugar adecuado para la negociación?	Have you chosen a suitable place for the negotiation?
19.	Ahora no es el momento de iniciar la negociación.	Now isn't the time to start negotiating.
20.	Estamos en la primera fase.	We're at the first stage.
21.	¿Estás bien preparado?	Are you well prepared?
22.	Conozco la oferta de memoria.	I know the offer by heart.
23.	La he leído detenidamente.	I've looked it over very carefully.
24.	Lo que pasa es que no conozco bien a la otra parte.	The thing is I don't know the other party well.
25.	¿Cuál es el objetivo de la negociación?	What is the aim of the negotiation?

Negotiations Translation List 4

1.	*Han retrasado el plazo.*	They've pushed back the deadline.
2.	*Quiero adelantar el plazo.*	I want to push forward the deadline.
3.	*¿Qué enfoque podemos utilizar?*	What approach shall we use?
4.	*¿Cómo lo podemos hacer?*	How shall we go about it?
5.	*¿Dónde está el orden del día para la reunión?*	Where is the agenda for the meeting?
6.	*¿Tienes las actas de la reunión?*	Do you have the minutes from the meeting?
7.	*Se discutieron muchas cosas.*	There was a lot of discussion.
8.	*Se convirtió en una discusión acalorada.*	It turned into an argument.
9.	*No te centraste en tus intereses.*	You didn't focus on your interests.
10.	*¿Cuáles son tus argumentos a favor?*	What are your arguments in favor?
11.	*Tengo una objeción.*	I have an objection.
12.	*¿Qué tienes en contra?*	What do you have against it?
13.	*¿Por qué no nos referimos a unos criterios objetivos?*	Why don't we refer to some objective criteria?
14.	*Con un poco de flexibilidad podemos ponernos de acuerdo.*	With a little flexibility, we can agree on something.
15.	*¡Necesito soluciones, chicos!*	I need solutions, guys!
16.	*Deja de quejarte.*	No ifs, ands, or buts.
17.	*Haré una concesión.*	I'll make a concession.
18.	*Estamos bloqueados.*	We're at an impasse.
19.	*¿Estamos de acuerdo?*	Do we agree?
20.	*Dime si estás de acuerdo o no.*	Tell me if you agree or not.
21.	*Sí, estoy completamente de acuerdo.*	Yes, I completely agree.
22.	*No, no estoy de acuerdo en absoluto.*	No, I don't agree at all.
23.	*Voté que no porque no estaba de acuerdo.*	I voted "no" because I didn't agree.
24.	*Si estuviera de acuerdo, lo firmaría.*	If I agreed, I would sign.
25.	*¿Os pondréis de acuerdo los dos o no?*	Will you (both) agree to it or not?

Negotiations Translation List 5

1.	Se ha roto la negociación.	The negotiation broke down.
2.	¿Cuáles son los factores de éxito en la negociación?	What are the factors for a successful negotiation?
3.	Tenemos una negociación en grupo.	We have a group negotiation.
4.	Negocié mucho durante la comida de trabajo.	I negotiated a lot during the business lunch.
5.	Es alguien que sabe los detalles de cortesía.	He's somebody who is really detailed about politeness.
6.	Trabaja mucho con negociaciones internacionales.	He deals with a lot of international negotiations.
7.	Conoce bien el protocolo para una situación así.	He really knows the protocol for such a situation.
8.	Es un buen negociador.	He's a good negotiator.
9.	Contempla la negociación como si fuera un desafío.	Think of the negotiation as if it were a challenge.
10.	Presenta tu oferta con claridad.	Present your offer clearly.
11.	¿Has conseguido captar el interés de la otra parte?	Did you manage to capture the other party's interest?
12.	Exprésate con convicción.	Show conviction.
13.	Sabe convencer a la gente.	He knows how to convince people.
14.	¿Sabes leer el lenguaje no verbal?	Do you know how to read non-verbal language?
15.	Busco una solución racional.	I'm looking for a rational solution.
16.	No creo que la otra parte sea de fiar.	I don't think the other side is trustworthy.
17.	¿Tienen de verdad la intención de firmar un acuerdo?	Are they really planning to sign an agreement?
18.	¿Cuáles piensas que son sus intenciones?	What do you think are their intentions?
19.	Tiene mucha habilidad para romper el hielo.	He's really good at breaking the ice.
20.	Quiero crear una atmósfera de confianza.	I want to create a setting with trust.
21.	Confío en ti.	I trust you.
22.	Ellos no han mostrado ninguna deferencia hacia nosotros.	They haven't shown any respect towards us.
23.	No comprenden nuestra posición.	They don't understand our position.
24.	Mira, no busco engañar a nadie.	Hey, I'm not looking to cheat anyone.
25.	No dejo nada al azar.	I don't leave anything to chance.

SECTION C
ADVANCED
BUSINESS TOPICS

[Dando el salto a un inglés
de negocios más avanzado]

CHAPTER 12

MARKETING

[Tu caja de herramientas del
Marketing en inglés]

MARKETING

Marketing entails communicating the value of a product or service to customers, with the objective of selling the product or service. It is an essential business function for attracting customers.

To entail -
To involve:
'involucrar'.

The marketing process includes analyzing marketing opportunities, choosing target markets, as well as understanding consumer buying behavior and providing value to customers, developing the marketing mix, and managing the marketing effort.

NEEDS, WANTS AND DEMANDS

The concepts of human **needs**, **wants** and **demands** are essential to marketing.

Needs are states of felt deprivation. Basic needs include physical needs for food, clothing, warmth and safety. Social needs include belonging and affection and individual needs include knowledge and self-expression.

Wants are desires derived from human needs as shaped by culture and individual personality.

When supported by buying power, wants become **demands**.

VALUE, SATISFACTION AND QUALITY

Value, **satisfaction** and **quality** are interrelated terms. Conveying them effectively to potential customers is essential to successful marketing.

Value is the ratio between what the customer gets and what they give. The customer gets benefits and gives costs.

Total Quality Management - A philosophy within an organization to constantly improve its ability to deliver high-quality products and services to customers.

Consumers choose products that they perceive to offer them the greatest value. The benefits a customer receives may be functional or emotional. The cost of products are not only monetary. They may also include investments of time and energy.

Marketing aims to provide value to customers by raising benefits and reducing costs.

Satisfaction is the customer's perceived performance from a product in relation to their expectations.

Quality is perception of product excellence by customers. It is linked to customer need satisfaction.

Many organizations implement the concept of **Total Quality Management (TQM)**, in which they work to continuously improve the quality of their products to achieve customer satisfaction.

Office Talk!

PISTA DE AUDIO 19

Aquí te ofrezco cinco frases típicas del uso corriente que puedes oír en una oficina donde se habla inglés. Tapa la columna de la derecha y traduce en voz alta las frases.

Vayamos a tomar un café antes de empezar.	**Let's go for a coffee before we get started.**
Nos hemos encontrado con más problemas de los que esperábamos.	**We've run into more problems than expected.**
Te reembolsarán todos los gastos mientras estés allí.	**They'll fully reimburse you for any expenses while you're there.**
¿Dónde te alojarán?	**Where will they put you up?**
Estoy seguro de que usan varios proveedores de servicios distintos.	**I'm sure they use a number of different service providers.**

MARKETING MANAGEMENT

Marketing management includes the analysis, planning and implementation of programs designed to build and maintain profitable relationships with buyers. This includes managing demand and managing customer relationships.

Demand management refers to how companies work to find a way to deal with different levels of demand.

Conventional marketing theory has typically focused on attracting new customers and making sales; however, **more and more** companies are putting increasing emphasis on retaining customers and building lasting relationships.

More and more:
'cada vez mas'.

 Remember:
Efforts to keep a customer or client are almost always cheaper than the efforts needed to find new ones.

STRATEGIC PLANNING

Formal planning can yield many benefits for all types of companies. Strategic planning refers to developing and maintaining a link between an organization's goals and capabilities and its changing marketing opportunities.

A **mission statement** serves to define the organization's purpose.

An effective mission statement guides people in the organization towards overall organizational goals. It helps employees understand the corporate, social end ethical values of the firm. Good mission statements should be market oriented, specific, realistic and motivating.

The business portfolio refers to the collection of businesses and products that comprise the company. An ideal portfolio should fit the company's **strengths** and **weaknesses** and recognize **opportunities** and **threats** in the market.

SWOT analysis

A SWOT analysis (an acronym for **S**trengths, **W**eaknesses, **O**pportunities, and **T**hreats) is a common tool for assessing business ventures or projects. It involves specifying the objective of the project and identifying the internal and external factors that are favorable and unfavorable.

The Boston Consulting Group developed a well-known portfolio planning method, known as the **growth-share matrix**, in which analysts **plot** points on a chart, ranking business units or products according to market share and growth rate. The **market growth rate** is a measure of market attractiveness, while relative **market share** indicates the company's strength within the market. Four types of business units (or products) are defined by the matrix.

To plot -
To position a point on a map or chart: 'trazar'.

Cash cows are products with high market share in a slow-growing industry. They usually generate good amounts of cash. Low investment is required to keep them profitable and companies are very happy to have as many of them as possible.

Break even: *'salir a la par'*.

Synergies: *'sinergias'*.

Return on Assets (ROA) - An indicator of company profitability relative to total assets. ROA shows how efficiently management is using its assets to generate earnings. ROA is displayed as a percentage and is calculated by dividing a company's annual earnings by its total assets.

Market share: *'cuota de mercado'*.

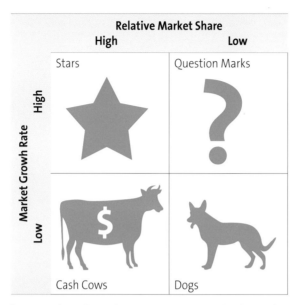

Relative Market Share

Stars | Question Marks | Cash Cows | Dogs

Market Growth Rate

Dogs are units with low market share in a mature, slow-growing industry. They typically **"break even"**, in terms of cash flow generated. These products may create jobs or **synergies** that help other business units, but they do not contribute to a company's **return on assets,** and are therefore often sold off by companies.

Question marks are business units with a low **market share** but operating in a high market growth environment. They are a starting point for most businesses. Question marks have a potential to gain market share and become stars, and eventually cash cows if market growth slows, or dogs if market share declines. Investing in question marks requires careful research and consideration.

Stars are units with a high market share in a fast-growing industry. They are former question marks that have become successful in a high growth sector. The hope is that stars become the next cash cows.

UNDERSTANDING THE MARKET AND YOUR CUSTOMERS

A careful analysis of customers is needed to understand their needs and wants in order to satisfy them and win customers from competitors.

Market segmentation involves dividing a market into groups with different characteristics who may require different products, services or marketing mixes. A **market segment** is defined as a group of consumers who respond in a similar way to a specific set of marketing stimuli.

Market targeting refers to the process of evaluating the attractiveness of each market segment and deciding on which segments to enter. Companies should target segments where they can generate sustained customer value. Small companies may enter only one segment, while other companies may be more suited to compete and be profitable in many different segments with a variety of products. General Motors, for example, claims it makes a car for every "person, purse and personality".

After deciding on the market segment (or segments) to enter, a company must decide what position it wants to take in each one.

The product's **position** is the place it occupies relative to competitors in consumers' minds. Products have to **stand out** in order to give consumers a reason to buy them.

Market positioning involves arranging for a product to occupy a clear distinctive and desirable place relative to competing products in the minds of target consumers.

To be successful, a company must do better than its competitors at satisfying target customers.

To stand out:
'destacar'.

THE MARKETING MIX

The "**marketing mix**" refers to the set of marketing tools that the firm blends to present the product as is wants in the target market. These marketing tools are collected into four groups of variables, known as "The Four Ps": Product, Price, Place and Promotion.

"Product" refers to the mix of goods and services offered to the market.

"Price" refers to the price customers have to pay for the product or service. Properly **pricing** products is often a challenging task and high or low pricing can greatly influence how potential customers perceive a product's level of quality.

To price - Here the word "price" is used as a verb.

"Place" includes the location where the company intends to make the product available to customers. The company has to consider how to best distribute its products to make them available to customers.

"Promotion" refers to the activities used to communicate the merits of the product and persuade target customers to buy it.

An effective marketing plan should blend the four Ps of the marketing mix to achieve the company's objectives and deliver value to consumers.

MARKETING RESEARCH

Marketing research is very important for companies to better understand their environment, customers' perception of products and services as well as opportunities and threats in the market.

The marketing research process involves:

- Defining the problem and research objectives
- Developing a research plan for collecting information
- Implementing the plan, collecting and analyzing the data
- Interpreting and reporting the findings

Focus group:
'grupo focal'.

Questionnaire:
'cuestionario'.

Survey: *'sondeo'*
o 'encuesta'.

Focus groups, questionnaires, telephone or computer interviews and **surveys** are among the many ways people's thoughts on products and services can be tested. The best method to use, of course, depends on the nature of the business, its products and budget available. Additionally, there are many ways the data can be analyzed and interpreted.

While marketing research is very important, a further discussion of it is beyond the scope of this book. I strongly recommend, however, further reading and study in this area.

PRODUCT POSITIONING

Product Positioning refers to the way the product is defined by consumers, that is the place it occupies in consumers' minds relative to competing products.

Since consumers try to choose products that give them the greatest value, companies try to develop a product positioning strategy which distinguishes their products or business units. For example, a company may promise 'high quality for a lower cost', or 'high quality with more after sale service'.

The product positioning **task** consists of three steps:

- Identifying possible competitive advantages
- Selecting the right competitive advantages
- Communicating and delivering the chosen position to the market

Task: *'tarea'.*

A **competitive advantage** refers to an advantage over competitors gained by offering greater value either by setting lower prices or providing more benefits that justify higher prices.

Selecting the right competitive advantages to promote can be challenging. Some marketers feel that companies should only promote one benefit to the target market, but others maintain that they should position themselves on more than one differentiating factor.

What is clear is that the company must carefully select the ways in which it will stand out from others. A difference is typically worth establishing if it makes the product superior, is important, distinctive and communicable to buyers. It should also be difficult to copy, affordable and of course, profitable for the company.

Most of the companies and brands we are most familiar with have achieved great success through innovation, strong business models and achieving a competitive advantage.

For example Google accessed tremendous revenue streams by linking highly specific search results and content with text advertisements. Gillette has been able to establish lifelong relationships with loyal customers based on its disposable razors and clever marketing of similar products.

The ultimate goal is to achieve a sustainable competitive advantage, which occurs when an organization possesses an attribute or combination of attributes that allows it to outperform its competitors. It is an advantage that is not easily copied and, thus, can be maintained over a long period of time.

No one has achieved a sustainable competitive advantage better than the Coca Cola Company.

The Coca Cola Company - Sustainable competitive Advantage

Coca Cola is arguably the world's most recognized brand. Almost 120 years after incorporation the company remains one of the most desired stocks on the New York Stock Exchange.

- A number of factors have helped Coke achieve and sustain its competitive advantage:
- Its unique and secret recipe.
- Coke's ability to constantly develop new products and re-invent old ones – Coca-Cola currently offers over 400 brands in 200 markets worldwide.
- The world's greatest distribution system brings Coca Cola to people even in the most remote parts of the world.
- Super-efficient production systems that minimize costs and maximize profit margins.

Who's who?

Do you know the names of different roles in the company?

Board of directors:

The **board of directors** is a group of elected or appointed individuals who oversee the activities of a company or organization. The people on this board are known as the "directors".

The "Inside directors" are those who are employees, officers, major shareholders, or someone similarly connected to the organization.

Typical inside directors include the CEO, who may also be chairman of the board, the CFO, large shareholders, representatives of other stakeholders such as labor unions and members of the community.

"Outside directors" are members the board who are not otherwise employed by or engaged with the organization.

The Chairman of the Board:

Presides over meetings of the board and acts as its representative or spokesperson outside of board meetings. The CEO is often the Chairman of the board.

CEO:

The Chief Executive Officer is the highest-ranking officer in charge of the company.

The CEO may also be referred to as the "Managing Director".

COO:

Chief Operations Officer, also known as "Director of Operations", is responsible for the daily operation of the company. Reports directly to the CEO. The COO may also be the President. The COO is usually more "hands-on" than the CEO.

CFO:

The Chief Financial Officer also reports to the CEO and is responsible for financial reporting and documenting budgets and expenses.

The President handles the day-to-day running of the company, and acts as a liaison between the management and the CEO, whom he or she reports to. The President technically ranks lower than a CEO on the corporate hierarchy. Presidents often hold the position of Chief Operations Officer as mentioned above.

In English, we use the word "Manager" a lot. It can mean *'gerente'*, *'director'* or *'jefe'*.

MARKETING TOOLS

If you run your own small business, or have influence over marketing decisions or strategy in your company, you will want to consider a variety of common marketing tools.

In the following section, I present some ideas to consider when making decisions about day-to day marketing activities.

1. The 30-second elevator **pitch**!

Pitch - Promotional wording, designed to persuade someone: 'argumento de venta'.

An important marketing tool is the 30 second "elevator pitch", which introduces your company and explains what you do. Think of a 30-second commercial on television. A good pitch will explain your business concept clearly and concisely in less than 30 seconds.

I call it the elevator pitch because it is the type of explanation of your business you could give in the time it takes to travel a few floors with someone on an elevator.

An effective elevator pitch should always include four things:

• The name of your business

• Your main product or service

• The customer group that uses your product or service

• One unique benefit to those customers of using your product or service

You never know when you are going to meet a potential customer. Some studies show that the human attention span, that is the amount of time a person will be truly focused and receptive to your business idea, can be as little as eight seconds! Having a good elevator pitch is essential for you to capture the attention of potential customers whom you have a brief opportunity to interact with.

Imagine you meet someone at a party and they introduce themselves as follows:

"Hi, my name is Sam Rockwell and I own "Beer Boss". We sell home beer brewing kits to beer lovers who don't necessarily have the time or expertise to make a great beer, but want to get started with a home kit and enjoy the cost savings. We set up the home brewing system, teach them how to use it and check in every week to see how they are doing."

This is an effective elevator pitch, because it explains what Sam does and is appealing to someone who might want to try making their own beer without giving too many details to someone who might not be interested.

Having a good elevator pitch is a great (and free) marketing tool which works well for businesses of all sizes. For small businesses gaining one good customer can often make a big difference in the success of the business. For larger companies, having a culture where employees know a focused 30-second pitch can help employees maintain a common understanding of the company's objectives as well as accumulate unexpected sales and interest in your products or services.

2. The tag line

A **tag line** is a short statement about your business. Usually it can be found above, below or next to the company's logo. A good tag line educates a potential customer in a tiny, neatly wrapped package of one line.

This tiny line can cause a potential customer to take immediate interest in your company, or realize that it isn't for them.

A recent study of 400 well-known corporate slogans analyzed by marketing experts rated the most influential taglines since 1948 according to longevity, the strength of their identity with the company, originality and other factors.

The top five results were as follows:

The Five Most Influential Taglines Since 1948

1.	"Got milk?"	California Milk Processor Board (1993)
2.	"Don't leave home without it."	American Express (1975)
3.	"Just do it."	Nike (1988)
4.	"Where's the beef?"	Wendy's (1984)
5.	"You're in good hands with Allstate."	Allstate Insurance (1956)

How many do you recognize?

There are four common types of tag lines:

Type 1: The benefit tag line:

This type of tag line tells customers why they should buy the product. It indicates how their lives will be improved thanks to the product (or service).

Imagine a tag line for a healthy salad dressing called Garden Fresh:

"When health matters, there's Garden Fresh!"

Type 2: The product or service-focused tag line:

This type of tag line is very simple and basically tells customers your key product or service. This tag line, while not fancy, helps people immediately understand what you do. This can be particularly helpful if your logo and company name don't make the nature of your business evident.

Imagine a tag line for *Motor Doctor*, who only specifically repair Volkswagens:

"Specializing in custom VW repairs and accessories"

Type 3: The customer-focused tag line:

This type of tag line is aimed at a very specific type of customer and describes your particular customer base. It helps reduce inquiries from people who are clearly not going to become customers.

Imagine a company, Wilson watercraft, which only produces canoes. The name could be confusing and could attract interest from people looking for other types of boats.

A good tagline for them to eliminate this ambiguity could be:

"Producing quality canoes since 1968"

Type 4: The vague idea tag line:

This is a common type of tag line, but is the least effective. This type of tag line tries to tell the reader about the company's philosophy but often fails to educate people on what the company actually does. You can often see these types of tag lines on highway billboards.

Imagine the following:

Diamond Technologies: "Building relationships every day".

What does this company do? We don't know. The tagline fails to clarify the objectives of the company or help readers understand who their typical customer might be.

If you are choosing a tagline for your business, consider the type that would be most appropriate for your business and your target market.

Once you have a tag line you can include it, along with your logo, in emails, business cards, your website, brochures, advertisements, **letterhead**, etc.

3. The business card

A good **business card** is essential to demonstrate the credibility of a new business. You can think of your business card as a mini brochure for your business.

A vCard is the electronic form of a business card that can be emailed to contacts instead of handed to them.

In addition to simply giving people your contact information, the business card gives an impression of the quality of your business. If you are operating your own small business, it is usually a good idea to invest in an attractive, professional looking card.

Remember, the main purpose of the card is to offer your contact information. Make sure you include as much of the following information as possible:

Name
Title
Business title
Logo
Tag line
Telephone number
Fax number
Mailing address
Email address
Website address

4. The website

A website is one of the most essential marketing tools available. Customers for many products will want to look at a company's website before making a purchase.

Creating your own website is relatively simple, involving the following four steps:

Letterhead - The heading at the top of a sheet of letter paper: *'membrete'*.

Business card: *'tarjeta de visita'.*

Step 1. Buy your domain

This step is very easy and should be done as soon as possible before someone else buys the name you are looking for. Some sites for purchasing domains are:

www.godaddy.com

www.namecheap.com

www.aplus.com

www.name.com

www.networksolutions.com

If the name you want is not available, you might want to look for creative alternatives. Instead of the normal *.com* or *.es* extensions, you can also look for the name you want with *.biz*, *.org*, *.net* or *.info*.

Step 2. Write the content

While there are a lot of pages and a lot of content you could have on your website, the main five content pages are:

The "Home" page – Gives a brief introduction of the company indicating how customers benefit from your products or services.

The "Products and Services" page – Offers a description of the products or services you sell along with photos and pricing.

TIP

Don't overwhelm readers with too much information. If necessary, have a sub-page with further details. Keep in mind that the reader may only spend seconds on the page.

A good idea is to use a bullet list detailing up to six or seven products or services. More points than that on a bullet list is visually unappealing.

The "Clients" page - Simply lists your past and current clients. It demonstrates credibility that you have a professional history. If you don't have any customers yet, just omit this page.

The "About Us" page - Tells the reader who you are, your philosophy and your way of doing business. It helps build legitimacy and rapport with the reader. It is also appropriate to include a Bio of the business's founding members or the current president or CEO.

The "Contact" page – Explains how people can find you. It may seem obvious, but it amazes me how some companies fail to provide complete information in this important section. If customers can't find you how can they buy your products?

Be sure to include:

The business name

- Logo
- Mailing address
- Telephone number
- Fax number
- Email address

The contact page should include a "call to action" statement, which encourages the reader to contact the company.

The typical "call now!" line seen on television commercials is a perfect example of this. If worded and placed properly, the call to action statement should create a sense of urgency to contact the company. Some examples that might work for you are:

- Call today to start enjoying.....
- Click here to visit our store:
- Receive a free sample by clicking here:

Etc.

There are many other pages you could include, such as a testimonials page or a career opportunities page, but with these basic five pages you have everything you need to have an effective online presence.

Step 3. Design the look of the pages

After your content has been prepared, you'll want to establish the layout of the page. Most of the host providers listed above provide templates to help you arrange your content, as well as countless other providers you can find online. They are a great option in terms of the time and cost required to develop a decent page. Of course, hiring a professional web designer is always an alternative and can help you get a more professional-looking page.

Step 4. Publish the site with a host

The domain providers listed above, as well as many others, can provide a hosting service, which is the actual service of publishing your site to the internet and making it available to be accessed 24 hours a day, seven days a week.

Many hosts also offer additional services, such as email and blog hosting, online sales options as well as domain name registration and design templates, as mentioned.

5. Pay-per-click advertising

Pay-per-click advertising allows your business to move to the top of search results on search engines, such as Google. You pay a small fee (a few cents) per click to have your website listed up among the easily seen "sponsored links" that appear in a search.

Typically, the higher ranked on the search results page, the more visitors it will receive from the search engine's users.

The process for setting up a pay-per-click account is fairly **straightforward**.

1. Choose a provider, (such as Google)
2. Set up an account with them online
3. Choose keywords that might be searched by potential customers.
4. Write the ad

When you write your pay-per-click ad, choose your words carefully. Usually the ad will be less than 25 words you'll want to catch the attention of potential customers.

Set a limit of how much you want to spend.

The beauty of this form of advertising is that you can spend as little or as much as you like. Through your account, choose how much you want to spend per month or day. Often you can also indicate where you want the ads to run geographically or at what times of day.

6. Search engine optimization

Search engine optimization, known as "SEO", is another way to improve your business's presence online. SEO refers to efforts made to increase the visibility of a website through a search engine's unpaid search results. It usually considers what key terms are most important and increases the presence of these terms on sites and in the coding of the sites in order to have the site appear more prominently in search results. Other, more complex tactics are also used.

7. Social Media Marketing

When done properly, marketing with social media can be very helpful to your business.

Social media marketing involves the sharing of industry-related content, videos and images for marketing purposes through social media platforms, such as Facebook, Google +, Pinterest, Twitter or LinkedIn.

Each site is different and the way people interact on each is distinct.

Facebook is a fairly casual, friendly online environment. You will need to create a Facebook Business Fan Page. Make the layout attractive and be sure to post content that is fun and interesting for readers.

Google + is essentially Google's rival to Facebook. Like most things Google, Google + is very forward thinking and offers some interesting features.

With Google+ circles, you can segment followers into smaller groups, and share information with some followers while not others. This can be helpful for offering discounts to certain people such as those who have made purchases in the past or who speak favorably about your product online.

Pinterest's image-centered platform is great for retail. It allows small businesses to **showcase** their own products while also developing their own brand's personality through unique "pinboards".

Twitter is a very powerful and popular social media marketing tool. If you follow tweeters in your industry or related fields, you should gain followers in return.

By mixing "official" tweets about specials, discounts, and news updates with fun, funny and interesting tweets you will gain followers and people will pay attention to the business related tweets when they do see them.

Be sure to answer people's questions when possible and retweet nice things that are said about you. Twitter is a great platform for interfacing directly with customers.

LinkedIn

LinkedIn is a very professional social media marketing site which we covered in the "Job Search" section of this book. By using LinkedIn Groups, you can have professional dialog with people in similar industries and share content with like-minded individuals.

Having customers or clients give your business a recommendation on their LinkedIn profile will make your business appear more credible and reliable for new customers.

Other social media platforms such as Reddit, Stumble Upon or Digg could be helpful for creating awareness for your brand as well. Look into your alternatives and decide what is best for the industry you are in and the type of marketing strategy you have, as well as the time you have available to dedicate to online promotion.

Every business should be involved in at least some form of social media. It is very low cost and when done properly can be very effective for creating brand awareness and stimulating sales.

8. The Brochure

The brochure is a very useful marketing tool. It can be mailed to potential clients, given out at trade shows or converted to a PDF file and emailed.

There are many formats you can consider, but a good standard one is the tri-fold, the size of an A4 piece of paper. When you fold the paper into thirds horizontally, you have six panels available to convey your company's information. The purpose of each panel can be the same as the pages on your website.

Be sure the cover stands out and that the information gets to the point. Remember, a brochure gives a quick overview, and encourages the reader to get more information by going to your website or contacting your company.

9. The Introductory Letter

Having a good letter to introduce your company and its products and services is a very important and inexpensive marketing tool. More and more, these letters will be emailed, rather than mailed normally.

An effective introductory letter will be short, typically no more than one page. Like with so many other things we have seen in this book, we have to think of the limited amount of time we have to capture the attention of the reader.

The **subject line** should usually be no more than eight words and explains a direct benefit to the customer. For example:

"More affordable printing solutions for your business"

or

"Healthy meals in just a few minutes."

In the body of the letter, it is common to begin by introducing a common problem that your typical customer has. By describing this problem in detail, the reader will identify with a need for your solution when you present it.

Now that you have the reader's attention, introduce your company and the solutions you offer to the specific problem mentioned by clearly explaining what your company does. In the next, very important paragraph, mention specific benefits to the customer. Explain how your product or service will help your customer save money, save time, live more comfortably, look younger, feel better, work more efficiently, or whatever it is that your products or services do to benefit customers.

Client or Customer?

Do you know the difference between a "Client" and a "Customer"?

While you say *'cliente'* for both in Spanish, in English:

A **client** is someone who buys a **service**.

A **customer** is someone who buys a **product**.

Similarly, we have the words "provider" and "supplier"
A provider provides services (to clients).
A supplier supplies products (to customers).

Be sure to end your letter professionally, with a respectful closing statement, ending with "sincerely" or "best regards" and including your full name, business name and title.

More marketing tools

Other than the marketing tools briefly mentioned here, there are many others that could be beneficial to you depending on the nature of your business and the types of customer you wish to access. There are many sources online to help you learn about blogs, newsletters, press releases and other marketing tools, as well as more information about the ideas mentioned in this book. Depending on your budget and resources, you may find professional help with certain marketing efforts to be a worthwhile investment.

Like with the other business topics to follow, this book does not attempt to cover the field of marketing in depth. Here we have presented some terminology and some of the many concepts relevant to the field of marketing. Marketing is a key element of any successful business and formulating a marketing strategy deserves careful thought and planning.

To further expand your base with some of the terminology from the world of marketing, I now offer some key vocabulary and five translation lists of common marketing language.

MARKETING VOCABULARY!
25 words you should know

PISTA DE AUDIO 20

1.	*Publicidad*	Advertising
2.	*Percepción*	Perception
3.	*Marca*	Brand
4.	*Competencia*	Competition
5.	*Presupuesto*	Budget
6.	*Deseos*	Wants
7.	*Demografía*	Demographics
8.	*Marketing directo*	Direct marketing
9.	*Distribución*	Distribution
10.	*Característica, distintivo*	Feature
11.	*Posicionamiento del producto en el mercado*	Market positioning
12.	*Países en desarrollo*	Developing countries
13.	*Población*	Population
14.	*Comportamiento de los consumidores*	Consumer behavior
15.	*Los componentes del marketing, Los elementos del marketing*	Marketing mix
16.	*Valor*	Value
17.	*Cuota de mercado*	Market share
18.	*Declaración, extracto, resumen*	Statement
19.	*Renta per cápita, ingreso per cápita*	Per capita income
20.	*Punto de venta*	Point-of-sale (POS)
21.	*Fidelidad a una marca*	Brand loyalty
22.	*Enfoque*	Focus
23.	*Escasez, falta*	Scarcity
24.	*Concesión, autorización*	Licensing
25.	*Utilidad*	Utility

Marketing Translation List 1

1.	*Muchos factores influyen en la conducta del cliente.*	**Many factors influence customer behavior.**
2.	*¿Cómo podemos influir en su comportamiento?*	**How can we influence their behavior?**
3.	*¿Cómo podemos conseguir que compren nuestros productos?*	**How can we get them to buy our products?**
4.	*¿Cuál es el ciclo vital de este producto?*	**What's the life cycle of this product?**
5.	*Las creencias y actitudes cambian con el tiempo.*	**Beliefs and attitudes change over time.**
6.	*Los líderes de opinión tienen una gran influencia.*	**Opinion leaders have great influence.**
7.	*Los matrimonios toman decisiones en conjunto.*	**Married couples make joint decisions.**
8.	*Vamos a preparar un tríptico.*	**We're going to prepare a three-page leaflet.**
9.	*La gente no entenderá el mensaje.*	**People won't understand the message.**
10.	*El tipo de letra es demasiado pequeño.*	**The print-type is too small.**
11.	*Vamos a llenar la ciudad de vallas publicitarias.*	**We're going to fill the city with billboards.**
12.	*No creo en la publicidad mediante vallas.*	**I don't believe in billboard advertising.**
13.	*¿Cuáles son las tarifas publicitarias?*	**What are the advertising rates?**
14.	*Las palabras representan una fuerza poderosa.*	**Words are a powerful force.**
15.	*¿Cómo puedo conseguir que este anuncio destaque?*	**How can I make this ad come alive?**
16.	*Tu anuncio tiene que ser más específico.*	**Your ad has to be more specific.**
17.	*Tu anuncio no debe sonar como un anuncio.*	**Your ad shouldn't sound like an ad.**
18.	*Tenemos que llegar a cuanta más gente mejor.*	**We have to reach as many people as possible.**
19.	*Nadie se va a fijar en tus vallas publicitarias.*	**Nobody is going to notice your billboards.**
20.	*Tenemos que hacernos notar.*	**We have to get ourselves noticed.**
21.	*Tenemos que conectar con la mente del cliente.*	**We have to connect with the mind of the customer.**
22.	*Esto os va a llevar a la ruina.*	**This is going to lead to your ruin.**
23.	*Dale lo que quiere en vez de lo que necesita.*	**Give him what he wants instead of what he needs.**
24.	*Los resultados de la campaña son desalentadores.*	**The results of the campaign are disappointing.**
25.	*Estoy decepcionado con los resultados.*	**I'm disappointed with the results.**

Marketing Translation List 2

#		
1.	*Nunca sigo sus consejos. (de él)*	I never follow his advice.
2.	*Hemos gastado millones en publicidad ineficaz.*	We've spent millions on ineffective advertising.
3.	*Eres incapaz de ver tus productos objetivamente.*	You're incapable of seeing your products objectively.
4.	*A nadie le interesa por qué eres el número uno.*	No one is interested in why you're number one.
5.	*Me da igual que hayan ganado un premio de publicidad.*	I don't care if they won an advertising award.
6.	*Elabora un manual de información del producto.*	Draw up a product information manual.
7.	*La gente no aprecia ciertas características clave.*	The people don't appreciate certain key features.
8.	*Este anuncio va a impresionar a la gente.*	This ad is going to impress people.
9.	*Van a hacer cola para comprar nuestro producto.*	They're going to line up (queue up) to buy our product.
10.	*¿Quién toma las decisiones en la familia?*	Who's the decision-maker in the family?
11.	*¿Quién influye en quien toma las decisiones?*	Who influences the decision-maker?
12.	*¿Quién tiene la autoridad final para tomar decisiones?*	Who has the final authority to make decisions?
13.	*Con cada compra de nuestro producto, puedes ganar un viaje a Disneylandia.*	With each purchase of our product, you can win a trip to Disneyland.
14.	*Siempre caen en la misma trampa.*	They always fall into the same trap.
15.	*Tu anuncio no es nada convincente.*	Your ad isn't convincing at all.
16.	*Estoy orgulloso del producto que vendo.*	I'm proud of the product I sell.
17.	*¿Cuál es el primer paso para hacer una venta?*	What's the first step in making a sale?
18.	*Quiero darte la enhorabuena por tu pequeño logro.*	I want to congratulate you on your small achievement.
19.	*El mensaje que transmites debe ser coherente.*	The message you convey should be consistent.
20.	*Hace falta mucha repetición para que la gente se acuerde de tu producto.*	It takes a lot of repetition for people to remember your product.
21.	*Un anuncio así activará una respuesta en la mente.*	An ad like this will trigger a response in the mind.
22.	*Estamos sin blanca.*	We're broke.
23.	*El producto fue un éxito de la noche a la mañana.*	The product was an overnight success.
24.	*Estamos comprometidos con la calidad.*	We're committed to quality.
25.	*Nuestro lema es "la calidad lo es todo".*	Our motto is "quality is everything".

Marketing Translation List 3

1.	Los enfoques lógicos a menudo fracasan.	Logical approaches often fail.
2.	Nos ha causado una honda impresión.	It made a deep impression on us.
3.	Gánate primero su corazón y después su mente.	Win their hearts first, and then their minds.
4.	¿Qué hace que un cliente quiera comprarle a usted?	What makes a customer want to buy from you?
5.	Tienen ustedes que destacar entre sus competidores.	You have to stand out among your competitors.
6.	Hay muchos clientes potenciales por ahí fuera.	There are a lot of prospective customers out there.
7.	Esto no es un buen uso de nuestro dinero.	This isn't a good use of our money.
8.	Saca el mayor provecho posible del dinero disponible.	Make the most of the available cash. (money)
9.	Tus preguntas han sido totalmente predecibles.	Your questions were totally predictable.
10.	Tienes que fijar tus prioridades primero.	You have to set your priorities first.
11.	¿Qué quieres sacar de esto, dinero o fama?	What do you want to get out of this, money or fame?
12.	Esto va a tener un impacto increíble en el mercado.	This is going to make an incredible impact on the market.
13.	Todo el mundo sonríe cuando oye el eslogan.	Everyone smiles when they hear the slogan.
14.	Estás intentando esquivar la pregunta.	You're trying to dodge the question.
15.	¿Cómo piensas medir el éxito de la campaña?	How do you plan to measure the success of the plan?
16.	¿Cuáles son los principios básicos de la publicidad?	What are the basic principles of advertising?
17.	Estos conceptos son válidos para todo el mundo.	These concepts are valid for everybody.
18.	Trata de visualizar a tus clientes como seres humanos.	Try to visualize your customers as human beings.
19.	Esto representa el 40% de las ventas.	This accounts for (represents) 40 percent of sales.
20.	¿Cómo influyen los unos en los otros en el proceso de compra?	How do people influence each other in the buying process?
21.	Quiero saber la edad y profesión de mis clientes.	I want to know the age and occupation of my customers.
22.	Clasificamos a la gente según sus tendencias de consumo.	We classify people according to their consumption tendencies.
23.	Ciertas personas tienen características de personalidad únicas.	Some people have unique personality traits.
24.	Mis actividades de ocio se centran en mi hogar.	My leisure activities center on my home.
25.	La gente está expuesta a muchos estímulos.	People are exposed to many stimuli.

Marketing Translation List 4

1.	*Los resultados avalan lo que yo sospechaba.*	The findings reinforce what I suspected.
2.	*¿De qué se preocupa la gente rica?*	What do rich people worry about?
3.	*¿Qué piensa el primer 1% de la gente?*	What do the top one percent of people think?
4.	*Los ingresos medios por familia aquí son altos.*	Average household incomes here are high.
5.	*La edad media de jubilación es de 64 años.*	The average retirement age is 64.
6.	*En este segmento, el patrimonio familiar supera los tres millones de euros.*	In this segment, the family estate (household net worth) exceeds three million euros.
7.	*Mucha gente está recortando gastos.*	A lot of people are cutting back on expenses.
8.	*¿Cuáles son las conclusiones de la encuesta?*	What are the conclusions of the survey?
9.	*Los ricos gastan en sí mismos.*	Wealthy people spend on themselves.
10.	*¿Qué hacen los ricos con su tiempo y su dinero?*	What do wealthy people do with their time and money?
11.	*Mucha gente busca el logro individual.*	A lot of people search for individual accomplishments.
12.	*Mucha gente también busca más tiempo de ocio.*	A lot of people also seek out more leisure time.
13.	*Pocos quieren una vida más emocionante y rápida.*	Few people want a more emotional and faster-paced life.
14.	*¿Qué estás intentando decirnos?*	What are you trying to tell us?
15.	*Estoy señalando un hecho importante.*	I'm pointing out an important fact.
16.	*Lo que funcionaba ayer ya no funciona hoy.*	What worked yesterday no longer works today.
17.	*Lo que antes funcionaba ya no funciona.*	What used to work doesn't work anymore.
18.	*Esa ropa ya no está de moda.*	Those clothes aren't in fashion anymore.
19.	*Abundan las reglas no escritas en la publicidad.*	Unwritten rules abound in advertising.
20.	*Nuestro anuncio televisivo ganó el premio Pearson.*	Our TV commercial won the Pearson award.
21.	*Quiero hablar en nombre de mi empresa.*	I want to speak on behalf of my company.
22.	*¿Estáis dispuestos a seguir adelante con esto?*	Are you willing to move ahead with this?
23.	*Soy el portavoz de mi empresa.*	I'm the spokesperson (spokesman) for my company.
24.	*Tienes que hacer las cosas con pasión.*	You have to do things with passion.
25.	*Les da igual qué clase de reloj lleves.*	They don't care what kind of watch you wear.

Marketing Translation List 5

#		
1.	La verdad es más importante que los hechos.	The truth is more important than the facts.
2.	¿Qué quieres decir con esa afirmación?	What do you mean by that statement?
3.	Nuestro jefe de comunicación preparará un comunicado.	Our PR manager will prepare an announcement.
4.	Vamos a fusionarnos con nuestro competidor.	We're going to merge with our competitor.
5.	Me encanta el expositor que habéis diseñado.	I love the display stand you designed.
6.	Esta es una herramienta de ventas interesante.	This is an interesting sales tool. (selling tool)
7.	Compramos la mayoría de ello a granel.	We buy most of it in bulk.
8.	Realizamos compras de gran volumen.	We make large-volume purchases.
9.	Nos hacen ciertos descuentos por volumen.	They give us certain volume discounts.
10.	Si no le gusta el producto, le devolvemos el dinero.	If you don't like the product, we'll give you a full refund.
11.	Ofrecemos una interesante variedad de referencias.	We offer an interesting variety of items.
12.	Fijamos nuestros precios por debajo de los de nuestros principales competidores.	We price below our major competitors.
13.	Ponemos anuncios en las revistas de mayor tirada.	We place ads in magazines with the greatest circulation.
14.	Esto no cubre costes.	This doesn't cover costs.
15.	Esto no deja margen de beneficio.	This doesn't leave a profit margin.
16.	El precio es tan alto que desanima a los compradores.	The price is so high that it discourages buyers.
17.	Todos nos esforzamos para asegurar la satisfacción del cliente.	All of us strive to assure customer satisfaction.
18.	Vamos a realizar una serie de entrevistas telefónicas.	We're going to conduct a series of telephone interviews.
19.	¿Cuánto cobran por sus servicios?	How much do they charge for their services?
20.	¿No crees que son un poco caros?	Don't you think they're a little expensive?
21.	¿Quieres un producto o una solución?	Do you want a product or do you want a solution?
22.	Si lo que quieres es una solución, entonces son baratos.	If you really want a solution, then they're cheap.
23.	Hay dos pasos a la hora de formular una estrategia.	There are two steps in formulating a strategy.
24.	Está mal ubicado.	It's in an inconvenient location.
25.	Tienes que saber cuáles son tus fortalezas y debilidades.	You have to know your strengths and weaknesses.

CHAPTER 13

FINANCE & INVESTING

[Una introducción al mundo financiero en inglés]

FINANCE & INVESTING

FINANCE

Finance is the science of money management, and the allocation of assets and liabilities over time. A key concept in finance is the **time value of money**, which is the idea that a unit of currency today is worth more than the same unit of currency tomorrow. Finance aims to price assets based on their **risk**, and expected **rate of return**. Here we will consider three different sub categories of finance: public finance, corporate finance and personal finance.

Public finance is a branch of economics which considers how government manages revenue, primarily received through taxation, and expenditure, and works to ensure economic stability in the country or region governed.

Corporate finance deals with how companies acquire the funds they need for the operation of their businesses.

Keeping in mind that the goal of management in a company is to maximize value to the **shareholders,** corporate finance considers the tools available to management. This involves **capital budgeting**, which deals with the section of profitable projects, and **capital structure** decisions, regarding the financing of the projects with **debt** or **equity capital**.

Debt financing involves raising money by selling bonds, bills or notes to investors. In return for their money the investor becomes a **creditor** and receives a promise that principle and **interest** on the debt will be repaid.

Equity financing involves issuing **shares**, representing partial ownership in the firm. The values of these shares will fluctuate in line with the overall value of the firm. We will explore concepts of stock market investing in the section below on personal finance.

Corporate finance also involves short-term management of the company's **current assets** and **current liabilities**; such as cash, inventories, and short-term borrowing and lending. You can find a more detailed discussion about many of these terms in the *Accounting* section.

Rate of return - Profit on an investment, expressed as a proportion of the amount. invested: *'beneficio sobre*

Shareholders - Individuals who own shares in a company: *'accionistas'.*

Debt capital - The capital that a business raises by taking out a loan: *'capital externo'.*

Equity capital - Capital invested in a company by shareholders, who then become part owners of the company: *'capital propio'.*

Shares - *'acciones'.*

Interest - A fee paid by a borrower to the lender as compensation: *'interés'.*

Current assets - Assets that are expected to be converted into cash within *a year: 'activos líquidos'.*

REMEMBER: In English we say to **give** a loan, or to **ask for** a loan.

We lend money TO others and borrow money FROM others.

Current liabilities - Debts payable within a year: *'pasivos líquidos' o 'pasivos'.*

Financial management in many ways overlaps with accounting; however, financial accounting is concerned with the reporting of past financial information, while financial management is more concerned with the allocation of resources to maximize shareholder value.

Personal finance refers to the financial decisions and management issues of individuals or families. This involves saving, budgeting, and investing.

Estate planning: *'planificacion patrimonial'.*

Taxation, retirement objectives and **estate planning** are all issues that must be considered.

Planning is essential for effectively handling personal finances. Accurately assessing one's current financial situation, setting realistic goals, creating a suitable plan, executing the plan, monitoring progress and making adjustments as necessary are all essential steps in the planning of one's personal finances.

Many concepts of personal finance are included in our next section, investing.

BUSINESS BITS

Office Talk!

PISTA DE AUDIO 26

Aquí te ofrezco cinco frases típicas del uso corriente que puedes oír en una oficina donde se habla inglés. Tapa la columna de la derecha y traduce en voz alta las frases.

¿Estás libre para comer el jueves que viene?	**Are you free for lunch next Thursday?**
Necesitamos planear una nueva estrategia.	**We need to map out a new strategy.**
Me lo llevaré a casa esta noche y lo repasaré.	**I'll take it home with me tonight to go over it.**
La gente de repente ha dejado de comprar.	**People have suddenly stopped buying.**
Escanéalo y envíamelo lo antes posible.	**Scan it and send it to me ASAP.**

INVESTING

A variety of options exist for personal investment. While we won't explore them in depth in this book, we can consider a few common products and concepts.

Securities - *'valores'.*

Most typical investment products can be referred to as **securities**, which are essentially a legal representation of the right to receive future benefits under stated conditions.

Common types of securities include:

Treasury bills (or notes)

These securities involve lending money to the government for a relatively short period (typically three months to one year). The level of risk on these investments is typically considered to be low to none, and therefore the return on investment is relatively low.

Long term bonds

In the case of long term bonds, the investor is again lending money either to a government or company issuing the bond. The borrower commits to making cash payments each year (known as **coupon payments**), until a predetermined maturity date. These payments include a repayment of a portion of the lender funds and an interest payment to compensate the lender.

Common shares

Common shares represent partial ownership of a company and entitle the holder to **dividend** payments. Dividends are typically declared quarterly and paid to shareholders.

Dividend: *'dividendo' (Ver explicación abajo).*

Preferred shares: *'acciones preferentes'*

Other types of shares exist including **preferred shares** which have priority over common shares in terms of receiving payment in the event of bankruptcy or liquidation of a company.

What are dividends?

Dividends are distribution of portions of a company's earnings that the company has decided to distribute to its shareholders. Dividends are usually granted in a dollar (or Euro) value per share and paid to shareholders who own the stock on a specified date.

Funds

An investment fund is a collection of investments pooled together and managed by professionals. The decisions to buy or sell those securities are made by the investment company behind the fund.

Mutual funds:
'fondos de inversión'.

Funds become an interesting investment option for people who are not interested in stock or bond picking and trading.

There are two main types of investment funds:

1. Open-ended funds, which can be bought or sold from/to the issuer at any time during the fund lifetime. Most **mutual funds** are open-ended funds. Mutual funds are a popular investment tool for those interested in investing in a diversified portfolio, managed by a professional. Mutual fund companies are compensated by collecting **management fees** from investors.

2. Closed funds, which have a finite number of units issued at fund creation, and last for the whole fund lifetime.

ETFs

Exchange Traded Funds, or "ETFs" are a relatively new and growing investment product.

They are a basket of stocks in many ways similar to a mutual fund, but they can be bought and sold like an individual stock on the market.

ETF's have the advantage over mutual funds that they carry significantly lower management fees.

Capital markets are the markets that exist for trading financial assets. When common shares are issued to raise capital for a company, an underwriter is typically used to facilitate the introduction of shares to the market. This sale of shares is known as an "initial public offering" or "IPO". The underwriter may be one or more investment banks who are confident they can profit from the share offering and buy the shares, then reissue them onto the secondary market, known as the **stock exchange**.

What the heck is a stock market?

Despite their global importance and usefulness in personal wealth creation, a surprising portion of adults don't really understand how stock markets work or even what purpose they really serve. If you fit into this group, read on!

Stock markets are **secondary markets**, where previously issued stocks are traded. This means that when stocks are bought on a stock exchange such as the New York Stock Exchange (NYSE), the London Stock Exchange or the Spanish Stock Exchange, the proceeds of sale go to the previous owner for the shares, and not the company, which already received money for the shares issued only at the time of their IPO. These secondary markets serve as a centralized meeting point for buyers and sellers of investments, which leads to better trading **liquidity** and more efficient pricing of investment products.

Brokerages are financial institutions that facilitate the buying and selling of investments. Often considered an activity for the rich, stock market investing has become increasingly accessible to average people as a result of **discount brokerage** firms. Discount brokers offer investment to their clients for lower fees than conventional full fee brokerages, which offer investment advice to their clients then charge commissions when shares are purchased on the advice of their professional advisors. Discount brokerages on the other hand do not offer advice, and are a cheaper way for individual investors to acquire the investments they have chosen through their own research.

The internet has popularized the trend towards online, discount trading, and many discount brokerages can sell stocks and other investments to investors like you for as little as a few dollars or Euros per transaction.

While the famous and chaotic trading floors depicted in the media and movies such as "Boiler Room" or "Wall Street" still do exist, most trading nowadays takes place through internet-based electric transactions.

INVESTMENT ANALYSIS:

Investors interested in participating in stock market investing can form a portfolio of stock investments they feel will increase in value. They can sell the stocks at a higher price and realize a profit known as a **capital gain**.

Capital markets: *'mercados financieros' o 'mercados de capital'.*

Secondary market - The financial market in which previously issued financial instruments such as stock's and bonds trade: *'mercado secundario'.*

Liquidity - The degree to which an asset or security can be bought or sold in the market: *'liquidez'.*

Brokerage: *'agencia de corredores'.*

Capital gain - The profit that results from the sale of an asset, having increased in value since the purchase: *'ganancias'.*

Diversification: *'diversificación'.*

Diversification is used within an investment **portfolio** to reduce risk. By investing in companies in a variety of sectors or even countries, one can reduce the vulnerability to negative price fluctuations affecting specific companies.

Risky business!

Diversification refers to the act of reducing risk by investing in a variety of assets. Generally speaking, when one asset goes down in price, other assets will not go down by the same amount. Some may even rise in value due to the same factors that cause another to fall.

By creating a diversified portfolio including investments of different types, in different industries, and based in different parts of the world, investors can significantly reduce the risk of an overall portfolio.

Portfolio: *'cartera de valores'.*

The "**asset mix**" refers to the allocation of investment money into different types of assets, or "**asset classes**". The appropriate asset mix for an investor depends on many factors, specifically, their age, income, risk tolerance and personal circumstances.

Don't put all your eggs in one basket!

Let's now consider potential asset mixes for three different investors.

1. John Alexander - A young, healthy single individual professional with medium investment knowledge and high risk tolerance and a long time horizon:

Cash: 5%
Fixed Income   25%
Equities   70%

John can put more money into equities because he has sufficient income to cover expenses and the time to endure market fluctuations over a long period of time.

2. Mary Matthews – A 71 year old with low income, and a low risk tolerance:

Cash: 8%
Fixed Income   62%
Equities   30%

Mary needs the income provided by fixed income investments, such as bonds and Treasury bills. While some investments in equity for growth are valued, she keeps cash on hand to meet immediate expenses.

3. Gary Gumbly – A middle-aged factory worker with three teenage children. He owns his home but is concerned about future employment:

Cash: 10%
Fixed Income   40%
Equities   50%

Gary appreciates the income from his fixed income investments, but still wishes to invest in equities to grow his wealth through equity investments.

Choosing investments or **"holdings"** for a portfolio can be challenging task and investors and investment professionals use countless concepts, models and strategies in an attempt to predict which investments will perform best over time and be best suited for inclusion in a particular portfolio. The two basic forms of investment analysis are technical analysis and fundamental analysis.

Technical analysis is often known as "*charting*" and is based on the idea that the future **trend** in prices can be predicted from charts of past records of prices and **trading volume**.

Holdings - The contents of an investment portfolio: '*valores en cartera*'.

Trend: '*tendencia*'.

Trading volume - The volume of shares bought and sold on a given day: '*volumen de transacciones*'.

Highs and lows:
'puntos altos y
bajos'.

Market breadth -
A technical
analysis measure
that assesses the
direction of the
overall market
by analyzing
the number
of companies
advancing
relative to
the number
declining.

Moving average -
A technical
analysis indicator
averaging prices
over a defined
number of
periods up to
the present. As
time progresses,
the oldest
observation
points are
removed from
the average as
new ones are
added: 'promedio
variable'.

**To break
through:** 'romper
(la tendencia)'.

To slope:
'inclinar'.

There are many different types of indicators that technical analysts attempt to interpret. Some of the most common ones include **stock price trend lines**, **volume changes**, breadth of market and new **highs and lows**.

Analysts use **moving averages** as a way to smooth out stock prices over a period of time. It helps analysts form a long term trend, which they often believe the stock price should return to. Trends are altered when the stock price **breaks through** the trend line on strong trading volume.

Accumulation (or "reversal") patters are formations on charts that usually precede significant increases in stock price.

One example of a common pattern recognized by technical analysts is the "bottom head and shoulders pattern", which is considered to be one of the most reliable patterns.

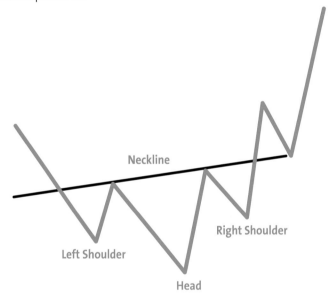

The bottom head and shoulders pattern is a chart formation in which a stock's price:

1. Rises to a peak and then declines.

2. Then, rises above the former peak and again declines.

3. And finally, rises again, but not to the second peak, and declines once more.

The first and third peaks are "shoulders", and the second peak forms the "head". With this pattern shown, since the **Neckline**" **slopes** upwards, analysts would expect prices to rise over time.

On the other hand, other patterns could give indication of coming declines in share price. This technical topic is beyond the scope of this book, but having a basic knowledge of the vocabulary you see here can help you research and learn more in this field.

Trading volume is often studied as high volume in changing prices can indicate how long prices might be expected to rise or fall. "**OBV**" or "**on balance volume**" is a line graph often found at the bottom of a stock price chart indicating trading volume.

Breadth of the market refers to the number of different stocks being traded in a given period. This is considered to be an important figure as it indicates what is happening to the supply and demand for all stocks, not just a few blue-chip companies.

Fundamental analysis studies many factors to determine how securities prices may change. Analysts assess the profitability of companies, their ability to pay dividends and the rate of growth of those dividends.

A variety of items and ratios are studied to assess the profitability and potential growth of companies and their share price.

 TIP

Take note! To understand the valuation tools often used, we should be aware that the value of an asset (including a stock) is defined as the present value of the expected future cash flows it will provide.

INVESTMENT VALUATION MODELS

There are many models used to attempt to determine the value of a stock. Here we see some of the most common ones.

The dividend discount model:

The dividend discount model is an essential model that relies on the principle mentioned earlier that the value of an asset, including a stock, is the present value of its expected future cash flows. As the dividends are the cash flows from the stock, its price should be the present value of the dividends paid to owner of the stock.

$$\text{Value of stock} = \frac{\text{Dividend per share}}{\text{Discount rate-Dividend Growth rate}}$$

The idea is that if the value obtained from the "DDM" is higher than what the shares are currently trading at, then the stock is undervalued.

EX

Example: Jim Morton's Donuts

Let's say we are looking at shares of Jim Morton's Donuts. Their stock pays an annualized dividend of $1.24 and a typical market rate of return for this industry is considered to be 8%. We expect their dividends to grow at a rate of 2% per year based on our analysis.

We could calculate the value of the Jim Morton's stock as follows:

Dividends per share = 1.24

Discount rate = r = 0.08

Dividend growth rate = g = 0.02

$$\text{Value of stock} = \frac{1.24}{0.08 - 0.02}$$

$$\text{Value of stock} = \frac{1.24}{0.06}$$

$$\text{Value of stock} = \$20.67$$

So we would calculate the value of the stock to be $20.67. If the current market price is below this, we may want to buy it, as we would expect it to rise in price to this level. Conversely, if it were selling above this level, we would likely want to sell the stock.

Of course the model has the drawback that it doesn't work for companies that don't pay dividends.

Earnings per share:

Earnings per share serves as an indicator of a company's profitability. It represents the portion of net income for a period attributable to a single share of a company.

Price / Earnings ratio (P/E):

This very important ratio shows price of a share divided by the earnings per share.

P/E ratios are often used to try to decide if a company's share price is "cheap" or "expensive" given the earnings a company has.

Compared to past levels or industry averages a high ratio can mean the price could be too high, or it could indicate that investors feel that the company will increase earnings in the future. Conversely, lower ratios could mean that a company could be undervalued at its current price or that analysts expect earnings to fall.

Undervalued / overvalued: 'infravalorado' / 'sobrevalorado'.

$$P/E\ ratio = \frac{\textbf{Market Value per Share}}{\textbf{Earnings per Share (EPS)}}$$

Return on Equity (ROE)

This ratio shows the amount of net income returned as a percentage of shareholders equity (assets minus its total liabilities). **Return on equity** is a popular measure of profitability as it shows how much profit a company generates with the money shareholders have invested.

ROE is expressed as a percentage and calculated as:

$$\textbf{Return on Equity} = \frac{\textbf{Net Income}}{\textbf{Shareholder's Equity}}$$

Return on equity: 'rentabilidad sobre recursos propios'.

The topic of investing and investment analysis is vast and extends well beyond the scope of this book. The following translation examples will help give you a more solid background of relevant terminology.

FINANCE AND INVESTING VOCABULARY!

25 words you should know

PISTA DE AUDIO 27

1.	*Mercado de valores, la bolsa*	The stock market
2.	*Accionista*	Shareholder
3.	*Deuda*	Debt
4.	*Bono*	Bond
5.	*Acciones, patrimonio*	Equity
6.	*Capital*	Capital
7.	*Ingresos*	Revenue
8.	*Interés*	Interest
9.	*Acciones*	Shares
10.	*Valores*	Securities
11.	*Letra del Tesoro*	Treasury bill, T-Bill
12.	*De larga duración, A largo plazo*	Long term
13.	*Dividendos*	Dividends
14.	*Comprar y vender en Bolsa, operar en Bolsa*	To trade
15.	*Agencia de corredores*	Brokerage
16.	*Diversificación*	Diversification
17.	*Cartera de valores*	Portfolio
18.	*Honorarios*	Fees
19.	*Presupuesto*	Budget
20.	*Liquidez*	Liquidity
21.	*Valores en cartera*	Holdings
22.	*Puntos altos y bajos*	Highs and lows
23.	*Plusvalía*	Capital gain
24.	*Rentabilidad sobre recursos propios*	Return on equity
25.	*Volumen de transacciones*	Trading volume

FINANCE AND INVESTING TRANSLATION LISTS

Finance and Investing Translation List 1

PISTA DE AUDIO 28

1.	¿Confías en tu asesor?	Do you trust your advisor?
2.	No tengo licencia para operar.	I'm not licensed to trade.
3.	¿Cuál es el precio de apertura?	What's the opening price?
4.	Mi hermana opera por internet.	My sister trades online.
5.	Ella paga comisiones muy bajas.	She pays very low commissions.
6.	¿Qué ratios son más importantes?	Which ratios are most important?
7.	Los mercados estaban recuperándose por la mañana.	The markets were rallying in the morning.
8.	El IBEX 35 ha subido un 18% este año.	The IBEX 35 has risen 18% this year.
9.	¿Qué haces con tus dividendos?	What do you do with your dividends?
10.	Tengo un plan de reinversión de dividendos.	I have a dividend reinvestment plan.
11.	La capitalización de mercado es de más de 2.000 billones de euros.	Their market capitalization is more than 2 billion euros.
12.	Tendrás que votar por poderes.	You'll have to vote by proxy.
13.	Ojalá estuviera en el consejo de administración.	I wish I were on the board of directors.
14.	Cotizan en la bolsa de Nueva York.	They're listed on the New York Stock Exchange.
15.	Antiguamente cotizaban en la bolsa de Londres.	They used to be listed on the London Stock Exchange.
16.	Enséñame el estado de flujos de caja.	Show me the statement of cash flows.
17.	Todos los índices están en números rojos.	All the indices are in the red.
18.	Ya han emitido acciones tres veces.	They've already issued shares three times.
19.	Tendremos que esperar a la memoria anual.	We'll have to wait for the annual report.
20.	Échale un ojo al balance de situación.	Take a look at the balance sheet.
21.	Sus activos fijos valen un montón.	Their fixed assets are worth a lot.
22.	¿Qué me dices de los activos intangibles?	What about the intangible assets?
23.	¿Ves una tendencia?	Do you see a trend?
24.	John opera con futuros.	John trades futures contracts.
25.	Trabaja en el parqué de operaciones.	He works on the trading floor.

Finance and Investing Translation List 2

1.	*Solía comprar fondos de inversión.*	**I used to buy mutual funds.**
2.	*Ya no los compro.*	**I don't buy them anymore.**
3.	*No me gusta pagar gastos de gestión.*	**I don't like paying the management expenses.**
4.	*Son un buen método de diversificar.*	**They're a good way to diversify.**
5.	*¿Cuál es el valor de tu cartera?*	**What's the value of your portfolio?**
6.	*La burbuja está a punto de explotar.*	**The bubble is about to burst.**
7.	*¿Quién subscribe la nueva emisión?*	**Who's underwriting the issue?**
8.	*El dealer está consiguiendo un beneficio enorme.*	**The dealer is making huge profit.**
9.	*Vamos a recortar nuestras pérdidas.*	**Let's cut our losses.**
10.	*Necesitamos aumentar capital.*	**We need to raise capital.**
11.	*Ya hemos emitido bonos.*	**We've already issued bonds.**
12.	*Estoy más preocupado por la seguridad del principal.*	**I'm more concerned with safety of principal.**
13.	*¿Qué hay de los ingresos?*	**What about income?**
14.	*¿Crees que nuestro sector está creciendo?*	**Do you think our sector is growing?**
15.	*¿Cuántos impuestos tendremos que pagar?*	**How much tax will I have to pay?**
16.	*Eso depende de las ganancias de capital y los dividendos.*	**That depends on capital gains and dividends.**
17.	*No te olvides de los ingresos por intereses.*	**Don't forget about interest income.**
18.	*No entiendo las leyes fiscales.*	**I don't understand the tax laws.**
19.	*Los impuestos sobre plusvalías pueden ser confusos.*	**Capital gains tax can be confusing.**
20.	*Supongo que tendré que pagar por recibir consejo profesional.*	**I guess I'll have to pay for professional advice.**
21.	*Podrías comprar bonos del Estado.*	**You could buy government bonds.**
22.	*¿Cuál es la evaluación de ese bono?*	**What's the rating on that bond?**
23.	*Éste está vendiendo con prima sobre la par.*	**This one is selling at a premium.**
24.	*Aquel está vendiendo bajo par.*	**That one is selling at a discount.**
25.	*Los tipos de interés están cayendo.*	**Interest rates are falling.**

Finance and Investing Translation List 3

PISTA DE AUDIO 30

1.	*David es nuestro Jefe de Inversión Estratégica.*	David is our Chief Investment Strategist.
2.	*Es solo un beneficio no realizable hasta que vendas.*	It's only a paper profit until you sell.
3.	*Los perfiles demográficos tienen una gran influencia.*	Demographics have a huge influence.
4.	*La generación del baby-boom tiene un montón para invertir.*	The baby-boomers have a lot to invest.
5.	*¿Cuál fue el precio de cierre?*	What was the closing price?
6.	*Tenemos que jugar con sus reglas.*	We've got to play by their rules.
7.	*Dice que los contables estaban equivocados.*	He says the accountants were wrong.
8.	*He oído que tienen avión privado de empresa.*	I've heard they have a corporate jet.
9.	*Tu casa puede ser el aval.*	Your house can be the collateral.
10.	*Los inversores están perdiendo optimismo.*	Investors are losing optimism.
11.	*¿Qué me dices de los activos intangibles?*	What about the intangible assets?
12.	*Su marca también vale un montón.*	Their brand is worth a lot too.
13.	*Eso es difícil de cuantificar.*	That's tough to quantify.
14.	*¿Cuánto se generó de actividades de explotación?*	How much came from operating activities?
15.	*¿Quiénes son sus competidores principales?*	Who are their main competitors?
16.	*Ese es un sector interesante.*	That's an interesting sector.
17.	*¿Cómo calcularon la depreciación?*	How did they calculate the depreciation?
18.	*Tendrás que preguntarle al contable.*	You'll have to ask the accountant.
19.	*Las acciones cayeron la friolera del 16%.*	The shares dropped a whopping 16%.
20.	*Tienen un nuevo presidente.*	They've got a new president.
21.	*He analizado su rentabilidad.*	I've analyzed their profitability.
22.	*Hay un montón de ratios que puedes calcular.*	There are a lot of ratios you can calculate.
23.	*Creo que la relación precio-beneficio es muy importante.*	I think the P/E ratio is very important.
24.	*Es difícil cuantificar el sentimiento del inversor.*	It's tough to quantify investor sentiment.
25.	*Se están abriendo nuevos mercados en Dubai.*	New markets are opening in Dubai.

ADVANCED BUSINESS TOPICS FINANCE & INVESTING 249

Finance and Investing Translation List 4

1.	Los tipos de interés están creciendo lentamente.	Interest rates are slowly rising.
2.	Somos un proveedor de servicios financieros diversificados.	We're a diversified financial services provider.
3.	Tenemos tasas hipotecarias atractivas.	We have attractive mortgage rates.
4.	El gasto de los consumidores ha aumentado.	Consumer spending has risen.
5.	El banco nacional no ha hecho ningún comunicado todavía.	The national bank hasn't made an announcement yet.
6.	¿Sabes cuál es tu código SWIFT?	Do you know your SWIFT code?
7.	Lo necesitarás para hacer transferencias internacionales.	You'll need it to make international transfers.
8.	Me gustaría transferir dinero a la cuenta de mi hermano.	I'd like to transfer money to my brother's account.
9.	Mi esposa y yo compartimos una cuenta.	My spouse and I share an account.
10.	Mi madre insiste en ir a la sucursal.	My mother insists on going into the branch.
11.	El problema es que cerramos todos los días a las 14:00.	The problem is we close every day at 14:00.
12.	Bueno, abrimos hasta las 18:00 los jueves.	Well, we're open until 18:00 on Thursdays.
13.	¿Tiene banca por internet? (ella).	Does she have internet banking?
14.	Ni siquiera tiene ordenador.	She doesn't even have a computer.
15.	Podría usar un cajero automático.	She could use the ATM machine.
16.	¿Qué me dice de la banca por teléfono?	What about your telephone banking services?
17.	¿Cuándo está disponible el servicio de atención al cliente?	When are the customer service representatives available?
18.	Trabajan de 9 a 5.	They work from 9 to 5.
19.	Hay un servicio de contestador automático disponible las 24 horas.	There's an automated answering service available 24 hours a day.
20.	Facturaremos al proveedor por eso.	We'll bill the supplier for that.
21.	¿No recibiste la factura?	Didn't you receive the invoice?
22.	¿Cuál es el tipo de cambio de hoy?	What's today's exchange rate?
23.	Quiero saber cuál es el tipo de cambio de hoy.	I want to know what today's exchange rate is.
24.	Los tipos de cambio han estado fluctuando mucho últimamente.	The exchange rates have been fluctuating a lot lately.
25.	Tenemos nuestros propios asesores financieros.	We have our own financial advisors.

Finance and Investing Translation List 5

1.	¿Estás interesado en bonos del Estado?	Are you interested in government bonds?
2.	Los tipos de interés están aumentando.	Interest rates are increasing.
3.	Este bono está vendiéndose por encima de la par.	This bond is selling at a premium.
4.	Tiene un rendimiento al vencimiento más alto.	It has a higher yield to maturity.
5.	Tratamos con muchos bancos extranjeros.	We deal with a lot of foreign banks.
6.	Podrías contratar un préstamo con un tipo de interés variable.	You could take out a floating rate loan.
7.	Éste estaba vendiendo a la par.	This one was selling at par.
8.	Los mercados extranjeros pueden ser complicados.	The foreign exchange markets can be complicated.
9.	Usamos contratos de futuros para protegernos del riesgo.	We use futures contracts to hedge against risk.
10.	Necesitarás una cuenta especial para eso.	You'll need a special account for that.
11.	Espera que le concedan un préstamo.	He hopes they'll grant him a loan.
12.	Está intentando financiar su nuevo negocio.	He's trying to finance his new business.
13.	Podrías estar acumulando intereses en tu dinero.	You could be accruing interest on your cash.
14.	Me van a dar una carta de crédito.	They're giving me a letter of credit.
15.	Quiere saber cuál es el saldo de la cuenta.	She wants to know what the account balance is.
16.	Aún estamos en números rojos.	We're still in the red.
17.	Esperamos estar consiguiendo beneficios antes del verano.	We hope to be making a profit before the summer.
18.	Simplemente están haciendo lo que es mejor para los inversores.	They're just doing what's best for the investors.
19.	Puede que haya una fusión de bancos en primavera.	There may be a bank merger in the spring.
20.	Hará que el precio de las acciones se mueva.	It will make the stock prices move.
21.	Podría ser una OPA hostil.	It could be a hostile takeover.
22.	Probablemente el precio de las acciones se moverá.	The share prices will probably move.
23.	Normalmente la empresa licitadora paga de más.	The bidding firm usually over-pays.
24.	El precio de su acción podría caer.	Their share price may fall.
25.	Buscarán sinergias y costes reducidos.	They'll look for synergies and reduced costs.

CHAPTER 14

ACCOUNTING

[Entender la contabilidad en inglés]

ACCOUNTING

Accounting is essentially the practice of recording, classifying, and summarizing business performance in terms of money.

There are two basic types of accounting; **managerial** or "management" **accounting** and **financial accounting**.

Managerial accounting is concerned with providing information to managers within an organization for the purpose of directing and controlling its operations and helping management make better financial decisions.

Financial accounting is concerned with providing information to shareholders, **creditors** and others who are outside the organization. It involves the preparation of documents for external reporting purposes.

Creditor - The person or company that money is owed to: *'acreedor'*.

Various bodies exist around the world to establish accounting rules, such as the **Generally Accepted Accounting Principles**, known as **GAAP**, in the United States and **International Financial Reporting Standards**, or **IFRS** used in Europe and over 100 countries worldwide.

Great efforts have been made in recent years towards the harmonization of international accounting practices, to allow "apples to apples" comparisons among the performance of businesses around the world.

More money phrasal verbs!

En esta tanda de "phrasal verbs", vamos a practicar dos verbos que se usan cuando hablamos de la devolución de dinero prestado, "to pay back" y "to pay off".

To pay back	*Devolver dinero*	**To return money owed to someone.**
To pay off	*Finalizar la devolución de dinero prestado*	**To finish paying all money that is owed.**

¡A practicar! Para ganar soltura con estas estructuras, tapa la columna de la derecha y contesta afirmativamente a las siguientes preguntas con respuestas completas. También escucha el audio e intenta contestar en voz alta con la voz grabada.

Did he pay you back in full	*Yes, he paid me back in full.*
Have you paid back your student loan?	*Yes, I've paid back my student loan.*
Do they always pay you back on time?	*Yes, they always pay me back on time.*
Will she pay me back before the end of January?	*Yes, she'll pay you back before the end of January.*
Did he pay the whole loan off?	*Yes, he paid off the whole loan.*
Have they finally paid off their mortgage?	*Yes, they've finally paid off their mortgage.*
Do they always pay off their phone bills immediately?	*Yes, they always pay off their phone bills immediately.*
Will you pay off your boat loan soon?	*Yes, I'll pay off my boat loan soon.*

FINANCIAL STATEMENTS

Businesses typically prepare three principal financial statements to report the results of their activities.

1. The Balance Sheet
2. The Income Statement
3. The Statement of Cash Flows

Additional statements such as the **statement of shareholders equity** are also important, but we will examine the three statements above for an overview of the relevant accounting terminology in English.

The income statement: *'cuenta de resultados' o 'cuenta de pérdidas y ganancias'.*

The statement of cash flows: *'estado de flujos de efectivo'.*

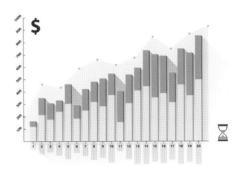

The balance sheet - 'el balance de situación'.

Snapshot - 'imagen actual'.

Owner's equity - The owner's investment in the business minus the owner's withdrawals plus the net income since the business began. 'patrimonio neto'.

The balance sheet, also known as the **statement of financial position**, presents a **snapshot** of the resources of a company, (their assets) and the claims on those resources (liabilities and **owner's equity**) at a particular moment in time.

The balance sheet represents the following balance, which is often known as the "accounting equation":

Assets = Liabilities + Owner's Equity

'Activos' = 'Pasivos' + 'Capital Propio'

Common balance sheet assets:

Cash	Currency available to the company including checking and savings accounts.
Temporary Investments	Short-term investments in other companies including shares, treasury bills or bonds.
Accounts Receivable	Amounts owed to the company as a result of credit sales to customers.
Inventory	Goods held for resale to customers.
Prepaid expenses	Expenses paid in advance but not yet used.
Capital Assets	Investments in land, buildings and **intangible assets** to be used over the long term. This includes **patents**, **trademarks** and **goodwill**.

Intangible assets: 'activos intangibles'.

Patent: 'patente'.

Trademark: 'marca registrada'.

Goodwill: 'fondo de comercio'.

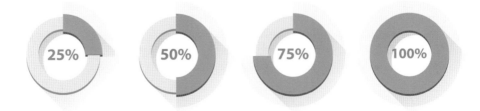

Common balance sheet liabilities:

Bank indebtedness	Amounts owed to the bank on short-term credit.
Accounts payable	Amounts owed to suppliers from the purchase of goods on credit.
Notes payable	Amounts owed to a creditor represented by a formal agreement (a note).
Dividends payable	Amounts owed to shareholders for dividends that are declared by management.
Accrued liabilities	Amounts owed based on expenses incurred but not yet due.
Taxes payable	Amounts owed to taxing authorities.
Long-term debt	Amounts owed to creditors over periods longer than one year.

Accrued-
Accumulated
over time:
'devengado',
'acumulado'.

Current assets and **current liabilities**, as mentioned in the finance section, are essentially relatively short-term use assets and liabilities. Current assets are reasonably expected to be converted into cash within one year in the normal course of business. These assets include cash, accounts receivable,

inventory, marketable securities, prepaid expenses and other liquid assets that can be readily converted to cash.

Similarly, current liabilities are essentially short-term debts or obligations that are due within one year. Current liabilities appear on the company's balance sheet and include short-term debt, accounts payable, accrued liabilities and other debts.

It is important for managers to pay attention to current assets and current liabilities, as they indicate the company's ability to deal with short-term cash obligations.

Liquidity is the ability to pay short-term obligations when they fall due. It is often expressed as a ratio.

The **current ratio** measures whether or not a firm has enough resources to

$$\text{Current ratio} = \frac{\textbf{Current Assets}}{\textbf{Current Liabilities}}$$

pay its debts over the next 12 months. It compares a firm's current assets to its current liabilities. It is expressed as follows:

The current ratio is an indication of a firm's market liquidity and ability to meet creditor's demands.

The ideal current ratio values vary from industry to industry. Usually, a current ratio of 2:1 is considered acceptable. The higher the current ratio is, the more capable the company is of paying its obligations.

The lower the ratio is, the greater the likelihood that it may have problems paying its bills on time.

More money phrasal verbs!

En esta tanda de "phrasal verbs", vamos a practicar dos verbos que se usan cuando hablamos de ahorrar dinero, "to save up" y "to put aside".

To save up	*Ahorrar*	To keep money for a large expense in the future.
To put aside	*Ahorrar dinero para algo especifico*	To save money for a specific purpose.

¡A practicar! Para ganar soltura con estas estructuras, tapa la columna de la derecha y contesta afirmativamente a las siguientes preguntas con respuestas completas. También escucha el audio e intenta contestar en voz alta con la voz grabada.

Did they save up for a new television?	Yes, they saved up for a new television.
Do you think they've saved up enough for their supplies?	Yes, I think they've saved up for enough for their supplies.
Do you save up a little bit of money every month?	Yes I save up a little bit of money every month.
Will they save up enough to buy a new car in three years' time?	Yes, they will save up enough to buy a new car in three years' time.

Did your grandparents put aside a little money every month?	Yes, my grandparents put aside a little money every month.
Has she put aside any money for college?	Yes, she has put aside some money for college.
Do they regularly put aside a certain percentage of sales?	Yes, they regularly put aside a certain percentage of sales.
Are you going to put aside a portion of what you earn each month?	Yes, I am going to put aside a portion of what I earn each month.

Consider the following example balance sheet for Krazy Kyle's T-Shirt Printing:

Krazy Kyle's T-Shirt Printing - Balance Sheet as of 31st December 2013

	2013 USD	2012 USD
ASSETS		
Non-current assets		
Property, plant & equipment	110,000	100,000
Goodwill	10,000	10,000
Intangible assets	60,000	50,000
	190,000	170,000
Current assets		
Inventories	12,000	10,000
Trade receivables	25,000	30,000
Cash and cash equivalents	8,000	10,000
	45,000	50,000
TOTAL ASSETS	235,000	220,000
EQUITY AND LIABILITIES		
Equity		
Share capital	100,000	100,000
Retained earnings	40,000	30,000
Revaluation reserve	15,000	10,000
Total equity	155,000	140,000
Non-current liabilities		
Long term borrowings	25,000	40,000
Current liabilities		
Accounts payable	25,000	15,000
Short-term borrowings	10,000	8,000
Current portion of long-term borrowings	15,000	15,000
Current tax payable	5,000	2,000
Total current liabilities	55,000	**40,000**
Total liabilities	80,000	**80,000**
TOTAL EQUITY AND LIABILITIES	235,000	**220,000**

Expenses:
'gastos'.

Revenues:
'ingresos'.

Net income, Net profit, "The bottom line" -
A company's total earnings (or profit). Net income is calculated by taking revenues and adjusting for the cost of doing business, depreciation, interest, taxes and other expenses:
'ingreso neto'.

Depreciation -
A method of allocating the cost of a tangible asset over its useful life:
'depreciación'.

Amortization -
The deduction of capital expenses over a specific period of time (usually over the asset's life):
'amortización'.

The Income Statement

The income statement, or "statement of profit and loss" (or P&L) in British English, documents a company's **revenues** and **expenses** during a particular period of time.

It shows how revenues are transformed into **net income** (the result after all revenues and expenses have been accounted for, also known as "**net profit**" or the "**bottom line**")

This statement shows the costs associated with generating revenues, in addition to costs and expenses, including **depreciation** and **amortization**. It helps managers and investors see whether the company made or lost money during the period being reported.

✔ **Notice how we say "to make money"**

Generally, we say:

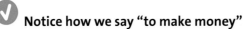

Companies **make** money

People **earn** money working

People **win** money at the casino

Unlike the balance sheet, which represents the company's financial position at a particular moment in time, the income statement reports performance over a particular period, typically a **quarter** or a **fiscal year**.

Common income statement items:

Sales revenue	The total amount of sales for a period.
Other income	Various types of revenues or income other than from sales.
Cost of goods sold	The cost of the units of inventory that were sold during the period.
Selling, General and administrative expenses	The total amount of other expenses of the company during the period that do not fit into any other category.
Amortization expense	The allocation of part of the cost of long-lived items like equipment.
Interest expense	The amount of interest incurred on the company during the period.
Income tax expense	Taxes on the profits of the company during the period.

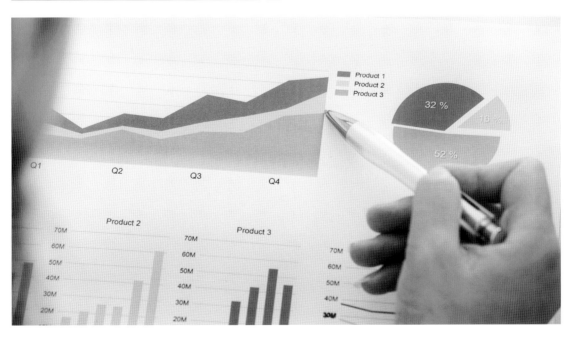

Consider the following example Income Statement for Krazy Kyle's T-Shirt Printing:

Krazy Kyle's T-Shirt Printing - Income Statement for the Year Ended 31st December 2013

	2013 USD	2012 USD
Revenue	90,000	70,000
Cost of Sales	(43,000)	(36,000)
Gross Profit	47,000	34,000
Other Income	16,000	9,000
Distribution Cost	(9,000)	(7,000)
Administrative Expenses	(16,000)	(14,000)
Other Expenses	(3,000)	(2,000)
Finance Charges	(1,000)	(1,000)
	(13,000)	(15,000)
Profit before tax	34,000	19,000
Income tax	(10,200)	(5,700)
Net Profit	23,800	13,300

The Statement of Cash Flows:

Also known as the "Cash Flow Statement", this is an important financial statement that indicates how changes in the balance sheet and income statement affect the amount of cash and cash equivalents.

Cash and other **liquid assets** are extremely important to businesses and are essential for businesses to meet their short-term financial obligations.

Liquid asset - An asset that can be easily and quickly converted to cash: *'activo líquido'.*

Cash flow problems

Managing cash flow and avoiding cash flow problems is extremely important, as poor cash flow is a very common reason for the failure of small businesses.

EX

Cash Crunch! - A practical example

Rick's Design Studio in Portland, Maine offers web and graphic design services in the Northeastern United States. They have been successful in recent years and have been able to hire four new employees, rent a larger office space and subscribe to a licensed software package that is somewhat expensive, but helps them do a great job in less time.

Recently, Rick accepted a new, very large and profitable contract with a big client. The client pays well, but Rick agreed to their terms, which allow them to pay after 90 days of completion of the job, which lasts 2 months, another 60 days.

Rick made the mistake of overlooking the fact that he will have to incur the costs associated with his payroll for the workers, rent, software subscription expenses and more for 150 days. During that period, he will have to pay these shorter term expenses, most of which have to be paid within 30 or 60 days.

Without adequate cash on hand, Rick has found it impossible to pay the company's bills and generally meet its short-term obligations. Despite doing more business than ever, the business was almost forced to close, and Rick was only able to save it thanks to the financial help from his family.

**This example shows how regardless of income into a business, serious problems can result if proper attention isn't paid to handling cash in such a way that ensures all short-term obligations can be met.

Consider the following sample statement of cash flows for Krazy Kyle's T-Shirt Printing:

Krazy Kyle's T-Shirt Printing - Statement of Cash Flows for the year ended 31st December 2013

	2013 USD	2012 USD
CASH FLOWS FROM OPERATING ACTIVITIES		
Profit before tax	34,000	19,000
Adjustments for:		
Depreciation	8,000	6,500
Amortization	6,000	5,500
Impairment losses	10,000	1,500
Bad debts written off	500	-
Interest expense	800	1,000
Gain on revaluation of investments	(18,000)	-
Interest income	(10,000)	(8,500)
Dividend income	(2,000)	(1,500)
Gain on disposal of fixed assets	(1,000)	(1,550)
	28,300	21,950
Working Capital Changes:		
Movement in current assets:		
(Increase) / Decrease in inventory	(2,000)	750
Decrease in trade receivables	5,000	1,400
Movement in current liabilities:		
Increase / (Decrease) in trade payables	10,000	(1,300)
Cash generated from operations	41,300	22,800
Dividend paid	(4,000)	(3,000)
Income tax paid	(12,000)	(10,000)
*Net cash from operating activities (A)	25,300	9,800
CASH FLOWS FROM INVESTING ACTIVITIES		
Capital expenditure	(80,000)	(65,000)
Dividend received	5,000	3,000

Interest received	3,500	**1,000**
Proceeds from disposal of fixed assets	18,000	**5,500**
Proceeds from disposal of investments	2,500	**2,200**
Net cash used in investing activities (B)	(25,700)	**(43,500)**
CASH FLOWS FROM FINANCING ACTIVITIES		
Issuance of share capital	200,000	-
Bank loan received	-	**50,000**
Repayment of bank loan	(50,000)	-
Interest expense	(1,300)	**(3,600)**
Net cash from financing activities (C)	123,000	**2,900**
NET INCREASE IN CASH & CASH EQUIVALENTS (A+B+C)	122,000	**(30,800)**
CASH AND CASH EQUIVALENTS AT START OF THE YEAR	1,200	**32,000**
CASH AND CASH EQUIVALENTS AT END OF THE YEAR	123,200	**1,200**

The Annual Report

The annual report is a larger document sent to all owners and parties interested in the company. A complete annual report includes the balance sheet, income statement and statement of cash flows for a company for a given period. It may also include a statement of retained earnings, notes to the financial statements and additional supporting documents.

BUSINESS BITS

Office Talk!

PISTA DE AUDIO 35

Aquí te ofrezco cinco frases típicas del uso corriente que puedes oír en una oficina donde se habla inglés. Tapa la columna de la derecha y traduce en voz alta las frases.

Me complace anunciar que nuestras ventas han estado creciendo de forma estable desde el pasado mayo.	**I'm happy to announce that our sales have been steadily improving since last May.**
Todo nuestro trabajo está empezando a dar su fruto.	**All our hard work is starting to pay off.**
El Sr. Peterson contestará preguntas después de su presentación.	**Mr. Peterson will be taking questions after his presentation.**
Sólo le importa el balance.	**He only cares about the bottom line.**
Las subidas de impuestos dificultarían las cosas para un negocio como el nuestro.	**Tax hikes would really make it tough on a business like ours.**

THE ACCOUNTING CYCLE

The accounting cycle is the process performed during the accounting period to analyze, record, classify, summarize and report financial information.

The **workflow** for accountants is often considered to be cyclical in that it follows a cycle which includes entering transactions, adjusting entries as necessary, closing the books at the end of the accounting period, and then starting the entire cycle again for the next accounting period.

The basic steps in the accounting cycle are detailed as follows:

1. Transactions

Transactions can include the sale of a product, purchase of supplies for business activities, or any other financial activity that involves the exchange of assets, the establishment or payoff of a debt, or deposit from or payout of money to the company's owners.

Account Entries

Accountants often use a system called the "**double entry**" or "**dual entry**" system where **T-accounts** are used to document any movements.

TIP

Please remember and understand the following rules:

...so you don't spend two months confused about key accounting concepts like I did in 1999 in my first accounting course with Ms. Tammy Crowell at Dalhousie University. I hated it until I learned the basics.

1. With the double entry system, every entry to an account requires an equal and opposite entry to a different account (or multiple accounts).

2. The left side of each T-account is known as the **debit** side and the right side as the **credit** side.

3. Asset accounts increase with a **debit** entry and Liabilities and Shareholder's Equity accounts increase with a **credit** entry.

Workflow: *'flujo de trabajo'.*

Double entry accounting - A bookkeeping system where every entry to an account requires an equal and opposite entry to a different account.

T- Account - A "T" shaped figure used for recording bookkeeping entries. Debits are listed on the left side and credits are listed on the right.

Debit - An entry to the left side of the ledger or T-account: *'débito'.*

Credit - An entry to the right side of the ledger or T-account: *'crédito'.*

For example, at a given moment, the T-account balances could look like this, for a fictitious company, "Snowbird Company":

Assets – Cash	
3,000	

Assets – Inventory	
2,500	

Liabilities – Accounts payable	
	2,500

Shareholder's Equity – Retained Earnings	
	0

Shareholder's Equity – Common Shares	
	7,500

Assets – Equipment	
4,500	

Assets – Accounts receivable	
0	

Remember: All debits must equal all credits.

2. Journal entries

The transaction is listed in the appropriate journal in chronological order.

3. Posting

The transactions are **posted** to the **general ledger** into the accounts that they impact. The ledger is a summary of all the business's accounts. The posting of journal entries can be done at the time the transaction is journalized; at the end of the day, week, or month, or as each journal page is filled.

Journal - The location of the first documentation of financial transactions. The journal shows the date, accounts affected and amount of the transaction: 'diario', 'libro diario'.

To post - To add entries to a ledger or other record: 'Actualizar', 'registrar'.

4. Trial balance

At the end of the accounting period (typically a month, quarter or year) a trial balance is calculated. The trial balance proves that the company's General Ledger is in balance, ensuring that the debits equal the credits.

5. Completion of adjusting entries

If the accounts do not balance, the accountant must look for errors and make corrections known as **adjustments**.

For accounting purposes, adjusting entries are journal entries made at the end of an accounting period. Adjusting entries allocate income and/or expenses to the period in which they actually occurred. The **revenue recognition principle** states that income and expenses must match. This is why adjusting entries need to be made under an accrual based accounting system. Based on this, revenues and associated costs are recognized in the same accounting period. However, the actual cash may be received or paid at a different time.

These adjustments are tracked on a worksheet.

6. Preparation of adjusted trial balance and financial statements

Accountants then prepare the balance sheet and income statement using the corrected account balances.

The process of preparing the financial statements begins with the adjusted trial balance, which requires "closing" the book and making the necessary adjusting entries to align the financial records with the true financial activity of the business.The process of preparing the financial statements begins with the adjusted trial balance. Preparing the adjusted trial balance requires "closing" the book and making the necessary adjusting entries to align the financial records with the true financial activity of the business.

7. Closing the books

The books are closed for the revenue and expense accounts and the entire cycle begins again with zero balances in those accounts.

There are four basic steps to closing the books.

General ledger - A complete record of financial transactions over the life of a company. It includes accounts for assets, liabilities, owners' equity, revenues and expenses: *'libro mayor' o 'libro mayor general'.*

1. Closing the revenue accounts, transferring the balances in the revenue accounts to a **clearing account** called **income summary**.

2. Closing the expense accounts, transferring the balances in the expense accounts to the income summary account.

3. Closing the income summary account, transferring the balance of the income summary account to the **retained earnings** account (also known as the capital account).

4. Closing the dividends account, transferring the balance of the dividends account to the retained earnings account.

This period's ending balance in the retained earnings account will be the beginning balance for for the next period's account.

Retained earnings - The portion of net earnings not paid out to owners, but kept by the company to be reinvested in its core business or to pay debt: 'ganancias retenidas'.

EX

THE ACCOUNTING CYCLE – A PRACTICAL EXAMPLE

Imagine you have recently decided to leave your current job and pursue your true love - yoga. You decide that Madrid's Lavapies neighborhood would be the perfect place to open your own yoga studio. Even better, your friend Adam, a certified instructor, has just moved to town and is willing to teach for you. You quickly prepare to open the studio, Ohm Yoga, on July 1.

Prior to opening the business (before July 1), you make the following transactions:

1. You contribute €4,000 in cash to start the business.
2. You purchase €500 worth of mats and other equipment for use during classes.
3. You purchase an additional €400 worth of mats, equipment, and clothing for sale at the studio.
4. You purchase liability insurance at a total cost of €1,200. The policy covers July 1 through December 31.

July

The following transactions take place during July:

1. You receive cash totaling €800 for classes.
2. Your instructor teaches classes for the month. You agree to pay €600 for the classes; €300 is paid on July 15, and €300 will be paid on August 3.
3. You pay rent for July of €1,000 on July 1.
4. You use utilities (electricity and water) totaling €200. This amount is payable on August 15.

August

The following transactions take place during August.

1. You receive €1,500 in cash for classes. Of this amount, €1,000 was for classes in August. The remainder is for 2-month passes allowing unlimited classes in August and September.
2. Your instructor again earns €600 teaching classes; €300 due on August 16 and €300 on September 1.
3. Utilities total €150, payable September 15.
4. You pay rent of €1,000 on August 1.
5. You sell inventory costing €150 for a revenue of €225.
6. You are worried about money, so your uncle Rafael makes you an offer. He agrees to loan you €2,000 in cash. You will need to repay him sometime later, but he doesn't say when.

7. A client is extremely dissatisfied with their class, and demands their money back. Reluctantly, you agree. The class cost €15.

8. After borrowing money, you decide to withdraw some of your investment in the studio to pursue other opportunities. You decide to withdraw €1,000.

Accounting Cycle – Step 1 – Recording of Transactions

Now, let's begin to look at the business from an accounting perspective, beginning the accounting cycle, by **recording the transactions.**

Let's look at how we would recognize and record the transactions involved in running Ohm Yoga.

Prior to opening the business, you make the following transactions:

1. You contribute €4,000 in cash to start the business.
Cash 4,000, Contributed Capital 4,000; Assets (+) = Equity (+)

2. You purchase €500 worth of mats and other equipment for use during classes.
Cash -500, Pre-Paid expenses 500; Assets (+), Assets (-) = 0

3. You purchase an additional €400 worth of mats, equipment, and clothing for sale at the studio.
Cash -400, Inventory 400; Assets (+), Assets(-) = 0

4. You purchase liability insurance at a total cost of €1,200. The policy covers July 1 through December 31.
Cash -1,200, Prepaid Insurance 1,200; Assets (+), Assets (-)

July - The following transactions take place during July.

1. You receive cash totaling €800 for classes.
Cash 800, Service Revenue 800; Assets (+) = Equity (+)

2. Your instructor teaches classes for the month. You agree to pay €600 for the classes; €300 is paid on July 15, and €300 will be paid on August 3.
Cash -300, Wage Payable 300, Instructor Expense 600

3. You pay rent for July of €1,000 on July 1.
Cash -1,000, Rent Expense 1,000

4. You use utilities (electricity and water) totaling €200. This amount is payable on August 15.
Utility Payable 200, Utility Expense 200

August - The following transactions take place during August.

1. You receive €1,500 in cash for classes. Of this amount, €1,000 was for classes in August. The remainder is for 2-month passes allowing unlimited classes in August and September.

Cash 1,500, Unearned Revenue 250, Service Revenue 1,250

2. Your instructor again earns €600 teaching classes; €300 due August 16 and €300 on September 1.

Cash -300, Wage Payable 300, Instructor Expense 600

3. Utilities total €150, payable September 15.

Utility Payable 150, Utility Expense 150

4. You pay rent of €1,000 on August 1.

Cash -1,000, Rent Expense 1,000

5. You sell inventory costing €150 for a revenue of €225.

a. Cash 225, Sales Revenue 225

b. Inventory -150, Cost of Goods Sold 150

6. You are worried about money, so your Uncle Rafael makes you an offer. He agrees to loan you €2,000 in cash. You will need to repay him sometime later, but he doesn't say when.

Cash 2,000, Loan Payable 2,000

7. A client is extremely dissatisfied with their class, and demands their money back. Reluctantly, you agree. The class cost €15.

Cash -15, Service Revenue -15

8. After borrowing money, you decide to withdraw some of your investment in the studio to pursue other opportunities. You decide to withdraw €1,000.

Cash -1,000, Contributed Capital -1,000

STEP 2 – Journal entries

Now we will record journal entries for the business transactions so they may later be used to create financial statements.

Each journal entry must have a debit and a credit (or multiple). Journal entries also include titles of the accounts debited and credited (credited account is indented several spaces to more easily see a visual distinction), the amount of each debit and credit, and an explanation of the transaction, also known as a narration. Journal entries should also be dated. To simplify for this example, we have numbered the entries.

Pre-opening:

Prior to opening the business, you make the following transactions:

1. You contribute €4,000 in cash to start the business.

Cash	4,000	
Contributed capital		4,000

2. You purchase €500 worth of mats and other equipment for use during classes.

Pre-Paid Expenses	500	
Cash		500

3. You purchase an additional €400 worth of mats, equipment, and clothing for sale at the studio.

Inventory	400	
Cash		400

4. You purchase liability insurance at a total cost of €1,200. The policy covers July 1 through December31.

Prepaid insurance	1,200	
Cash		1,200

July - The following transactions take place during July.

1. You receive cash totaling €800 for classes.

Cash	800	
Revenue		800

2. Your instructor teaches classes for the month. You agree to pay €600 for the classes; €300 is paid on July 15, and €300 will be paid on August 3.

Wage expense	600	
Cash		300

Wage payable 300

3. You pay rent for July of €1,000 on July 1.

Rent expense	1,000	
Cash		1,000

4. You use utilities (electricity and water) totaling €200. This amount is payable on August 15.

Utility expense	200	
Utility payable		200

August - The following transactions take place during August.

1. You receive €1,500 in cash for classes. Of this amount, €1,000 was for classes in August. The remainder is for 2-month passes allowing unlimited classes in August and September.

Cash	1,500

Revenue		1,250
Unearned revenue		250

2. Your instructor again earns €600 teaching classes; €300 due on August 16 and €300 on September 1.

Wage expense	600	
Cash		300
Wage payable		300

3. Utilities total €150, payable September 15.

Utility expense	150	
Utility payable		150

4. You pay rent of €1,000 on August 1.

Rent expense	1,000	
Cash		1,000

5. You sell inventory costing €150 for a €225.

Cash	225	
Revenue		225
Cost of goods sold		150
Inventory		150

(These can be combined into a single entry if you choose.)

6. You are worried about money, so your Uncle Rafael makes you an offer. He agrees to loan you €2,000 in cash. You will need to repay him sometime later, but he doesn't say when.

Cash	2,000	
Loan payable		2,000

7. A client is extremely dissatisfied with their class, and demands their money back. Reluctantly, you agree. The class cost €15.

Revenue	15	
Cash		15

or

Refund expense	15	
Cash		15

8. After borrowing money, you decide to withdraw some of your investment in the studio to pursue other opportunities. You decide to withdraw €1,000.

Contributed capital	1,000	
Cash		1,000

STEP 3 – Posting

In this step we will post the journal entries from the journal into the ledger accounts.

Pre opening

Cash			Pre-Paid Expenses	
$4,000			$500	
	$500			
	$400		$500	
	$1,200			
$1,900				

Pre-Paid Insurance			Contribured Capital	
$1,200				$4,000
$1,200				$4,000

Inventory	
$400	
$400	

July

Cash		Pre-Paid Expenses		Utility Payable		Revenue		Utility Expense	
$1,900		$500			$200		$800	$200	
$800	$300								
	$1,000								
$1,400		$500			$200		$800	$200	

Pre-Paid Insurance		Accumulated dep, PPE,		Contributed Capital		Wage Expense		Insurance Expense	
$1,200			$20		$4,000	$600		$200	
	$100								
$1,000			$20		$4,000	$600		$200	

Inventory		Wage Payable		Retained Earnings		Rent Expense		Depreciation Expense	
$400			$300	$1,220		$1,000		$20	
$400			$300	$1,220		$1,000		$20	

Step 4 – The Trial Balance

The trial balance proves that the company's general ledger is in balance, ensuring that the debits equal the credits.

Now, let's prepare a trial balance for Ohm Yoga as follows:

1. You contribute €4,000 in cash to start the business.
   Cash 4,000, Contributed Capital 4,000

2. You purchase €500 worth of mats and other equipment for use during classes.
   Cash -500, PPE 500

3. You purchase an additional €400 worth of mats, equipment, and clothing for sale at the studio.
   Cash -400, Inventory 400

4. You purchase liability insurance at a total cost of €1,200. The policy covers July 1 to December 31.
   Cash -1,200, Prepaid Insurance 1,200

The trial balance for debits will be:
4,000 (cash) + 500 (PPE) + 400 (inventory) + 1,200 (prepaid insurance) = 6,100

The trial balance for credits will be:
4,000 (contributed capital) + 500 (cash) + 400 (cash) + 1,200 (cash) = 6,100

The calculation will be the same for the next two periods in the example, including any necessary adjustments.

Step 5 - Adjusting Entries

Income and expenses must be allocated to the period in which the transaction actually occurred, which may not coincide with when cash was actually received or paid.

Transactions needing adjustment in later periods:

July

a. Recognize insurance expense
   Prepaid Insurance -100, Insurance Expense 100

b. Depreciation of €20/month
   Accumulated Depreciation 20, Depreciation Expense 20

August

a. Recognize insurance expense
   Prepaid Insurance -100, Insurance Expense 100

b. Depreciation @ €20/month
   Accumulated Depreciation 20, Depreciation Expense 20

c. Pay wages from July
   Cash -300, Wage Payable -300

d. Pay utilities from July
   Cash -200, Utility Payable -200

The journal entries to record these transactions would be as follows:

July

a. Expiration of insurance

Insurance expense.. 200
   Prepaid insurance...200

b. Depreciation on studio equipment (500 for 25 months = 20/month)

Depreciation expense.. 20
   Accumulated Depreciation...20

August

a. Expiration of insurance

Insurance expense.. 200
   Prepaid insurance...200

b. Depreciation on studio equipment (500 for 25 months = 20/month)

Depreciation expense.. 20
   Accumulated Depreciation...20

c. Pay wage from July

Wage payable.. 300
   Cash...300

d. Pay utility bill from July

Utility payable.. 200
   Cash...200

6. Preparation of adjusted trial balance and financial statements

Adjustments are posted to the appropriate accounts after a trial balance shows that they will balance properly. Then we can prepare the financial statements for the period in question.

Let's see the Income statements and Balance Sheets for Ohm Yoga for July and August:

July

Ohm Yoga - Balance Sheet: July 31, 2013

Current Assets	
Cash	1,400
Prepaid Insurance	1,000
Inventory	400
Total Current Assets	**2,800**
Long term Assets	
Property, Plant and Equipment	500
Accrued Depreciation - PP&E	-20
Property, Plant and Equipment (net)	480
Total Long term Assets	**480**
Total Assets	**3,280**
Liabilities and Owner's Equity	
Wages payable	300
Utilities Payable	200
Total Liabilities	500
Contributed Capital	4,000
Retained earnings	1,220
Total Equity	**2,780**
Total Liabilities and Owner's Equity	**3,280**

Ohm Yoga - Income Statement - July 31, 2013

Revenue	800
Wage expense	600
Rent expense	1,000
Utility expense	200
Insurance Expense	200
Depreciation Expense	20
Total Operating Expenses	**2,020**
Net Income	**(1,220)**

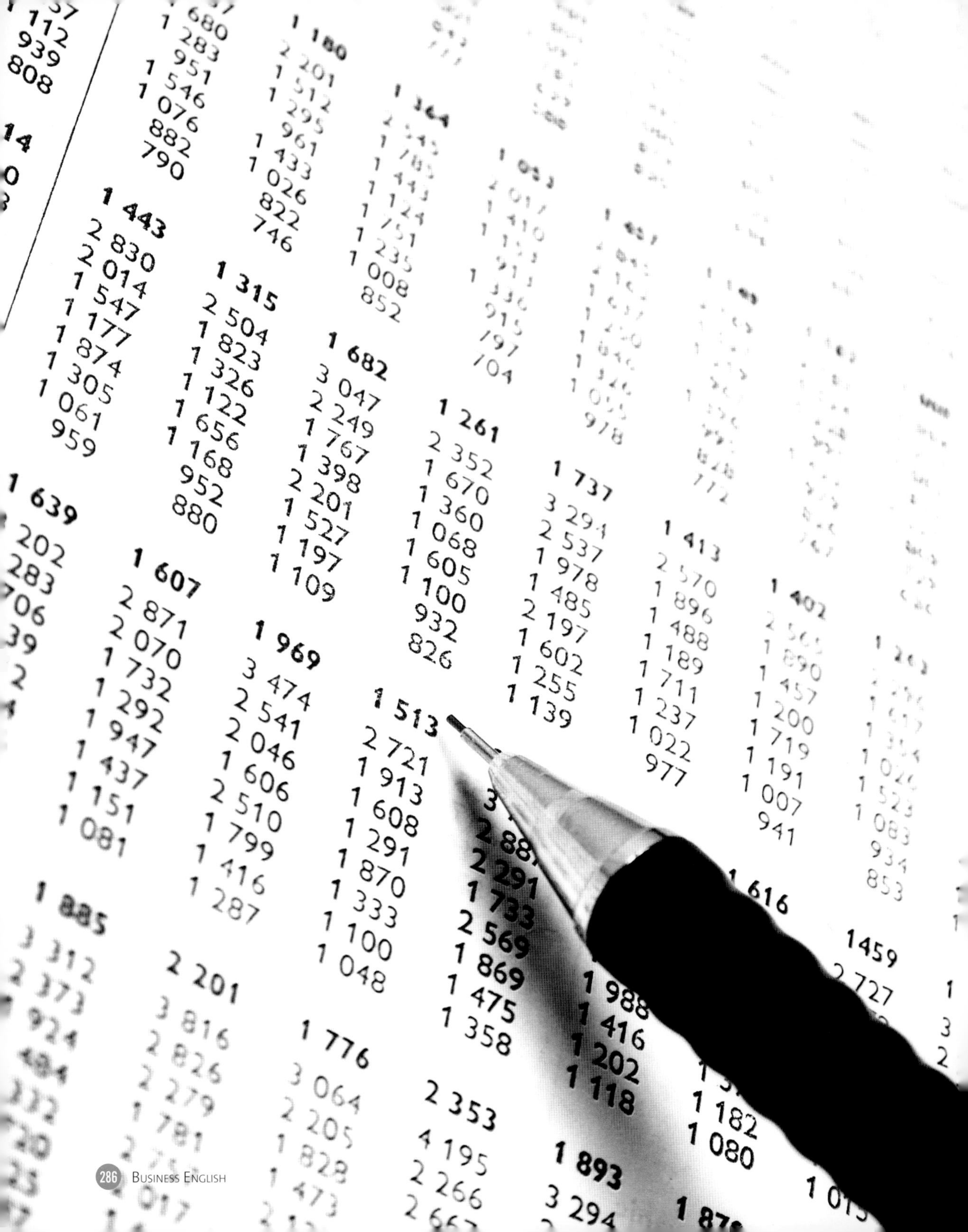

August:

Ohm Yoga - Income Statement - August 31, 2013

Current Assets	
Cash	2,310
Prepaid Insurance	800
Inventory	250
Total Current Assets	**3,360**
Long term Assets	
Property, Plant and Equipment	500
Accrued Depreciation - PP&E	-40
Property, Plant and Equipment (net)	460
Total Long term Assets	**460**
Total Assets	**3,820**
Liabilities and Owner's Equity	
Wages Payable	300
Utilities Payable	150
Unearned Revenue	250
Total Current Liabilities	**700**
Long Term Liabilities	
Loan Payable	2,000
Total Liabilities	**2,700**
Contributed Capital	3,000
Retained earnings	-1,880
Total Equity	**1,120**
Total Liabilities and Owner's Equity	**3,820**

Ohm Yoga - Income Statement - August 31, 2013

Revenue	1,460
Cost of Goods Sold	150
Wage expense	600
Rent expense	1,000
Utility expense	150
Insurance Expense	200
Depreciation Expense	20
Total Operating Expenses	**2,120**
Net Income	**-660**

7. Closing the books

The books are closed for the revenue and expense accounts and the entire cycle begins again with zero balances in those accounts.

To reset our accounts to zero for the next reporting period, we close the *revenue* and *expense* accounts, transferring their balances to the *income summary* account.

Finally, we will close the *income summary* account transferring its balance into the *retained earnings* account which will roll-over, having this period's ending balance be the beginning balance for the next period.

The closing entries for July and August for Ohm Yoga would be as follows:

July

Closing journal entry

Revenue	800	
Retained Earnings	1,220	
Wage Expense		600
Rent Expense		1,000
Utility Expense		200
Insurance Expense		200
Depreciation Expense		20

August

Closing Journal Entry

Revenue	1,460	
Retained Earnings	660	
Cost of Goods Sold		150
Wage Expense		600
Rent Expense		1,000
Utility Expense		150
Insurance Expense		200
Depreciation Expense		20

Now, after closing the books on these periods we can begin September with zero balances and repeat the process.

ACCOUNTING VOCABULARY!
25 words you should know

1.	Activos	Assets
2.	Pasivos	Liabilities
3.	Ingresos	Revenues
4.	Gastos	Expenses
5.	Ingresos netos	Net income
6.	Depreciación	Depreciation
7.	Amortización	Amortization
8.	Trimestralmente	Quarterly
9.	Anual	Annual
10.	Cuentas a pagar	Accounts payable
11.	Cuentas por cobrar	Accounts receivable
12.	Principios de contabilidad	Accounting principles
13.	Efectivo	Cash
14.	Coste de los bienes vendidos	Cost of goods sold
15.	Solvencia	Solvency
16.	Deuda	Debt
17.	Acciones	Equity
18.	Activos líquidos	Current assets
19.	Pasivos líquidos	Current liabilities
20.	Fondo de comercio	Goodwill
21.	Patente	Patent
22.	Derechos de autor	Copyright
23.	Marca registrada	Trademark
24.	Acumular, devengar	To accrue
25.	Libro mayor general	General ledger

ACCOUNTING TRANSLATION LISTS:

Accounting Translation List 1

1.	Va a haber una Junta General la semana que viene.	There's going to be an annual general meeting next week.
2.	¿Quién lleva la contabilidad en tu departamento?	Who runs accounting in your department?
3.	¿Qué clase de ajustes de precio se necesita realizar?	What kind of price adjustments need to be made?
4.	Es muy importante seguir las reclamaciones de los clientes.	It's very important to keep track of customer complaints.
5.	Están agotadas las existencias en el almacén.	They're out of stock in the warehouse.
6.	Sólo hay un socio minoritario.	There is only one limited partner.
7.	No se presentó a la reunión del Consejo de Administración.	He didn't show up at the board of directors' meeting.
8.	Quita ese apunte del balance.	Take out that item from the balance sheet.
9.	Creo que los accionistas mayoritarios están en contra de las condiciones establecidas.	I think the majority shareholders are against the set terms.
10.	No consigo cuadrar el debe y el haber.	I can't get the asset and liability sides to add up.
11.	Mándaselo a Carmen en la facturación.	Send it to Carmen in billing (invoicing).
12.	Prepara un informe de las cuentas a pagar.	Prepare a report on accounts payable.
13.	Van a liquidar los terrenos e inmuebles.	They are going to liquidate the land and buildings.
14.	¿Ha aumentado la rotación de inventario?	Has the inventory turnover increased?
15.	Dile que el valor añadido es insignificante.	Tell him that the added value is negligible.
16.	No permitas a ese cliente más adelantos.	Don't give that customer any more advances.
17.	¿Cuándo tendrán los resultados del análisis del balance?	When will they have the balance-sheet analysis?
18.	Quiero que hagas la lista del inventario.	I want you to make a list of the inventory.
19.	Para las operaciones del día al día, dependo de Miguel.	For day-to-day transactions, I report to Miguel.
20.	Ese auditor externo era muy minucioso.	That outside auditor was very thorough.
21.	La subasta tendrá lugar el jueves próximo.	The auction will take place next Thursday.
22.	Tienen un problema gordo con los pasivos devengados.	They have a big problem with accrued liabilities.
23.	Puede que la amortización se quede en el 14,7%.	Depreciation might stay at 14.7%.
24.	Hubo una gran malversación de fondos.	There was a serious misappropriation of funds.
25.	Las cifras sobre las previsiones de ventas resultaron útiles.	The sales forecast estimates turned out to be useful.

Accounting Translation List 2

1.	*Por favor, imprime los extractos del mes pasado.*	Please print last month's financial statements.
2.	*Te entregaré el análisis del presupuesto mañana.*	I'll have the budget analysis for you tomorrow.
3.	*Le vamos a poner en nómina.*	We are going to put him on the payroll.
4.	*¿Cuándo es el último día para declarar el impuesto sobre la renta?*	When is the last day for filing income taxes?
5.	*¿Hemos recibido la devolución ya?*	Have we received the tax rebate yet?
6.	*Si el prestatario rompe el acuerdo, no podemos seguir.*	If the borrower breaches the agreement, we can't proceed.
7.	*Va a garantizar el pago con un pagaré.*	He'll guarantee his payment with an IOU.
8.	*Su participación vale el 12% del capital.*	His holding is worth 12% of the equity.
9.	*¿Cuánto son las ganancias capitalizadas?*	What are the retained earnings?
10.	*El saldo deudor actual es mayor que el del año pasado.*	The current debit balance is higher than last year's.
11.	*No estás autorizado a emitir tal número de acciones.*	You are not authorized to issue such a number of shares.
12.	*Según los estatutos sociales, se requiere un tercero.*	According to the charter, a third party is required.
13.	*¿Cómo van a repartir el capital social?*	How are they going to allocate the capital stock?
14.	*Multiplica por la base ajustada para obtener la deducción.*	Multiply by the adjusted basis to obtain the deduction.
15.	*¿Tienen la autoridad exclusiva para decidirlo?*	Do they have the sole authority to decide?
16.	*En esta crisis no se puede garantizar los dividendos.*	Dividends can't be guaranteed during this crisis.
17.	*¿Tiene él derecho previo a un dividendo anual de 10$ por acción?*	Does he have prior claim to an annual $10 per share dividend?
18.	*Se presenta la distribución de los dividendos en la siguiente tabla calculada.*	The dividend distribution is presented in the following tabulation.
19.	*Se han saltado tres pagos ya.*	They've already missed three payments.
20.	*Si la empresa quiebra, se acabó lo que se daba.*	All bets are off if the company goes bankrupt.
21.	*Necesito hablar con él personalmente para emitir el documento de poderes.*	I need to speak to him personally to issue the proxy form.
22.	*Eso no forma parte del capital desembolsado.*	That's not part of the paid-in capital.
23.	*A la liquidación, tienen derecho a recibir 105$ por acción.*	Upon liquidation, they are entitled to receive $105 per share.
24.	*La declaración de dividendos está publicada en el informe anual.*	The dividend declaration is published in the annual report.
25.	*Reconoció que no podía encontrar una carencia en el inventario para justificar el superávit.*	He admitted he couldn't find an inventory shortage to account for the surplus.

Accounting Translation List 3

1.	Necesitamos identificar las tendencias en los gastos.	We need to identify trends in expenditure.
2.	¿Cómo podemos dar empuje rápidamente a la rentabilidad?	How can we quickly boost profitability?
3.	¿Cómo podemos evitar la escasez de efectivo?	How can we avoid cash shortages?
4.	Estoy compilando un informe de ingresos.	I'm putting together an income statement.
5.	Si nos audita, Hacienda querrá los recibos.	If we get audited, the tax people will want receipts.
6.	¿Tenemos una prueba de pago?	Do we have proof of payment?
7.	No contratamos los servicios de un contable externo con regularidad.	We don't use an outside accountant on a regular basis.
8.	El valor de las existencias sujetas a impuestos supera los 18.000$.	The value of the taxable supplies exceeds $18,000.
9.	Han contactado con la Unidad de Gestión de Deudas.	They've contacted the Debt Management Unit.
10.	Ya hemos solicitado una prórroga de un año.	We've already applied for a first-year extension.
11.	Es posible pagar a plazos durante 4 meses.	It's possible to pay in installments over 4 months.
12.	Incluso las empresas rentables pueden quebrar.	Even profitable companies can go bankrupt/bust.
13.	¿Cuáles son los ingresos de caja y los gastos reales?	What is our actual cash income and expenditure?
14.	¿Cuánto dinero en efectivo necesitamos para ser solventes?	How much cash do we need to be solvent?
15.	La dirección quiere saber cuánto debe de verdad.	Management wants to know how much they really owe.
16.	Tenemos que convertir la cuenta de resultados a dólares.	We have to convert the financial statements to dollars.
17.	Proporcionan una formación en contabilidad para operar los programas.	They provide accounting training to operate the programs.
18.	Considera utilizar las hojas de cálculo y las bases de datos.	Consider using spreadsheets and databases.
19.	Las modernizaciones continuas permiten la afluencia de dinero.	Constant upgrades keep the money flowing in.
20.	Internet ha cambiado el modelo de contabilidad comercial.	The internet has shifted the business accounting model.
21.	Este programa da seguimiento a la actividad del vendedor.	This program keeps track of the vendor's activity.
22.	¿Cuánto gasta esa ONG en gastos generales?	How much does that NGO spend on overhead?
23.	Si uno no se puede fiar de las cuentas, no consigue inversores.	If you can't trust the books, you can't get investors.
24.	No ha habido tantas fusiones y adquisiciones desde los años noventa.	Not since the '90s have there been so many mergers and acquisitions.
25.	Con un buen plan de estrategia podemos conseguir el mejor resultado.	With a good strategic plan we can get the best outcome.

Accounting Translation List 4

1.	Eso supone un riesgo para nuestro negocio.	That poses a risk for our business.
2.	Tenemos que centrarnos en la ética y en los informes fiables.	We need to focus on ethics and reliable reporting.
3.	Consideramos el impacto de que fracasara el acuerdo.	We considered the impact were the deal to fail.
4.	Esa empresa no utiliza los métodos de seguimiento adecuados.	That company doesn't use the right tracking methods.
5.	Esas empresas están poco preparadas para gestionar riesgos de seguridad.	Those companies are ill-equipped to manage security risks.
6.	Esta previsión ofrece análisis y proyecciones minuciosas.	This forecast offers in-depth analyses and projections.
7.	El tiempo es oro.	Time is money.
8.	Cuanto más complejo es el negocio, más compleja es la gestión de las reclamaciones.	As business becomes more complex, so does claims management.
9.	Cualquiera está en peligro de estafa de cuentas.	Anyone is at risk from check fraud.
10.	Cada vez es más difícil convencer a las empresas para que tomen compromisos de alto riesgo.	It's getting harder to convince companies to make high-risk commitments.
11.	Si tienes un negocio, es tu responsabilidad protegerlo.	If you own a business, your responsibility is to protect it.
12.	¿Cuáles son los indicadores de rendimiento más relevantes?	What are the most relevant performance indicators?
13.	¿Tenemos una crisis de flujo de fondos?	Are we having a cash-flow crisis?
14.	¿Somos tan rentables como podríamos ser?	Are we as profitable as we could be?
15.	¿Cómo podemos implementar eficazmente las estrategias corporativas?	How can we effectively deploy corporate strategies?
16.	Queremos más beneficios y una mano de obra más estable.	We want better profits and a more stable workforce.
17.	Se habla de llevar a cabo un despido masivo.	There's talk of executing a massive layoff.
18.	Quieren recortar drásticamente costes como los de I+D.	They want to slash costs such as R&D.
19.	Necesitamos innovación para generar grandes beneficios.	We need innovation to produce big rewards.
20.	Estamos empezando a presentar previsiones más fiables.	We're starting to produce more reliable forecasts.
21.	Si centralizamos las operaciones, podemos ahorrar en costes.	If we centralize operations, we can save on costs.
22.	Ahora trabajamos en una economía mundial.	We are now operating in a global economy.
23.	Mover este capital a otra jurisdicción implica impuestos.	Moving this capital to another jurisdiction means taxes.
24.	Presupuestar bienes es una herramienta esencial para la dirección.	Budgeting properly is an essential tool for management.
25.	Los pagos trimestrales tocan mañana.	The quarterly payments are due tomorrow.

Accounting Translation List 5

#		
1.	Esa consultoría nos ayudará a recortar y reorganizar costes.	That consultancy will help us trim and reorganize costs.
2.	Es una herramienta para mejorar los informes de cuentas.	It's a tool for improving balance reporting.
3.	No está dentro de nuestros medios invertir a corto plazo.	It's not within our means to invest in the short term.
4.	¿Por qué no introducimos paulatinamente pequeños cambios en el presupuesto?	Why don't we phase in small budget changes?
5.	Esta aplicación hace más eficiente el proceso de presupuestos.	This application streamlines the budgeting process.
6.	Su programa para recopilar datos financieros es incompatible con el nuestro.	Their financial record program is incompatible with ours.
7.	¿Cuáles son los riesgos y oportunidades de esa compra (de una empresa)?	What are the pitfalls and opportunities of that buyout?
8.	Necesitamos decidir entre alquilar o comprar.	We need to decide between leasing and buying.
9.	Estoy preparando ahora la declaración de 2014.	I'm preparing the 2014 return now.
10.	Implantemos las estrategias para disminuir nuestra obligación fiscal.	Let's implement strategies to lessen our tax liability.
11.	Utilizamos programas con tecnología punta para la contabilidad.	We are using state-of-the-art accounting software.
12.	Es esencial que se lleven cuentas pendientes de manera rápida y sin problemas.	It's critical that receivables are handled quickly and smoothly.
13.	No es un buen momento para negociar el crédito a largo plazo.	Now is not a good time to negotiate long-term credit.
14.	Una valoración ahorrará tiempo y dinero en caso de liquidación.	A valuation will save time and money in case of liquidation.
15.	Esas cifras del rendimiento de la Empresa son incorrectas.	Those are inaccurate company performance figures.
16.	Las empresas de hoy invierten más en activos intangibles.	Companies today invest more in intangible assets.
17.	No es fácil hacer más eficaz el proceso de previsión.	Making the forecast process more efficient is no small task.
18.	Registra la operación financiera por pequeña que sea.	Record the financial transaction no matter how small.
19.	Desarrolla un enfoque sistemático para el seguimiento de los pagos.	Develop a systematic approach to keep track of payments.
20.	Conserva los documentos por motivos fiscales.	Keep the documents for tax purposes.
21.	Intenta hacer cuadrar las cuentas.	Try to balance the accounts.
22.	¿Sabemos qué cobran los proveedores de servicio?	Do we know what fees the service providers charge?
23.	Prepare las cuentas para el informe de fin de mes.	Get your books ready for end-of-the-month reporting.
24.	¿Tienes una factura para justificar este asiento?	Do you have an invoice to back up this book entry?
25.	Localiza los fallos en el balance de prueba.	Track down the errors in the trial balance.

CHAPTER 15

INSURANCE

[Términos básicos del mundo
de los seguros en ingles]

INSURANCE

Here we offer a short section about insurance. While this topic isn't a major focus of the book, a basic understanding of insurance and some associated vocabulary will help you gain a balanced base of business terms.

WHAT IS INSURANCE?

Insurance is the transfer of risk from one entity to another in exchange for payment.

Policies are sold to insurance entities seeking coverage, and **premiums** are charged to them according to the amount of coverage they seek.

The insured party receives a contract, called the **insurance policy**, which details the conditions and circumstances under which the insured will be financially compensated.

Insurance involves **pooling** funds from many insured entities (known as "exposures") to pay for the losses that some may incur.

Policy: *'póliza'.*

Premium - The money charged by a company for active insurance coverage: *'prima'.*

Insurance policy: *'póliza del seguro'*

To pool - To collect together: *'juntar'.*

TYPES OF INSURANCE

There are many types of insurance. Following are a few of the most common ones:

Coverage - Insurance protection: *'cobertura'*.

Auto insurance:

This insurance typically covers the vehicle itself from damage or theft and liability **coverage** for injury to property damage to others in the event of an accident. It also provides medical coverage in the event of the accident.

Health insurance

Health insurance provides for the payments of benefits as a result of sickness or injury. It includes insurance for losses from accident, medical expense, disability, or accidental death.

Casualty Insurance

This insurance relates to accidents and is not necessarily linked to any specific property.

This can include auto insurance and worker's compensation. It may also cover a variety of less common risks including earthquakes, political risks or terrorism.

Property Insurance

Property insurance provides protection against risks to property, such as fire, theft or weather damage.

Liability Insurance

This form of insurance covers claims against the insured. These policies can cover payment on behalf of the insured party, known as "**indemnification**", to settle a lawsuit. These policies cover the negligence of the insured; that is, unintentional acts causing harm to another party.

Lawsuit:
'demanda',
'proceso'.

Credit insurance

This insurance repays loans in the event that the insured party becomes unable to make payments. Credit card payment protection plans and mortgage insurance are examples of credit insurance.

Life Insurance

Life insurance provides benefit to the family of the deceased. This insurance may provide income for burial and other final expenses.

Payments to the family can be in the form of a lump sum, one-time payment or annuities. Annuities may be paid monthly and provide income for the family member, typically a spouse who has outlived his or her partner and their financial resources.

More money phrasal verbs!

En esta tanda de "phrasal verbs", miramos dos verbos que usamos cuando tienes que empezar a usar tus ahorros. Veremos los verbos "to dip into" y "to break into".

To dip into	Empezar a usar tus ahorros	To spend part of your saved money.
To break into	Empezar a usar tus ahorros	To start to use money that you have saved.

¡A practicar! Para ganar soltura con estas estructuras tapa la columna de la derecha y contesta afirmativamente a las siguientes preguntas con respuestas completas. También escucha el audio e intenta contestar en voz alta con la voz grabada.

Did she dip into her college savings?	Yes, she dipped into her college savings.
Has your brother dipped into his savings recently?	Yes, he has dipped into his savings recently.
Does the company often dip into the emergency fund?	Yes, the company often dips into the emergency fund.
Will they dip into the emergency fund if they have to?	Yes, they'll dip into the emergency fund if they have to.
Did she break into the money her mother gave her?	Yes, she broke into the money her mother gave her.
Have the kids broken into their allowance money?	Yes, the kids have broken into their allowance money.
Do they always break into their savings at this time of year?	Yes, they always break into their savings at this time of year.
Will she need to break into her emergency funds?	Yes, she will need to break into her emergency funds.

WHOLE VS. TERM LIFE INSURANCE

Whole life insurance, sometimes known as "permanent life insurance" policies, exist until the holder actually dies. This increases the likelihood of payment by the insurance company to almost certainty, causing these policies to be much more expensive.

Term life insurance is a cheaper form of insurance. With this type of insurance, the premiums are guaranteed to stay the same during the period covered by the policy. If you die during the period of coverage, the death benefit is paid to the beneficiaries.

Whole life
insurance:
'seguro de vida integral'.

Term life
insurance:
'seguro de término fijo'.

Know your culture - time

Knowing how to schedule your day is important to doing business.

It is good to know how other cultures value time and plan their days so that you can deal with them effectively.

In Spain, being a bit late can be acceptable in many social circumstances, but this is not so much the case in English speaking countries or northern Europe.

While the Spanish tend to eat lunch at 2:00 and dinner at 9:00 or later, most English speakers will eat at lunch 12:00 and have dinner between 5:30 and 7:30.

INSURANCE VOCABULARY!

25 words you should know

PISTA DE AUDIO 43

#		
1.	*Póliza*	Policy
2.	*Prima*	Premium
3.	*Compensación monetaria*	Monetary compensation
4.	*Beneficiario/a*	Beneficiary
5.	*Causar, provocar un accidente*	To cause an accident
6.	*Optar por*	To opt for
7.	*Daños*	Damages
8.	*Siniestro*	Claim, loss
9.	*Cumplir los requisitos para*	To qualify for
10.	*Echarle la culpa a alguien*	To put the blame on someone
11.	*Exclusión*	Exclusion
12.	*Provisión*	Provision
13.	*Valorar*	To appraise
14.	*Demandar por*	To sue for
15.	*Poner pleito*	To file a lawsuit
16.	*Plazos mensuales*	Monthly installments
17.	*Descontar, retener*	To deduct
18.	*Un peligro para la salud*	A health hazard
19.	*Abolladura*	Dent
20.	*Responsabilidad CIVIL patronal*	Employers' liability
21.	*Robo*	Theft
22.	*Hacer muchos cálculos*	To crunch numbers
23.	*Incurrir en delito*	To commit a crime
24.	*Sindicato, consorcio*	A syndicate, a consortium
25.	*Riesgo*	Risk

INSURANCE TRANSLATION LISTS

Insurance Translation List 1

PISTA DE AUDIO 44

1.	*Preferiría la franquicia más baja posible.*	I'd like the lowest deductible possible.
2.	*¿Tengo derecho a solicitar un suplemento?*	Am I eligible for an endorsement?
3.	*Lo único que tenía era un seguro de propiedad.*	All she had was a homeowner's policy.
4.	*Cuanto más alta sea la franquicia, más baja es la prima.*	The higher the deductible, the lower the premium.
5.	*Al menos ésa es nuestra regla general.*	At least that's our rule of thumb.
6.	*Nuestra póliza para propietarios de negocios lo cubre.*	Our business owner's policy covers that.
7.	*Su póliza podría ser mejor a largo plazo.*	Their policy might be better in the long run.
8.	*Las tasas de explotación de los trabajadores han aumentado de manera espectacular.*	Workers' compensation rates have increased dramatically.
9.	*Steve dijo que mantendrá una reunión el miércoles.*	Steve said he's holding a meeting on Wednesday.
10.	*Él nos resumirá los cambios.*	He's going to brief us on the changes.
11.	*Las instalaciones eléctricas defectuosas causan la mayoría de estos incendios.*	Faulty wiring causes most of these fires.
12.	*El sistema de rociadores tampoco funcionaba.*	The sprinkler system didn't work either.
13.	*¿Puedes informarme sobre el seguro de Pérdida de Beneficios?*	Can you tell me about business interruption insurance?
14.	*Podríamos tener que trasladarnos o incluso paralizar la actividad.*	We might have to relocate or even shut down.
15.	*Solemos tener muchas reclamaciones en esta época del año.*	We usually get a lot of claims this time of year.
16.	*Preferiría tratarlo con un proveedor directo.*	I'd rather deal with a direct provider.
17.	*Recuérdale que puede llamarnos de forma gratuita.*	Remind him that he can call us toll-free.
18.	*Estás cubierto hasta 2.500 $ por los daños.*	You're covered for damages up to $2,500.
19.	*Presta atención a todas las condiciones del contrato.*	Pay attention to all the terms in the contract.
20.	*¿Cuándo se cancela la póliza?*	When does the policy lapse?
21.	*Éste es un contrato legal, ¿sabes?*	This is a legal contract, you know.
22.	*No estoy seguro de si el reclamante contrató la póliza con nosotros.*	I'm not sure if the claimant bought her policy from us.
23.	*Nunca se han saltado un pago.*	They've never skipped a payment.
24.	*Ron es actuario.*	Ron is an actuary.
25.	*Estamos en un sector verdaderamente competitivo.*	We're in a really competitive industry.

Insurance Translation List 2

1.	*A lo mejor podríais utilizar un árbitro.*	Maybe you could use an arbitrator.
2.	*Trabajamos como mutua de seguros.*	We operate as a mutual insurance company.
3.	*Los tomadores de las pólizas eligieron a nuestro Consejo de Administración.*	Policyholders elected our board of directors.
4.	*El huracán ha costado miles de millones de dólares a los reaseguradores.*	The hurricane has cost reinsurers billions of dollars.
5.	*No lo vieron venir.*	They didn't see it coming.
6.	*Creo que ella va a ser una comercial de primera clase.*	I think she's going to be a top-notch salesperson.
7.	*Enviemos a un perito.*	Let's send in an adjuster.
8.	*¿Trabajan a comisión?*	Do they work on commission?
9.	*¿Tienen un período de gracia en caso de que no paguen sus primas?*	Do they have a grace period if they don't pay their premiums?
10.	*Creo que deberíamos darles dos semanas antes de que la póliza se cancele.*	I think we should give them two weeks before the policy lapses.
11.	*¿Firmaste la declaración?*	Did you sign the declaration?
12.	*Ella quiere saber si firmaste la declaración.*	She wants to know if you signed the declaration.
13.	*¿Puedes hacerme una cotización?*	Can you give me a quote?
14.	*Quizá una empresa de construcción con experiencia podría darte una estimación.*	Maybe an experienced contractor could give you an estimate.
15.	*Tus primas se reducirían si instalaras una alarma antirrobo.*	Your premiums would be reduced if you installed a burglar alarm.
16.	*¿Puedo pagar la prima por internet?*	Can I pay my premium on the internet?
17.	*Han estado negociando con una aseguradora extranjera.*	They've been dealing with a foreign insurer.
18.	*Ella solicitó una ampliación de la póliza.*	She's asked for a policy extension.
19.	*¿No me pueden reembolsar los gastos médicos?*	Can't I be reimbursed for medical expenses?
20.	*Necesitarás cobertura de indemnización profesional.*	You'll need professional indemnity coverage.
21.	*¿Te acuerdas donde pusimos su póliza (de ellos)?*	Do you remember where we put their policy?
22.	*Ella ha estado asegurada desde el 16 de julio de 1996.*	She has been insured as of July 16, 1996.
23.	*Ella ha pagado todas las primas desde entonces.*	She's paid all her premiums since then.
24.	*Estaríamos en un verdadero lío sin nuestra póliza.*	We'd be in a real mess without our policy.
25.	*¿Quién es el tomador del seguro?*	Who's the policyholder?

Insurance Translation List 3

1.	*¿Puedes decirme quién es el tomador de la póliza?*	Can you tell me who the policyholder is?
2.	*Las comisiones que cedes se han incrementado en un 5%.*	Your ceding commissions have increased by 5%.
3.	*Asegúrate de que tienes cobertura.*	Make sure you're covered.
4.	*Tenemos derecho a rechazar tu oferta.*	We have the right to reject your offer.
5.	*¿Cuál es tu riesgo total?*	What's your total exposure?
6.	*¿Sabes cuál es tu riesgo total?*	Do you know what your total exposure is?
7.	*Tenemos alrededor de 400.000 $ de riesgo en este momento.*	We have about $400,000 at risk now.
8.	*Eso es, todavía, menos que la capacidad.*	That's still lower than capacity.
9.	*¿Cuál es el año de finalización de la póliza?*	When does the policy year end?
10.	*Todos contribuimos al pool.*	We all contribute to the pool.
11.	*Eso no está en nuestra mano.*	That's out of our hands.
12.	*No tengo autorización para vender ésos.*	I'm not licensed to sell those.
13.	*¿No tienes un abogado?*	Don't you have a lawyer?
14.	*Suerte que tienes cobertura.*	Good thing you're covered.
15.	*Los precios han subido bruscamente (repentinamente).*	Prices have risen sharply.
16.	*Estamos vendiendo más pólizas que nunca.*	We're selling more policies than ever.
17.	*El incendio comenzó justo después de medianoche.*	The fire started just after midnight.
18.	*Puedes llamar a cualquiera de nuestras oficinas.*	You can call any one of our branches.
19.	*Ésa es una póliza temporal.*	That's a term policy.
20.	*Vale la pena comparar precios.*	It pays to shop around.
21.	*Ésta tiene una cobertura de colisión más extensa.*	This one has more extensive collision coverage.
22.	*¿Estás aportando a un plan de pensiones?*	Are you paying into a pension plan?
23.	*¡Por supuesto! No puedo permitirme no hacerlo.*	Of course! I can't afford not to.
24.	*Hemos invertido en acciones preferentes.*	We've invested in preferred shares.
25.	*Necesitaré todos los detalles.*	I'll need all the details.

Insurance Translation List 4

1.	*No tenemos tantos agentes como antes.*	We don't have as many agents as we used to.
2.	*¿Has corregido la póliza recientemente?*	Have you amended the policy lately?
3.	*Están tratando de reducir los costes de adquisición.*	They're trying to reduce acquisition costs.
4.	*Los gastos del corredor son demasiado elevados.*	Broker fees are too high.
5.	*La cobertura no era tan completa como yo esperaba.*	The coverage wasn't as comprehensive as I hoped.
6.	*Había riesgos de gran escala desde el principio hasta el final.*	There were large-scale risks from start to finish.
7.	*Estamos tratando de eliminar lagunas en tu cobertura.*	We're trying to eliminate gaps in your coverage.
8.	*Ése es un problema típico cuando tienes múltiples pólizas.*	That's a typical problem when you have multiple policies.
9.	*Los suscriptores aún están haciendo sus cálculos.*	The underwriters are still making their calculations.
10.	*Fijaremos nuestras tasas de prima en base a sus conclusiones.*	We'll set our premium rates based on their findings.
11.	*¿Cómo analizan toda la información?*	How do they analyze all the information?
12.	*Nuestros suscriptores se unirán a nosotros en la reunión de hoy.*	Our underwriters will be joining us in today's meeting.
13.	*Haremos una presentación a clientes potenciales.*	We'll be making a presentation to prospective clients.
14.	*Realmente podríamos aprovechar este negocio.*	We could really use this business.
15.	*Espero que no se fijen en mi historial de conducción.*	I hope they don't look at my driving records.
16.	*No estamos especializados en seguros de vida.*	We aren't specialized in life insurance.
17.	*Asegúrate de leer la letra pequeña.*	Make sure you read the fine print.
18.	*No podemos predecir tus pérdidas.*	We can't predict your losses.
19.	*Los de la generación del baby boom están comprando muchas coberturas.*	The baby-boomers are buying a lot of coverage.
20.	*¿No podemos compartir el riesgo de alguna manera?*	Can't we share the risk somehow?
21.	*Somos una compañía cedente.*	We're a ceding company
22.	*Nunca habíamos reasegurado antes.*	We've never reinsured before.
23.	*¿Tengo que pasar un examen médico?*	Do I have to take a medical exam?
24.	*¿Quién es el tercero?*	Who's the third party?
25.	*¿Cuál es la probabilidad de pérdida?*	What's the likelihood of a loss?

Insurance Translation List 5

1.	¿Quién es el beneficiario?	Who's the beneficiary?
2.	Hay estatutos para promover la libre competencia.	There are statutes to promote free competition.
3.	Eso podría ser considerado un incumplimiento de contrato.	That could be considered a breach of contract.
4.	No estoy seguro de que todavía tengas cobertura.	I'm not sure if you're still covered.
5.	Estamos buscando reaseguro en ese negocio.	We're looking for reinsurance on that business.
6.	¿Quién es el gestor de grandes cuentas?	Who's the key account manager?
7.	¿Cuál es la desviación estándar sobre la media?	What's the standard deviation from the mean?
8.	No he estudiado mucha estadística.	I haven't studied much statistics.
9.	Bueno, son importantes para nuestro sector.	Well, they're important for our industry.
10.	Tenemos agentes de ámbito nacional.	We have agents nationwide.
11.	Nuestra red es la más extensa del país.	Our network is the most extensive in the country.
12.	¿Podríamos reasegurar el riesgo cedido por su compañía?	Could we reinsure the risk ceded by his company?
13.	Tiene una póliza de vida de 1.500.000 $.	She's got a $1,500,000 policy on her life.
14.	¿Deberíamos darles un periodo de gracia?	Should we give them a grace period?
15.	Definitivamente internet ha hecho las cosas más fáciles.	The internet has definitely made things easier.
16.	Revisa su solicitud cuidadosamente.	Review his application carefully.
17.	Eso no es negociable.	That's non-negotiable.
18.	Yo no pongo las primas.	I don't set the premiums.
19.	Incumplieron sus obligaciones contractuales.	They didn't fulfill their contractual obligations.
20.	¿No puede un comercial venir a mi casa?	Can't a salesperson come to my home?
21.	No soy una persona a la que le guste correr riesgos.	I'm not much of a risk taker.
22.	Hemos tenido algunos empleados deshonestos a lo largo de los años.	We've had some dishonest employees over the years.
23.	Yo diría que constituye un incumplimiento de garantía.	I'd say that constitutes a breach of warranty.
24.	¿Quién suscribe la póliza?	Who's underwriting the policy?
25.	Bueno, creo que vamos a suscribir al 50%.	Well, I think we're going to underwrite 50%.

CHAPTER 16

ECONOMICS

[Una vista general de la
economía en inglés]

ECONOMICS

Economics is the social science that analyzes the production, distribution, and consumption of goods and services. It is the study of the use of scarce resources to satisfy human wants as well as possible.

Microeconomics:
'microeconomía'

Microeconomics examines specific elements in the economy, such as individual households and firms or as buyers and sellers.

Macroeconomics analyzes the entire economy and the issues affecting it, including unemployment, inflation, economic growth, and monetary and fiscal policy.

Macroeconomics:
'macroeconomía'

TIP

Adam Smith

Scottish philosopher and economics pioneer Adam Smith is considered by many to be the "Father of modern economics", best known for publishing *The Wealth of Nations*. Smith believed that self-interest and competition can lead to economic prosperity.

He created the metaphor of the "invisible hand" to describe the self-correcting nature of the marketplace for goods and services. He saw the free market as a place where competition channels ambition toward socially desirable ends, a concept central to neoclassical economics.

SUPPLY AND DEMAND

The concept of supply and demand is central to economics and the idea of a market economy.

Demand refers to how much of a product or service is desired by buyers. The quantity demanded is the amount of a product people are willing to buy at a certain price.

Supply represents how much of a particular good or service the market has to offer. The quantity supplied refers to the amount that producers are willing to supply when receiving a certain price.

The relationship between price and quantity demanded is known as **the demand relationship**, whereas the relationship between price and how much of a good or service is supplied to the market is known as the **supply relationship**.

Market price, therefore, is a reflection of supply and demand.

The relationship between demand and supply underlies the forces behind the allocation of resources.

Market economy theories state that demand and supply will allocate resources in the most efficient way possible.

The Law of Demand

The **law of demand** states that, if all other factors remain equal, the higher the price of a good, the less people will demand that good. The higher the price, the lower the quantity demanded.

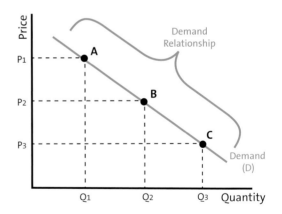

The Law of Supply

Like the law of demand, the **law of supply** demonstrates the quantities that will be sold at a certain price. But unlike the law of demand, the supply relationship shows an upward slope since higher the prices result in a higher the quantity supplied.

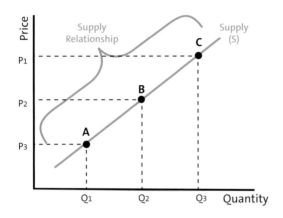

Equilibrium

The economy is said to be at **equilibrium** when supply and demand are equal. At this point, the allocation of goods is at its most efficient because the amount of goods being supplied is the same as the amount of goods being demanded.

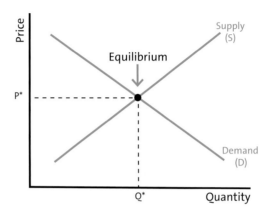

In the real marketplace equilibrium can only ever be reached in theory, so the prices of goods and services are constantly changing in relation to fluctuations in demand and supply.

Shifts vs. Movements

Movements and shifts in relation to the supply and demand curves often occur and represent very different market situations.

A **movement** refers to a change along a curve. On the demand curve, a movement denotes a change in both price and quantity demanded from one point to another on the curve. The movement implies that the demand relationship remains consistent.

A **shift** in a demand or supply curve occurs when a good's demanded or supplied quantity changes even though price remains the same. Shifts in the demand curve imply that the original demand relationship has changed, meaning that quantity demand is affected by a factor other than price.

Obviously, this basic overview of the topic for the purpose of introducing terminology is very limited, and further study is recommended to gain a true understanding of the intricacies of the supply and demand relationship.

Key learning!

Price elasticity of demand

An important concept to understand if you sell products or services is that of the price elasticity of demand, which shows the responsiveness, or "elasticity", of the quantity demanded of a good or service to a change in its price.

It measures how much the quantity demanded decreases for a given increase in price.

Understanding how your demand will change if you increase or decrease your sale price is essential to determine appropriate pricing and maximize the profitability of your business.

Gross domestic
product (GDP) -
The value of
final goods
and services
produced within
a country in
a year. GDP
per capita is
considered
an important
indicator of
a country's
standard of
living: 'Producto
Interior Bruto
(PIB)'.

GROSS DOMESTIC PRODUCT

A concept central to macroeconomics is that of **gross domestic product**, or "**GDP**", which is the value of all goods and services produced in a year. It is the key measure of a country's economy.

GDP is calculated as follows:

GDP = Consumption + Investment + Government Expenditure + Net Exports

Consumption refers to private consumption, in other words the final purchase of goods and services by individuals.

Investment is the gross private domestic investment, which includes replacement purchases plus net additions to capital assets plus investments in inventories.

Government Expenditure refers to government consumption and investment but excludes transfer payments made by a state.

Net exports is calculated by subtracting the value of total imports from the value of total exports.

THE BUSINESS CYCLE

Over time, economies tend to grow. In the short, and medium term they fluctuate, shrink and progress in a series of patterns known as the **business cycle.**

The cycle includes the following stages:

Expansion: A time of normal growth where the economy is steadily expanding, inflation is stable and demand for products and services is growing. Stock market activity is strong.

Peak: After demand for many products and services has been met, wages will have increased and *inflation* risen, interest rates will rise causing investment and purchases of expensive items, such as houses, to decline. Stock prices and market activity decline.

Recession or "Contraction":

The economy is in recession when economic activity begins to decline. Companies with unwanted inventory reduce production, postpone

Inflation - The sustained trend or rising prices: 'inflación'. (Ver explicacion en la página 323).

investment and reduce personnel. Lower incomes and confidence causes consumers to spend less, which further reduces sales and magnifies the problem.

A recession generally lasts from six to 18 months, and interest rates usually fall during these months to stimulate the economy as lower rates encourage borrowing and spending.

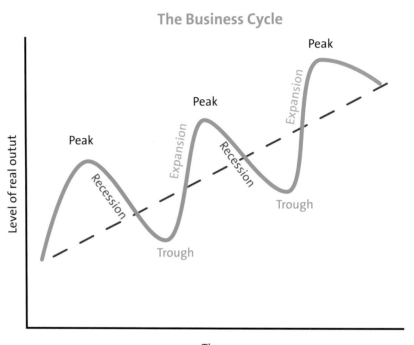

The Business Cycle

Trough: The trough is reached when consumers who postponed purchases during the recession are now encouraged by lower interest rates and begin to purchase to satisfy their demand. This causes sales and stock prices to climb.

Recovery: The recovery is the period when GDP returns to its previous peak. The recovery begins with a revival of interest rate sensitive items such as cars and houses. Companies stop laying off workers. When the economy passes its previous peak, a new expansion begins.

INTERNATIONAL TRADE

Given the realities of globalization and international trade, economies have become more interdependent. A country's interactions with the rest of the world are recorded in its balance of payments.

Balance of payments:

The balance of payments has two components: The current account and the capital account

The **current account** represents all payments between members of a given country and foreigners for goods, services, interest and dividends.

The **capital account** documents funds borrowed from foreigners to pay for items for which members of the country lack foreign receipts to cover.

Current and capital accounts must therefore balance, meaning that a current account deficit implies an equal and opposite capital account surplus.

Balance of payments: 'balanza de pagos'.

Current account: 'cuenta corriente'.

Capital account: 'cuenta de capital'.

INFLATION

Inflation is an extremely important indicator for the economy and for business and investment markets. Inflation is defined as the sustained trend of rising prices. It arises from having too much money chase too few products or services.

Many economists believe that the money supply as controlled by central banks is the cause of inflation, and that if supply remains constant prices must increase to be in line with inflation as more money is available to pursue the same goods and services.

Interest rates: 'tipos de interés'.

INTEREST RATES

Interest rates are essentially the "price of money", or the price of credit. Interest rates are probably the most important financial variable. Changes in interest rates affect the demand and supply for credit and debt.

Higher interest rates raise the cost of capital for business investments, reducing the overall number of profitable investments. Higher interest rates encourage saving, which in turn decreases spending. These rates also increase the portion of household income needed to service debt, including mortgage payments.

Inflation, foreign influences, demand and supply of capital and central bank operations are among the factors that influence interest rate levels.

ECONOMIC POLICY - MONETARY POLICY AND FISCAL POLICY

Monetary policy is implemented by central banks which exist to facilitate the functioning and flexibility of a country's financial system.

More specifically they serve several purposes including:

- To regulate credit and currency in the best interest of the nation

- To control and protect the value of the nation's currency

- To smooth fluctuations in the general level of production, trade and prices in the economy

- To generally promote the economic welfare of the nation

Central banks are responsible for issuing bank notes. Holding deposits of gold, administering government accounts, and managing the government's debt are some of its other functions.

A county's national debt is the total of all federal **deficits** less **surpluses**. Central banks hold auctions for **treasury bills** and **bonds** to issue debt when desired in order to raise funds.

Fiscal policy refers to the government's influence on the economy through taxation, spending and borrowing. Typically governments try to smooth out the business cycle by spending more and taxing less when the economy is weak and spending less and taxing more when the economy is strong.

Government spending can occur in a number of ways including building roads or transferring money to citizens to spend themselves via social security payments.

Taxes occur in many forms and discourage the type of activity being taxed. Income taxes reduce the incentive to work, payroll taxes reduce the incentive to hire and sales taxes reduce the incentive to spend.

A deficit occurs when spending exceeds revenue. A surplus is the opposite of a deficit.

Like the other sections of this book, we have only scratched the surface of the topic of economics here. Economics and politics are closely linked and typically any government decision can be considered from an economic perspective, and rightfully so. There are also many more business topics that could have been addressed in this book. Hopefully this brief introduction at least provides a base of knowledge and stimulates interest in further research and study of business topics.

Monetary policy - The process of controlling the money supply and adjusting interest rates in order to promote economic growth and stability: *'política monetaria'*

Deficit - *A state in which income doesn't reach the level of expenditure for a given period:* 'déficit'.

Surplus - A state in which income exceeds the level of expenditure for a given period: 'excedente'.

Treasury bill (T-Bill): *'letra del tesoro'*

Bond: *'bono'*

Fiscal policy - The government's policy of taxation and spending: *'política fiscal'*

ECONOMICS VOCABULARY!
25 words you should know

1.	Demanda	Demand
2.	Oferta	Supply
3.	Bienes y servicios	Goods and services
4.	Equilibrio	Equilibrium
5.	Elasticidad	Elasticity
6.	Producto Interior Bruto (PIB)	Gross domestic Product (GDP)
7.	Consumo	Consumption
8.	Inversión	Investment
9.	Utilidad	Utility
10.	Capital	Capital
11.	La tasa de desempleo	The unemployment rate
12.	A largo plazo	In the long run
13.	Ajustar	To adjust
14.	Medio de cambio	Medium of exchange
15.	Gasto público	Government Expenditure
16.	Sueldo, salario	Wages
17.	Exportaciones netas	Net Exports
18.	Una subida, aumento	An increase
19.	Cíclico	Cyclical
20.	Inflación	Inflation
21.	Balanza de pagos	Balance of payments
22.	Cuenta corriente	Current account
23.	Cuenta de capital	Capital account
24.	Recesión	Recession
25.	Política monetaria	Monetary policy

ECONOMICS TRANSLATION LISTS

Economics Translation List 1

PISTA DE AUDIO 50

1.	Los bienes son productos tangibles y los servicios son intangibles.	Goods are tangible products and services are intangible.
2.	La economía está relacionada con el comportamiento humano.	Economics is related to human behavior.
3.	La macroeconomía está enfocada en economías nacionales o regionales en total.	Macroeconomics deals with national or regional economies as a whole.
4.	La microeconomía se centra en el comportamiento de consumidores y empresas individuales.	Microeconomics focuses on the behavior of individual consumers and firms.
5.	PIB significa Producto Interior Bruto.	GDP stands for gross domestic product.
6.	El PIB es un indicador económico importante.	GDP is an important economic indicator.
7.	Es el valor total del mercado de todos los bienes y servicios producidos en un país durante un año.	It is the total market value of all goods and services produced in a country during a year.
8.	El periodo de informe del PIB suele ser de un año.	The reporting period for GDP is usually a year.
9.	El consumo, la inversión y el gasto público están incluidos.	Consumption, Investment and Government Expenditure are included.
10	Las exportaciones netas están incluidas también.	Net exports are added as well.
11.	Las exportaciones netas están calculadas restando las importaciones totales de las exportaciones totales.	Net exports are calculated by subtracting total imports from total exports.
12.	Este número puede ser positivo o negativo.	This number could be positive or negative.
13.	Las empresas reportan según el año fiscal.	Corporations report based on their fiscal year.
14.	El consumo incluye el gasto privado.	Consumption includes private spending.
15.	Eso incluye todo en lo que la gente se gasta.	That includes everything that people spend money on except new housing.
16.	La inversión en bruto es dinero invertido en inversión de capital fijo.	Gross Investment is money invested in capital expenditures.
17.	Las pensiones representan un gasto para el gobierno.	Retirement pensions represent an expense for the government.
18.	La palabra "gasto" se suele asociar a la inversión.	The word "expenditure" is usually associated with investments.
19.	El gasto público es un componente del PIB.	Government spending is a component of GDP.
20.	Los sueldos de los funcionarios están también incluidos en el gasto público.	Salaries of civil servants are also included in government expenditure.
21.	Todos los países importan y exportan.	Every country has imports and exports.
22.	La diferencia es la balanza comercial.	The difference is the trade balance.
23.	Si la balanza comercial es negativa, el país tiene un déficit comercial.	If the trade balance is negative, the country is running a trade deficit.
24.	Si la balanza comercial es positiva, el país tiene un excedente comercial.	If the trade balance is positive, the country is running a trade surplus.
25.	La economía está mejorando.	The economy is improving.

Economics Translation List 2

1.	*Podría haber un excedente o déficit.*	There could be a surplus or a deficit.
2.	*La oferta doméstica no llega a la demanda.*	Domestic supply can't meet demand.
3.	*Por este motivo, tenemos un déficit.*	For this reason, we're running a trade deficit.
4.	*La balanza de pagos es otro término macroeconómico importante.*	The balance of payments is another important macroeconomic term.
5.	*Estamos importando más que nunca.*	We're importing more tan ever.
6.	*Las remesas de dinero a parientes en el extranjero no aparece en la balanza comercial.*	Money transfers to relatives abroad doesn't appear in the trade balance.
7.	*No están considerados como bienes o servicios.*	They aren't considered to be goods or services.
8.	*El IPC significa Índice de Precios al Consumo.*	CPI stands for Consumer Price Index.
9.	*Indica niveles de precio de una cesta de bienes.*	It indicates price levels of a basket of goods.
10.	*Los cambios del IPC indican cambios en el coste de vida.*	Changes in CPI indicate changes in the cost of living.
11.	*Cuando mucho dinero compra pocos productos, tenemos inflación.*	When too much money chases few products, we have inflation.
12.	*Los precios suben cuando los proveedores no están fabricando lo suficiente para llegar a la demanda.*	Prices go up when suppliers aren't producing enough to meet consumer demand.
13.	*Esta inflación se suele controlar mediante el aumento de las importaciones.*	This inflation is often controlled by increasing imports.
14.	*La demanda sube los precios.*	Demand raises prices.
15.	*Estamos importando de China más que nunca.*	We're importing from China more than ever.
16.	*La competición por precio es alta dentro de la Unión Europea.*	Price competition is high within the European Union
17.	*Si la demanda por nuestros bienes es muy alta, podemos subir los precios.*	If the demand for our goods is high, we can raise prices.
18.	*Cuando tenemos demasiado inventario, deberíamos bajar precios.*	When we have too much inventory, we should lower prices.
19.	*Los precios suben y bajan según la demanda y oferta.*	Prices rise and fall according to supply and demand.
20.	*Política fiscal se refiere a impuestos y gastos del gobierno.*	Fiscal policy refers to taxation and government spending.
21.	*Una subida de impuestos baja el gasto y ralentiza la economía.*	An increase in taxes lowers spending and generally slows the economy.
22.	*La teoría económica keynesiana es prevalente en la mayoría de las escuelas.*	Keynesian economic theory is prevalent in most schools.
23.	*Los gobiernos dan poder a un banco central.*	Governments give power to central banks.
24.	*Cuando la economía se ralentiza demasiado, el paro sube.*	When the economy cools too much, unemployment rises.
25.	*Cuando los impuestos están más bajos, la gente tiene más dinero para gastar.*	When taxes are lower, people have more money to spend.

Economics Translation List 3

1.	*Demasiado gasto lleva a la inflación.*	Too much spending leads to inflation.
2.	*La política monetaria tiene que ver con los tipos de interés y la cantidad de moneda en la economía.*	Monetary policy has to do with interest rates and the amount of currency in the economy.
3.	*Los keynesianos creen que el gobierno debería usar la política fiscal para estabilizar la economía.*	Keynesians feel that governments should use fiscal policy to stabilize the economy.
4.	*Ajustan los impuestos para influir en el gasto.*	They adjust taxation to influence spending.
5.	*La política monetaria incluye el ajuste de los tipos de interés por parte de los bancos centrales.*	Monetary policy includes the adjustment of interest rates by central banks.
6.	*Los cambios de tipo de interés y suministro de dinero afectan a los préstamos y gastos.*	Changes in interest rates and money supply affect borrowing and spending.
7.	*Cuando los tipos de interés están bajos, la gente tiende a pedir más préstamos.*	When interest rates are low, people tend to borrow more.
8.	*Los tipos de interés más altos disuaden el préstamo y alientan al ahorro.*	Higher interest rates discourage borrowing and encourage saving.
9.	*Los economistas de la escuela austriaca dicen que necesitamos aumentar el ahorro.*	Austrian School economists say that we need to increase savings.
10.	*Sin ahorros no habrá capital para invertir en nuevos negocios.*	Without savings there is no capital to invest in new businesses.
11.	*Menos gobierno significaría impuestos más bajos.*	Less government would mean lower taxes.
12.	*A veces la gente gasta por encima de sus posibilidades.*	Sometimes people spend beyond their means.
13.	*Los tipos de interés son básicamente el coste de dinero.*	Interest rates are essentially the cost of money.
14.	*Cuando la gente ahorra, implica que prefieren el futuro consumo que el presente consumo.*	When people save, it implies that they prefer future consumption to present consumption.
15.	*Cuando ahorras, aplazas el consumo para el futuro.*	When you save, you defer consumption for the future.
16.	*Los ahorros tienen que ser acumulados antes de que puedan ser prestados.*	Savings must be accumulated before they can be lent.
17.	*El dinero es un objeto de comercialización.*	Money is a commodity.
18.	*El dinero tiene que ser reconocible, divisible, portátil y tener un valor estable.*	Money must be recognizable, divisible, portable and have a stable value.
19.	*La gente necesita sentir que su capacidad de comprar no se erosionará con el tiempo.*	People need to feel that their purchasing power won't erode over time.
20.	*Mucha gente gasta más de lo que gana.*	A lot of people spend more than they earn.
21.	*¿Usas tarjeta de crédito?*	Do you use a credit card?
22.	*Los economistas modernos tienden a asumir que el gasto estimula el crecimiento.*	Modern economists tend to assume that spending stimulates growth.
23.	*Creen que cuando haya deflación, la gente pospondrá sus compras.*	They believe that when deflation is present people will postpone purchases.
24.	*Podemos discutir este asunto.*	We could argue this point.
25.	*La deflación se describe como un declive total de precios según pasa el tiempo.*	Deflation is described as the overall decline of prices over time.

Economics Translation List 4

1.	*La gente no necesita ser persuadida para gastar.*	People don't need to be persuaded to spend.
2.	*La demanda de la gente no tiene fin.*	Human demand is essentially endless.
3.	*Si la gente no gasta, quizás una caída de precio sería el tratamiento perfecto.*	If people aren't spending, maybe a price drop would be the perfect cure.
4.	*No mucha gente se podía permitir comprar una televisión de pantalla plana cuando salieron a la venta.*	Not many people could afford flat-screen TVs when they first came out.
5.	*Según caían los precios, más gente se podía permitir comprarlas.*	As prices fell, more people could afford to buy them.
6.	*Los beneficios subieron.*	Profits rose.
7.	*¿Es tan mala la deflación?*	Is deflation really that bad?
8.	*Los políticos que buscan la reelección suelen querer tipos de interés más bajos.*	Politicians seeking re-election generally want lower interest rates.
9.	*Los tipos bajos no recompensan a los ahorradores.*	Low rates don't reward savers.
10.	*Los Estados Unidos se han transformado de una nación de ahorradores a una nación de gastadores.*	The United States has been transformed from a nation of savers to a nation of spenders.
11.	*El dinero necesita representar una reserva de valor.*	Money needs to represent a store of value.
12.	*Los precios de la vivienda no eran sostenibles.*	Housing prices weren't sustainable.
13.	*El metro de Nueva York fue construido principalmente por empresas privadas.*	The New York subway was mainly built by private companies.
14.	*Fue gestionado fuera del control de la ciudad durante casi cuatro décadas.*	It was managed outside of city control for almost four decades.
15.	*Las primeras monedas estaban respaldadas por oro.*	Early currencies were backed by gold.
16.	*El oro se ha usado como dinero durante miles de años.*	Gold has been used as money for thousands of years.
17.	*Un patrón oro es una sistema en el cual el dinero está basado en una cantidad fija de oro.*	A gold standard is a system in which the currency is based on a fixed quantity of gold.
18.	*Los Estados Unidos abandonaron el patrón oro en 1971.*	The US left the gold standard in 1971.
19.	*Desde entonces el dólar ha perdido aproximadamente el 90% de su poder adquisitivo.*	Since then the dollar has lost about 90% of its purchasing power.
20.	*Las monedas fiat no están respaldadas por oro.*	Fiat currencies are not backed by gold.
21.	*Su valor viene de la regulación del gobierno y las leyes.*	Their value comes from government regulation and law.
22.	*El dólar americano todavía es la moneda de reserva del mundo.*	The US dollar is still the world's reserve currency.
23.	*Durante una recesión, los precios tienen que bajar para reequilibrar la economía.*	During a recession, prices need to fall to rebalance the economy.
24.	*Si los precios bajan lo suficiente, la gente empezará a gastar otra vez.*	If prices fall enough, people will start spending again.
25.	*Los tipos de interés bajos pueden mantener los precios artificialmente altos.*	Low interest rates can keep prices artificially high.

Economics Translation List 5

1.	Hoy en día parece que todo está hecho en China.	Everything these days seems to be made in China.
2.	El renminbi es la moneda oficial de China.	The renminbi is the official currency of China.
3.	El yuan es la unidad básica del renminbi.	The Yuan is the basic unit of the renminbi.
4.	El dólar canadiense está dividido en céntimos.	The Canadian dollar is divided into cents.
5.	¿Me puedes dar cambio de un billete de 50 euros?	Can you make change for a 50 Euro note? (bill)
6.	La moneda china está vinculada al dólar americano.	The Chinese currency is pegged to the US dollar.
7.	Esto requiere que los chinos mantengan una parte de sus ahorros en dólares americanos.	This essentially requires the Chinese to hold a portion of their savings in US dollars.
8.	Hay demasiada gente en paro.	There are too many people unemployed.
9.	Un país con un excedente comercial vende más de lo que compra.	A country with a trade surplus sells more than it buys.
10.	Eso crea una demanda internacional por su moneda.	This creates an international demand for its currency.
11.	Si quieres sus cosas, necesitas su moneda.	If you want its stuff, you need its currency.
12.	Con la demanda, el valor de la moneda sube.	With demand, the currency value rises.
13.	Según sube la moneda, sus productos llegan a ser más caros.	As the currency rises, its products become more expensive.
14.	Esto da una oportunidad a países con monedas más débiles a vender sus productos.	This gives an opportunity to countries with weaker currencies to sell their products.
15.	Los economistas utilizan el término "utilidad" para referirse al placer que viene del consumo.	Economists use the term "utility" to refer to the pleasure that comes from consumption.
16.	La utilidad es subjetiva.	Utility is subjective.
17.	Depende de las preferencias de cada individuo.	It depends on each individual's preferences.
18.	El objetivo de cada consumidor es maximizar la utilidad total.	The consumer's objective is to maximize total utility.
19.	A la gente le gusta consumir.	People like to consume.
20.	La tasa de desempleo es alta.	The unemployment rate is high.
21.	Estamos intentando reducir nuestra deuda.	We're trying to reduce our debt.
22.	¿Qué me puedes decir de las hipotecas?	What can you tell me about mortgages?
23.	Voy a contratar a un contable.	I'm going to hire an accountant.
24.	A lo mejor deberías contratar a un abogado también.	Maybe you should get a lawyer too.
25.	¿Y qué sabemos de los precios?	And what do we know about prices?

VOCABULARY INDEX

VOCABULARY INDEX

		Page
The bottom line	*El resultado final*	185
Theft	*Robo*	305
To accrue	*Devengar, Acumular(se)*	259
To act	*Actuar*	29
To address	*Dirigirse a*	28
To adjust	*Ajustar*	272
To administer	*Supervisar, administrar*	28
To allocate	*Distribuir, repartir a, asignar*	29
To analyze	*Analizar*	29
To appraise	*Tasar, Evaluar*	29
To assemble	*Montar*	28
To assign	*Asignar*	28
To audit	*Auditar*	29
To author	*Crear, escribir*	28
To balance	*Cuadrar*	29
To budget	*Presupuestar*	29
To calculate	*Calcular*	29
To cause an accident	*Causar/provocar un accidente*	305
To commit a crime	*Cometer un delito*	305
To consolidate	*Consolidar*	28
To contract	*Contratar*	28
To coordinate	*Coordinar*	28
To create	*Crear*	29
To crunch numbers	*Hacer muchos cálculos*	305
To deduct	*Descontar, Retener*	305

		Page
To delegate	*Delegar*	28
To design	*Diseñar*	29
To develop	*Desarrollar*	28
To direct	*Dirigir*	28
To edit	*Revisar, Editar*	28
To engineer	*Diseñar, Ingeniar*	29
To establish	*Establecer*	29
To file a lawsuit	*Poner una demanda, Entablar un pleito*	305
To forecast	*Prever*	29
To illustrate	*Ilustrar, Demostrar*	29
To introduce	*Presentar*	30
To invent	*Inventar*	30
To maintain	*Mantener*	29
To motivate	*Motivar*	28
To negotiate	*Negociar*	28
To operate	*Operar*	29
To opt for	*Optar por*	305
To organize	*Organizar*	28
To overhaul	*Revisar exhaustivamente*	29
To perform	*Llevar a cabo*	30
To persuade	*Persuadir*	28
To plan	*Programar*	28
To project	*Prever, estimar*	29
To publicize	*Hacer publicidad, Publicitar*	28
To put the blame on someone	*Echarle la culpa a alguien*	305

		Page
To qualify for	*Cumplir los requisitos para*	305
To raise money	*Recaudar dinero*	43
To research	*Investigar*	29
To revitalize	*Revitalizar*	30
To shape	*Dar forma a*	30
To showcase	*Exhibir*	222
To solve	*Resolver*	29
To sue for	*Demandar por*	305
To supervise	*Supervisar*	28
To trade	*Comprar y vender en bolsa / Operar*	246
To train	*Entrenar, Formar*	29
To translate	*Traducir*	28
To upgrade	*Actualizar*	29
To write	*Escribir*	28
Total Quality Management (TQM)	*Gestión de Calidad Total*	206
Trade fair	*Feria de muestras*	20
Trademark	*Marca registrada*	258
Trading volume	*Volumen de transacciones*	241
Treasury bill, T-Bill	*Letra del Tesoro*	246
Undervalued	*Infravalorado*	244
Utility	*Utilidad*	331
Value	*Valor*	205
Wages	*Sueldo, salario*	326
Wants (economic)	*Deseos (económicos)*	205
Whole life insurance	*Seguro de vida*	303

AUDIO INDEX

AUDIO INDEX

Puedes encontrar las siguientes pistas de audio en la web
http://audios.vaughantienda.com (sigue las instrucciones de la página 8 de este libro):